A Psychology with a Soul

Jean Hardy has been a teacher in universities and polytechnics for over twenty years, mainly teaching sociology and social policy to social workers and community workers. Most recently she taught political philosophy and social policy at Brunel, University of West London and is now a freelance writer and teacher. In the course of a search for an alternative framework to psychoanalytic theory for social work practice, she found psychosynthesis, which has been of great personal as well as academic value to her. Jean Hardy is also the the author of *Values in Social Policy* (1981).

A Psychology with a Soul

Psychosynthesis in Evolutionary Context

Jean Hardy

ARKANA

ARKANA

Published by the Penguin Group
27 Wrights Lane, London W8 5TZ, England
Viking Penguin Inc., 40 West 23rd Street, New York, New York 10010, USA
Penguin Books Australia Ltd, Ringwood, Victoria, Australia
Penguin Books Canada Ltd, 2801 John Street, Markham, Ontario, Canada L3R 1B4
Penguin Books (NZ) Ltd, 182–190 Wairau Road, Auckland 10, New Zealand

Penguin Books Ltd, Registered Offices: Harmondsworth, Middlesex, England

First published by Routledge & Kegan Paul 1987
Published by Arkana 1989
10 9 8 7 6 5 4 3 2 1

Contents

'Call the world if you Please "The Vale of Soul-making". Then you will find out the use of the world. . . . I say *"Soul making"* Soul as distinguished from an intelligence − There may be intelligence or sparks of the divinity in millions − but they are not Souls till they acquire identities, till each one is personally itself. I(n)telligences are atoms of perception − they know and they see and they are pure, in short they are God − How then are Souls to be made? How then are these sparks which are God to have identity given them − so as ever to possess a bliss peculiar to each ones individual existence? How, but by the medium of a world like this? . . . I will call the *world* a School instituted for the purpose of teaching little children to read − I will call the *human heart* the *horn Book* used in that School − and I will call the *child able to read, the Soul* made from that *school* and its *horn-book.* Do you not see how necessary a World of Pains and troubles is to school an Intelligence and make it a soul? A Place where the heart must feel and suffer in a thousand diverse ways! . . . As various as the Lives of Men are − so various become their souls, and thus does God make individual beings, Souls, Identical Souls of the sparks of his own essence − This appears to me a faint sketch of a system of Salvation which does not affront our reason and humanity.'

Letter from John Keats
to his brother George
21 April 1819

Foreword

by Piero Ferrucci

As far as I know, Roberto Assagioli is the only individual who has participated personally and actively in the unfurling of two distinct and fundamental revolutions in twentieth century psychology.

The first revolution was the birth of psychoanalysis and depth psychology in the beginning of the century: Assagioli, then a young medical student, presented his MD dissertation on psychoanalysis, wrote in the official *Jahrbuch* side by side with Freud and Jung, and was part of the Zurich Freud Society, the group of early psychoanalytical pioneers. The idea of unconscious processes in the mind made a lasting impression on him, an impression which he later developed into a variety of hypotheses well beyond the boundaries of orthodox psychoanalysis.

The second revolution in which Assagioli participated was the creation of humanistic and transpersonal psychology in the 1960s. A. H. Maslow was the pioneer of these new developments. The main idea was simple: rather than focusing on pathology in order to define the human being (as psychoanalysis had all too often done), or on the structural similarities between the human and the animal nervous system (as behaviourism suggested), the humanistic and transpersonal point of view, while not denying the findings of the other schools, put the main emphasis on the organism's striving for wholeness, on the human being's potential for growth, expansion of consciousness, health, love and joy.

Richness in contacts and interchanges was quite important in Assagioli's background: consider such diverse acquaintances (some of them brief, others lasting) as Italian idealist Benedetto Croce, Russian esotericist P. D. Ouspensky, German philosopher Hermann Keyserling, Indian poet Rabindranath Tagore, Sufi mystic Inhayat Khan, Zen Scholar D. T. Suzuki, Tibet's explorer Alexandra David Neel, plus psychologists Viktor Frankl, the founder of logotherapy, Robert Desoille, creator of the guided daydream, and C. G. Jung himself, before and after his break with psychoanalysis. Such contacts, coupled with a life of experimentation and reflection, provided an undoubtedly wide perspective for

Assagioli's creation, which he called psychosynthesis. Many contributions in this system are worth mentioning:

- the multi-polar model of the human psyche, with its various 'subpersonalities' (as opposed to depth psychology's bi-polar or tri-polar traditional structure);
- the central position of the self as focus of coordination and integration of the personality;
- the importance of the will, and of being a conscious centre capable of choice and purpose, in the midst of the apparently chaotic and contradictory events of life;
- the existence of the transpersonal realm: the higher unconscious as source of inspiration, ecstasy, creativity, intuition, and illumination; *chapter 4.*
- the pathology of the sublime: the occurrence of psychological disturbances of a spiritual, rather than psychological, origin and nature;
- the use of a wide range of active techniques for everybody to use on his or her own to further their personal and spiritual development;
- the use of imagery for the exploration of the unconscious, the transformation of neurotic patterns, and the expansion of awareness;
- the concept of a natural tendency towards synthesis and 'syntropy' (the opposite of entropy), that is, towards the spontaneous organization of meaningful and coherent fields within the psyche.

This is all abundant material for investigation and discussion. However, psychosynthesis has not won to date an academic acknowledgment equal to its success among those in the helping professions who look for effective tools with minimum working hypotheses, and among seekers who look for a religiously neutral, psychologically oriented approach to the higher realms of consciousness. The reason for this difference lies probably in the pragmatic orientation of psychosynthesis: in its outlook, results (educational, therapeutic, spiritual) are what counts. Nonetheless, practical success should be balanced by a clear understanding of the place of psychosynthesis in contemporary psychology and in the history of ideas. For this reason *A Psychology with a Soul* is to be welcomed as a most needed contribution.

In reading this book one is struck – among other things – by an apparent contradiction: psychosynthesis claims to be an experimentally and scientifically based psychology; on the other hand, it appears to have an affinity with the esoteric traditions – a perspective widely divergent, if not opposite, to the scientific approach. How can this contradiction be explained? The answer is simple. Esotericism and empirical science are undoubtedly at two ends of a spectrum: esotericism starts with universal statements about reality, and ends up with the particular and the contingent. Empirical science, instead, starts from the particular and the contingent and ends up in the universal, i.e. in general laws and principles. Esotericism is based on faith and intuition. Science is based on experience. The two outlooks are, in fact, symmetrically opposed.

Psychosynthesis follows the attitudes and the methods of science, insofar as science can be applied to the study of human consciousness. Psychosynthesis has been slowly and gradually built up through experiment and observation; people approaching it will not find in it a credo, rather a set of techniques and hypotheses. No unquestioning acceptance is required, nor the following of a teacher. Only personal experience is the guiding principle here. And whereas esotericism and religion offer specific directions for one's conduct in life, psychosynthesis views its task as that of merely enabling an individual to envisage a wider range of choices and values; what to pick is up to him or her alone.

One point here needs to be made, however: it is commonly accepted by those who study scientific methodology that scientists (even those in the hard sciences) use all kinds of hypotheses, analogies, and visual images to support their investigations. In the field of psychology, for instance, Freud was inspired by Greek tragedy; Jung found alchemy a useful heuristic device. However, psychoanalysis is not Greek tragedy and analytical psychology is not the same as alchemy. Assagioli was interested in the great spiritual insights and teachings of all times: this influence certainly had a deep effect on his perspective and his choices; it was a source of inspiration, and helped him emphasize the spiritual element, the 'soul' or Self, in the development of psychosynthesis. However, this spiritual or transpersonal perspective was subject to empirical verification in the lives of everyone; it was a way of expanding the scope of observed phenomena, not an imposed dogma nor a compulsory key for interpreting reality. Assagioli always made it clear that he considered psychosynthesis a development of twentieth century psychology, and, as such, independent of any religious or esoteric belief: people of all backgrounds (including atheists) could use it to live more satisfactorily and develop their potential.

If we keep this point in mind we can fully appreciate the novelty of psychosynthesis and its endeavour to introduce mystical and spiritual – or as Assagioli calls them, 'transpersonal' – experiences as a legitimate object of inquiry in the field of psychology.

A Psychology with a Soul provides an excellent framework for understanding these issues and many others. We should be grateful to Jean Hardy for providing a comprehensive view of the relationship of psychosynthesis with contemporary culture as well as with ageless traditions. Comfortably and competently moving in such diverse fields as philosophy, mysticism, esotericism, psychology, and the history and methodology of science, she has given a vivid picture of the rich background into which psychosynthesis was born.

Piero Ferrucci
Florence, April 1986

Acknowledgments

I would first of all like to acknowledge the value of my whole experience of psychosynthesis, within the Trust for the Furtherance of Psychosynthesis and Education in London. I am especially grateful for the constant support and friendship given to me, particularly by Diana Whitmore, the founder of the present Trust, Judith Firman and Kunderke Kooijman on the staff, and for the companionship and generosity of my fellow students, too numerous to mention by name. Many thanks for that period 1981–85.

In writing this book I have received great encouragement from Dr Piero Ferrucci, who read much of the material as it was being produced, giving me constructive comments and corrections, and who has steadily backed me. He also arranged for my visit to Dr Assagioli's library in Florence. Dr Nikolas Rose of Brunel University encouraged me to develop the arguments and conclusions of the study, and has thus helped clear my path through many complex and thorny areas.

Dr Eugene Smith of Boston, Massachusetts, has given me invaluable factual information for Chapter 1 – he is writing a biography of Roberto Assagioli. Dr Geoffrey Ahern helped me, one stormy and dramatic August day in 1985, on the mystical material – it was most appropriate weather for our subject. Chris Robertson from the London Institute of Psychosynthesis pushed me into looking more rigorously at the evolving nature of psychosynthesis at the present time. Michal Eastcott kindly gave me something of her personal knowledge of Dr Assagioli and his visits to England.

I have discussed this material at different times with many people, and all have given me ideas and raised questions. I would like to thank particularly Dr Josephine Klein, Dr Colette Ray, Dr Len Davis, and a variety of classes at Brunel University, London University, at the Trust for the Furtherance of Psychosynthesis and Education, and in the Society of Friends (Quakers).

I would like to thank Jo Campling, and Eileen Campbell of Routledge & Kegan Paul, for their patience and help in getting the material published in the UK and America: and Frank Kevlin and Felix Erkelens for their enthusiastic assistance in publishing the study in Dutch.

Finally, I was most lucky that Andrea Hummel, one of the graduates of the Trust, was able to type the final draft. Not only has she produced a beautiful typescript, but she has edited the material with a meticulousness and care which I have greatly appreciated. Joyce May and Mary Furnell willingly typed the bibliographies and the references, and Nick Rimmer helped with the index.

Grateful acknowledgment is also made to Thorsons Publishing Group Ltd for permission to quote material from *What We May Be* by Piero Ferrucci and from *Psychosynthesis* and *The Act of Will* by Roberto Assagioli; and to David Higham Associates Ltd for material from *Dante The Divine Comedy* translated and introduced by Dorothy L. Sayers.

General introduction

Psychosynthesis is a transpersonal, or spiritual, psychotherapy, a phenomenon of the twentieth century Western world. It is a theory and practice of individual development and growth, though with a potential for wider application into social and indeed world-wide settings; and it assumes that each human being is a soul as well as a personality.

It was founded by Roberto Assagioli, an Italian living in Florence for much of his long life from 1888 to 1974. Dr Assagioli was a psychiatrist who was involved in the development of psychoanalytic theory at the very beginning of his career, but who worked out his framework for psychosynthesis simultaneously and independently.

Psychosynthesis was initially described in outline in Assagioli's paper 'La psicologia delle idee-forza e la psicagogia' in 1908. He worked as a psychiatrist and doctor in the First World War, and in 1926 set up the Istituto di Cultura e Terapia Psichica in Rome. He survived Mussolini's years of power in Italy with some hardship, being once imprisoned in 1938 and forced to flee to the countryside. He continued developing his theories, writing articles and practising as a psychiatrist after the Second World War, but it was only in the 1960s that psychosynthesis became internationally known. In 1961, the Istituto di Psicosintesi was founded in Florence. Centres have now been developed all over the world and the theory and practice is well known and respected in the humanistic/transpersonal field.

Roberto Assagioli was a 'thief' (he said) in his use of the many fields of study with which he was conversant. He lists many of these in his book *Psychosynthesis* published in 1965 – the psychodynamic movement (Janet, Freud, Adler, Jung, Rank, Horney), psychosomatic medicine, psychology, psychiatry and anthropology; also the psychology of religion (William James, Evelyn Underhill) and the investigations of the 'superconscious' and 'holism' (Bucke, Ouspensky, Maslow, Progoff, Smuts, Keyserling); and the study of parapsychology, though he was careful to use this material with discretion. He was most interested in the many techniques of individual psychotherapy, and psycho-synthesis is well known for its flexible use of a large number of techniques: these include Gestalt, guided fantasy, meditation, group psychotherapy, use of art, music and writing, work on meaning and purpose as well as on problems.

The sources that he lists in *Psychosynthesis* are those which he regarded as scientific. Like Freud, and indeed most psychiatrists today, he was determined that his work should pass muster and be accepted as a respectable scientific theory. In the twentieth century, a scientific study of the unconscious has just begun. But psychosynthesis, like psychoanalysis, was developed outside the universities, in a 'school'; it is still not widely accepted or known by academics whose work is based firmly in the scientific tradition, the predominant paradigm of formal knowledge for the past 300 years in Western society: there is a clear and unbridgeable distinction between sciences and religion.

Assagioli's work, however, in its assumption of the existence of the soul, harks back to a wide-ranging literature of religious and spiritual mysticism, both Western and Eastern, to neoplatonic theory, to the many mystics of the Middle Ages in Christian and Jewish thought – Dante, Eckhart, St John of the Cross, the Kabbalah, to the schools of knowledge founded in the West before the split between science and religion, to Buddhism and Hinduism, and to classical Greek philosophy, particularly Plato. At the beginning of the twentieth century, and also in the last twenty years, there has been access to and fascination with many forms of hitherto generally hidden knowledge, now made widely available. Assagioli was brought up in sympathy with this wide range of material – his mother became a follower of theosophy, an esoteric school founded in America in 1886, with a branch founded in Italy in 1902. And the twin commitments to scientific work with the unconscious, and religious and mystical knowledge based on personal experience, were present from his first writings.

He explicitly kept these mystical interests separate from psychosynthesis, but clearly his wide knowledge of many centuries of spiritual · thought is relevant to the theory and practice eventually developed in psychosynthesis – though this is rarely acknowledged in his therapeutic writing. This split has made the job of tracing the influences on psychosynthesis quite difficult, and sometimes speculative.

The immediate question that this study addresses concerns the origin of the ideas in the psychosynthesis framework. Where do the underlying ideas come from? How does Assagioli come to incorporate the idea of a soul into his psychology? What are the basic assumptions of the many techniques used in the system, emphasizing symbol, myth and imagery? Why did his notion of the unconscious develop so differently from that of psychoanalysis? So the tracing of ideas from his own account, from experience of psychosynthesis training, and from a study of his own library which is still open to the public in Florence, is the first piece of detective work that is attempted here.

The second question is on the nature of the knowledge in psychosynthesis. Is it scientific, as Assagioli maintained? How far can therapy be 'scientific' in any case, and what does the word mean in this context? What is the significance of Assagioli's life-long interest in spiritual material, and how far can that be related to the theory and practice of psychosynthesis? Are there different kinds of knowledge incorporated into such a system? And how can we understand these questions within the framework of the history of ideas, which attempts to trace the social and intellectual origins and movement of thought?

Finally, how is it that a transpersonal, or spiritual, psycho-therapy comes to exist and then to develop in the twentieth century? Is this the *only* time that such a phenomenon could have occurred? What is its significance? And can the twentieth century split between psychology on the one hand and theology on the other be healed through such a framework? Or is the attempt an inauthentic one, in the sense that it cuts across the boundaries of disciplines which are widely accepted as different? And what is the connection between Assagioli's theory and practice of personal therapy and his notion of the 'synthesis' of humanity, the vision of a 'whole' world as well as a healed person?

A question for a researcher of the origins of the theory, which combines in such a magpie way so many concepts from all parts of the world and from most historical epochs, is its authenticity. Keen, in an article on 'The golden mean of Roberto Assagioli' published in *Psychology Today* in December 1974, asked frankly whether psychosynthesis 'is a marriage of the best in modern psychology or an eclectic mishmash that boils down to a game of words?' My own judgment is now, on the basis of both my research and my personal experiences of psychosynthesis, that out of his wide reading in mysticism and his own mystical experience, his capacity for feeling and work with people, and his originality of mind, Assagioli has woven a theory that makes deep and sane sense.

Assagioli produced two books, *Psychosynthesis*, published in 1965 and composed largely of a series of articles, and *The Act of Will*, published in 1974. There are also numerous unpublished papers written throughout his life and mostly undated. His own writing, however, does not really convey the width and origins of his work, or set it forward in any systematic way. And because of his predominantly psychological and practical approach to psychosynthesis, the most deeply philosophical issues are just not discussed in his work – the practice is presented as an already created whole, without much explanation of the context of ideas which are so wide and deep. This present study, in examining this context, should at least provide the beginnings of a study of the wider framework, which is in its own right most fascinating, and significant to our present situation.

Keen, in his article, contrasts the self-confidence and optimism of psychosynthesis with the Christian tradition, which accepts the 'fallen' nature of mankind, and comments, 'in the Christian tradition healing comes from accepting our brokenness, not from synthesizing our parts into a perfect whole.' He adds, 'the idea of wholeness, realizing the full human potential, transcending contradictions, achieving enlightenment, intrigues me.' The potential involved in the theory *is* intriguing, both in practice and in the roots from which it springs. But Keen offers an unreal distinction, because the theory of psychosynthesis postulates that in accepting and working with our brokenness and fragmentation, we have the means of becoming whole.

Both the concepts of transcendence (God being experienced as the 'other') and immanence ('the God within') are drawn on in psychosynthesis, and both, Assagioli believed, could work towards the fuller potential of the individual. The more the person becomes what he or she could be, the more the unique individual becomes truly part of the whole. These elements are found in all mystical religions, with some placing more emphasis on transcendence and dualism (the differentiation of spirit and matter, and the journey towards contact with the spirit being the goal of the aspiring person), and others on immanence and monism (the recognition and realization of the Self, the soul within). Assagioli insisted that psychosynthesis was religiously non-specific, and both concepts are implicit in the theory and practice.

Psychosynthesis, then, can be thought of both as part of the development of scientific theories of the nature of the person in psychology and psychotherapy, and as part of the long mystic tradition, traceable over thousands of years. It is in tracing this material that I attempt to answer the questions raised earlier.

This research into psychosynthesis was triggered by my considerable curiosity about the origins of the ideas in the framework Assagioli presents but which he does not explain: as the spiritual origins of much of the source material became clearer, and more intriguing, the relationship between Assagioli's self-identification as a scientist and a clinician and this material became most interesting, and the relationship between science and mysticism became part of my search: the emergence of 'trans-personal psychotherapy' seemed to me more clearly a twentieth century rewriting of much older patterns, tackling a split that now exists between psychology and religion. This search has led me into fields of knowledge I did not know existed, and has uncovered to me older frameworks of theory and experience, which throw much light on our present struggling theories of the nature of the person, and maybe of the development of the human race. Perhaps it is true that in the twentieth century we have forgotten much of what people in the past once knew. The idea and experience of 'synthesis' may have compelling relevance to us on many levels of understanding and over many historical periods.

I
Psychosynthesis:
History and Concepts

Introduction

Psychosynthesis is rooted in the early part of the twentieth century. It was founded on the theory of the person based on drives and instincts which was current at that time, and on the discoveries about working with unconscious material promulgated by Freud and Jung in their great psychoanalytic international conferences held before the First World War. But from the beginning, both Jung and Assagioli held that the unconscious is potential as well as problem, and that the two are related: it is in working through the past, the defences that are no longer useful, and the Shadow, that the potential can be reached: creativity springs from these areas beyond the rational and the everyday mind.

Psychosynthesis, like any other living theory, has developed over time and will continue to evolve. The term 'psychosynthesis' had been used before Roberto Assagioli adopted it as the most appropriate description of his scheme of transpersonal, personal and social therapy. In the Freud/Jung letters,[167:47] Jung mentions the first system of psychosynthesis, advanced by Bezzola and reported to the Amsterdam Psychoanalytic Conference in the year 1907. Freud irritably remarked that this earlier version of psychosynthesis was just the same as psychoanalysis – 'after all,' he wrote, 'if we try to analyse to find the repressed fragments, it is only in order to put them together again'.[167:18F] Assagioli used the Italian 'psicosintesi' when he opened his first Institute in 1926, but in English he translated the term as 'psychosynthesis'. His synthesis is distinguished from almost all other therapies, including Jungian, by its specific and explicit techniques to put the 'repressed fragments' back together again.

In Chapter 1, I will describe first of all Assagioli's life-story as it relates to the formulation of psychosynthesis as a method of working – the early years in contact with the beginnings of the psychoanalytic movement; the long period of time working in Italy founding and developing the theory and practice, from about 1913 to the mid-1950s, forty years at least, in relative obscurity; and the final flowering from the late 1950s to his death in 1974.

Psychosynthesis continues to flourish in its many centres around the world, and some of its old forms give way to new ones, influenced most particularly by new theories of scientific knowledge, and a renewed acknowledgment of the feminine.

The next three chapters (Chapters 2 to 4) give the 'egg-shaped diagram', the picture of the nature of the person that Assagioli used from at least the 1930s onward, and which has links both with the Kabbalah and with the philosopher's stone. I am presenting this material following as closely as possible the way that Assagioli gave it, but am throughout concerned to pick up the assumptions contained in this work, and both the roots of these assumptions and how they may be changing. Chapters 3 and 4 similarly go on to consider in more detail the theory of subpersonalities and of the superconscious energies, looking at the origins of the models and their developing use.

Chapters 5 and 6 move more explicitly to a consideration of 'the unconscious' as a concept: the way it has developed, and its roots in symbols, dreams and fairy-tales, and then the use of particular techniques used over time to get in touch with this material, from projective techniques to Gestalt. The development of so many techniques is an indication of a technological and scientific age – though spiritual disciplines have always been used throughout history as a method of self-development and guides along the spiritual path.

The final chapter in this section is on the idea of synthesis as developed by Assagioli – not only personal self-development, but the extension of the idea to social forces, in couples, families, groups, whole societies, and, in fact, the whole of the human race in its relationship with the world in which it lives. This vision is always implicit in Assagioli's material and springs from his wide reading in spiritual views of the universe. This whole account of psychosynthesis, contained in Chapters 2 to 7, is a description given, as it were, from the inside. The purpose is not to evaluate the theory at this point, but to offer it as a starting point for the investigation of its roots, and of its significance as a framework for understanding and working with the human situation.

By the end of this part of the work, the two strands of mysticism and spirituality, and science and technology, will already have appeared. The next part of the book will go on to investigate some of the deep roots of these two strands of thought as they most influenced Assagioli, and as they stretch back through the centuries.

1

The history and development of psychosynthesis

The early period 1888–1926

Roberto Assagioli was born Roberto Grego on 27 February 1888 in Venice. His mother was Elena Kaula (1863–1925), who married Grego or Greco (Christian name unknown); Grego died when Roberto was very young, and his mother married Alessandro Assagioli, whose surname Roberto assumed. He was often known, in fact, as Roberto Grego Assagioli.

He was brought up in a cultured upper-middle-class Jewish family. His education was a typically classical one, including five years of Greek and eight of Latin, together with the study of several other languages. In his own home, Italian, French and English were all spoken and he was always comfortably trilingual. He also undertook German when he was 8, and Russian and Sanskrit at the University of Florence after 1906. Like all Italian schoolchildren, he was very familiar with Dante Alighieri's work, particularly the *Divine Comedy*, and it is recorded that he was particularly impressed by his teacher of Dante. The influences of Plato and Dante show directly in psychosynthesis, and were a constant source of inspiration to him throughout his life.

He lived in Venice until he went to medical school in Florence in 1906. Throughout his childhood he was devoted to his parents, who encouraged him to visit many European countries, including Russia. It was to this early exposure to many great cultures and ways of living that he felt he owed the width and depth of his own perception. His mother became a Theosophist, and this opened up to him the fields of spiritual and esoteric knowledge early in his life. He was interested in Jewish culture and continued to receive Jewish newspapers and belong to Jewish organizations for most of his life. He also became a mountain climber – a key image in psychosynthesis.

Assagioli trained as a medical student in Florence from 1906 and lived for much of his life in this city. Both in Venice and in Florence, the great artistic achievements of the Middle Ages and the Renaissance constantly surround the citizen. That particular synthesis of Greek, humanistic and religious ideas, resulting in supreme painting, sculpture and architecture, encouraged his strong appreciation of music, art and nature. It was also a synthesis he attempted in his own work.

In an article, which is undated and unsigned, on the history of psychosynthesis, it is stated that Assagioli was writing and publishing articles on psychological disciplines and therapies in the early 1900s. He was also studying Max Muller's translations of mystical and Theosophical writing at this time. His first article we know of, written in 1906, was entitled 'Gli effetti del riso e le loro applicazioni pedogagiche' – 'On the effects of laughter and its relation to education': this later became known as his paper 'Smiling wisdom'. At this time Assagioli seems to have been working on the boundaries of medicine, education and religion, a combination of interests which were to form the basis of psychosynthesis. It is recorded that he attended international conferences on the history of religions (William James's book on the varieties of religious experience had come out in 1902) and on moral education, in England in 1908, and his contributions were reported in the review *Scientia*. He met there many orientalists including Coomarasswamy. In that year he also gave a paper at the International Congress for Philosophy on the similarities between the German mystic J. G. Hamann and Ralph Waldo Emerson, the American transcendentalist.

The early years of the century were an exciting time in the development of knowledge. Religions and religious knowledge were being re-examined: scientific and technological knowledge was burgeoning in every field – Einstein was just beginning to publish material; education was being questioned and re-assessed by people such as Froebel, Montessori, and later Steiner; Eastern philosophies and religions were recognized by some groups as having an ancient wisdom to offer the West; and the nature of the person was being investigated, and the unconscious being scientifically studied, particularly of course by Freud. The first International Congress for Psychiatry was held in Amsterdam in September 1907. Throughout his life Assagioli used material from an enormous range of disciplines and interests, and this seems consistent with the great growth of new knowledge in many fields which he experienced during this formative period.

That Assagioli was clearly among the people identified with psychoanalysis at this early stage is confirmed in the Freud/Jung letters. Jung wrote to Freud in 1909,

The birds of passage are moving in, i.e. the people who visit one. Among them is a very pleasant and perhaps valuable acquaintance, our first Italian, a Doctor Assagioli from the psychiatric school in Florence. Professor Tanzi assigned him our work for a dissertation. The young man is *very* intelligent, seems to be extremely knowledgeable and is an enthusiastic follower, who is entering the new territory with proper brio. He wants to visit you next spring.[167:151J, n.3]

There are further reports of Assagioli in the letters. In 1909 he contributed an abstract to the *Jahrbuch für Psychoanalytische und Psychopathologische Forschungen*, the psychoanalytic journal, on psychoanalytic activity in Italy; in 1910, Freud reports that he had 'received a letter from Assagioli in Florence, in perfect German, incidentally',[167:171F] and later on in the year Jung reported both that Assagioli would contribute to the *Jahrbuch*, and also that he formed one of his 'group' of nineteen members, which acted as a study group.

In 1910 Assagioli produced his doctoral thesis, a critical study of psychoanalytic theory, presumably the dissertation assigned to him by Tanzi: this, Assagioli later said, was received 'with benign indifference'. In the obituary printed after his death in 1974, it is stated:

In 1910 Assagioli, the young medical student, introduced the important discoveries of Sigmund Freud to his professors in Florence . . . he simultaneously – in 1910 – laid the groundwork for a critique of that same psychoanalysis. He saw that it was only partial. . . . Assagioli's purpose was to create a scientific psychology which encompassed the whole of man – creativity and will, joy and wisdom, as well as the impulses and drives. Moreover, he wanted psychology to be practical – not merely an understanding of how we live, but an aid to helping us live better, more fully, according to the best which is within us.[23]

After taking his doctoral degree, Assagioli trained in psychiatry with Bleuler. Eugen Bleuler was the Director of the Burghölzli, a huge hospital in Zürich at which Jung had worked (also under Bleuler) from 1900. Bleuler and Jung had a rather wider range of patients here than Freud, as the hospital took all classes of people and was residential. Bleuler was the director, with Freud, of the aforementioned *Jahrbuch*, with Jung as editor; in 1911 he coined the word 'schizophrenia' to denote the 'splitting of the mind' as it was then perceived.

At the time when Assagioli was training with Bleuler, Bleuler was increasingly critical of Freud. It is worthwhile quoting one of Bleuler's letters to Freud, as the letters indicate something of the schisms of the early psychoanalytic movement, and of issues about the nature of the knowledge that was being produced in psychoanalysis. Bleuler wrote to Freud on being pressed to rejoin the International Psychoanalytical Association,

> There is a difference between us which I decided I shall point out to you, although I am afraid it will make it emotionally more difficult for you to come to an agreement. For you evidently it became the aim and interest of your whole life to establish firmly your theory and to secure its acceptance. . . . For me, the theory is only one new truth among many truths. . . . For me, it is not a major issue, whether the validity of these views will be recognized a few years sooner or later. I am therefore less tempted than you to sacrifice my whole personality for the advancement of the cause.

Within a few months he was to add that while

> . . . . the principle of all or nothing is necessary for religious sects and for political parties . . . for science I consider it harmful. . . .

Two years later he was to be even more specific.

> Scientifically, I still do not understand why for you it is so important that the whole edifice (of psychoanalysis) should be accepted. But I remember I told you once that no matter how great your scientific accomplishments are, psychologically you impress me as an artist.[57:293-4]

This theme of the validity and basis of psychotherapeutic knowledge was thus an issue, and seen as one by some adherents, from the start. Freud, Jung and Assagioli all believed themselves to be scientists; and yet their theories, even without the added complication of spiritual knowledge, have also been called elaborate metaphors, drawing on a different kind of truth from the rational Western tradition. There is considerable evidence to say that Freud wished at all costs to protect his theory *in toto*; Jung was more speculative throughout; and Assagioli accepted that his whole theory was provisional. The nature of the knowledge at the base of all psychodynamic theories has throughout this century been contentious.

After his training, Assagioli practised as a psychiatrist in Italy, where he continued to develop his particular understanding of therapy. From 1912 to 1915 he published a series of articles in *Psiche*, a Florence-based journal which he founded and which stopped publication in 1915 because of the war. After the war he published most of his work in the journal *Ultra*. It is stated in the paper on the history of psychosynthesis that his articles tended to have a somewhat 'explosive' effect on the culture of the time.

During the First World War, Assagioli served as a doctor and non-combatant. He lived in Rome during the period between the two wars. He met and married his wife, Nella, a Roman Catholic and a Theosophist, in the 1920s. They were married for forty years and had one son, Ilario.

The consolidation of ideas up to the Second World War

Assagioli continued his own wide research throughout the period between the wars; he was in touch with, amongst others, Croce, Tagore and Inayat Khan, a Sufi leader. He was influenced by Steiner, Suzuki and Ouspensky. He grew particularly close to Alice Bailey, an English spiritual leader, and they formed part of a circle of friends committed to a study of the spiritual basis of life.

Throughout the 1920s and 1930s, Assagioli was meeting or in touch with such leading thinkers as Jung, Keyserling and Buber, to whom he felt particularly close. His concerns grew outward from individual therapy and education to concern with the social situation of the world. The forces of fascism and war were gathering, and from 1922 to 1943 Italy was ruled by Mussolini.

In 1926 the Istituto di Cultura e Terapia Psichica – the Institute of Psychic Culture and Therapy[27] – was founded by Assagioli in Rome. It was based on psychosynthesis for individual therapy and in relation to education, 'to foster new guidelines in the field of education'.

In 1927 the Institute published a book in English called *A New Method of Treatment – Psychosynthesis*. The historical article already quoted gives an outline of the aims, which are addressed 'in particular to all those who suffer in mind or body'. This includes those with physical ailments who can combine psychosynthesis with other treatment; people with neurotic or nervous symptoms; 'the shy, the sensitive, the emotionally polarised, the despondent and the discouraged who aspire to become calmer, stronger and more courageous'; those who wish to 'strengthen the memory' and also to exert more awareness and control over their own feelings; those disturbed by drug-taking or addictions, or those tempted to suicide; and 'those desirous of learning how better to educate their children or pupils'.

The motto for psychosynthesis at that time was 'Know thyself – possess thyself – transform thyself'. Annual courses of lectures were given at the Institute: the 1928 theme was 'The energies latent in us and their use in education and medicine', which was about the possible reconciliation of the conflicting elements in the personality, being then harnessed to a higher synthesis. The interests in the relationship of mind, body and spirit, and in education, have continued in the psychosynthesis centres up until the present.

The work continued in the 1930s. Assagioli published two major articles during these years which later became the first two chapters of his book *Psychosynthesis*. The *Hibbert Journal*, a prestigious quarterly review of religion, theology and philosophy, published in England and making available the work of many well-known writers in these fields, offered both these articles in English.

'Dynamic psychology and psychosynthesis' appeared in the edition of 1933–4.[4(4)] Assagioli describes something of the last forty to fifty years of the small but growing group of people investigating 'the phenomenon and mysteries of the human psyche'. He discusses Janet, Freud, Adler and Jung ('who even admits a transcendental self between the ordinary and subconscious selves') and their exploration of unconscious material. He is also interested in describing developments in psychobiology, in investigations of psychic phenomena, in William James and Evelyn Underhill and their publications on religious experience and mystic states, and in Keyserling with his synthesis of Eastern and Western thinking.

It is in this article that his 'egg-shaped diagram' of the human psyche was first published in English: this picture of the nature of the person is used up to the present time in psychosynthesis and is fully described and discussed in the next chapters. In the diagram he clearly links together work with the unconscious with a realization of the Self, a continuing dominant theme in psychosynthesis. He offers psychosynthesis as a framework for people who want to live their lives with freedom and control and 'who refuse to submit passively to the play of psychological forces which are going on within them'. He extends his analysis from the individual to the social:

Thus, inverting the analogy of a man being a combination of many elements which are more or less coordinated, each man may be considered as an element or cell of a human group; this group, in its turn, forms associations with vaster and more complex groups from the family group to town and district groups and to social classes; from workers' unions and employers' associations to the great national groups, and from these to the entire human family.

His emphasis throughout is on synthesis rather than analysis.

'Spiritual development and its attendant maladies' appeared in the *Hibbert Journal* in 1937–8.[4(24)] In this article Assagioli discusses the alternative to 'letting yourself live' by searching for a meaning and a spiritual awakening. He describes the traps (such as being led into psychic investigations) and the despair that can attend the searcher's journey: he describes the melancholy that can be experienced, 'the dark night of the soul', but also the potentiality of a vision of glory. Assagioli writes that there is a possibility of therapy at every stage of this journey. It is a journey that many people, trapped by an uninspiring model of normality in our present society, will not make; but the search for meaning in every human being is fundamental and can be activated – often by pain and loss – and aided. This article later became the chapter 'Self-realization and psychological disturbances' in the book *Psychosynthesis*.

At this time, of course, the fascist organizations were well in power in Italy and Germany. In 1936 the Istituto di Cultura e Terapia Psichica, also known as the Istituto di Psicosintesi, aroused the suspicions of the Italian government, 'whose growing hostility towards his humanitarian and international activities made his work increasingly difficult and eventually forced him to close the Istituto in 1938.'[20] Freud was forced to leave Vienna in 1938, and psychoanalytic organizations were closed down. Assagioli, also Jewish, now in his fifties and living under an increasingly repressive regime, had at times to take refuge from the Italian authorities. He was imprisoned in 1938 for a month because of his interest in peace and internationalism, and both he and his son Ilario had to hide for a period in the Italian countryside. His son died in the early 1950s from tuberculosis of the bones, probably contracted during this period.

From the end of the Second World War up to 1974

From 1946 psychosynthesis became more international, both in terms of conferences and of internationally published articles. From the selected list in *Psychosynthesis*, Assagioli published work in Italy, America and France during the 1950s. In 1958, the Psychosynthesis Research Foundation was opened in the USA at Valmy near Delaware, teaching and publishing psychosynthesis material until 1976. The Istituto di Psicosintesi resumed its work, this time based in Florence, with branches in Rome and Bologna. In 1959 and 1960, conferences were held in Paris and London, with Assagioli attending and speaking.

In 1960, the Greek Centre for Psychosynthesis was founded by Triant Triantafyllou, and publication of material began in Greece. In 1960 also, the first international week of psychosynthesis took place in Switzerland, with representatives from nine nations present. In 1961, the new Institute in Florence took an active part in the Fifth International Conference of Psychotherapy in Vienna, with Assagioli giving a paper on 'Psychosynthesis and existential psychotherapy' and chairing a symposium on psychoanalysis. The second international week of psychosynthesis was held later in 1961, followed by a third a year later.

Psychosynthesis seems to have been more classically psycho-dynamic in technique in the 1950s and 1960s than it is now. However, a considerable range of techniques were then being developed and were clearly of interest to other therapists during this period. In an incident in 1954 mentioned by Laura Huxley in her introduction to Piero Ferrucci's book *What We May Be*,[81] her patient freely entered into some mystical state. Laura Huxley knew that Assagioli was an expert in the relationship of the soul to the personality.

One indication of the difference in emphasis and range, comparing the 1920s psychosynthesis with that of the 1950s and 1960s, is the statement of aims of the old and new Italian Institutes. In 1961, the work was to be systematized into five different fields:

 (i) individual culture, constituting the necessary preparation for functioning in all other fields;
 (ii) the psychotherapeutic field: as a training for doctors and therapists;
 (iii) the educational field: for parents and teachers, concerned with better and more modern educational matters;
 (iv) the field of interpersonal relations: particularly relating to couples – marriage, parent and child, teacher and pupil, therapist and patient;
 (v) the field of group and social relations: concerned with polarities between individual and group, between different

social groups, 'having in view the psychosynthesis of the whole of humanity'.[27]

This could still be a description of the concerns of psychosynthesis. Work with the individual is the most thoroughly developed, but the wider concerns are clearly there. Assagioli was increasingly concerned with the state of the world as well as with the individual, with seeing the relationship between the two problems.

In his contact with the United States in the 1960s, Assagioli came to know of and sympathize with the work of such therapists and writers as Fromm, Rogers and Maslow. His work became more international in every sense. At the end of his life he really seems to have experienced an extended Indian summer, and an appreciation of his work greater than he had so far received. As his obituary states: 'it was only in the late sixties that, with the suddenness born out of great and massive need, his book and other writings were taken up by thousands.' The reason for this and for the sudden growth of psychosynthesis will be part of the discussion at a later point in this study.

In the mid-1960s, an international conference was held by the Institutes on the education and problems of young people and particularly very able children: Assagioli was particularly gifted in working with children. Centres in psychosynthesis were also opened at this time in India, Japan and Argentina.

Several attempts seem to have been made to set up an Institute in England, following conferences in London and Assagioli's frequent visits to England. In 1964–65, a centre called 'Psychosynthesis in Education, An Association for Personal and Spiritual Integration,' was established in London by Dr Bill Ford Robertson, but this seems to have been quite limited. Involved in this first attempt to establish psychosynthesis in England were Dr Martin Israel, Geoffrey Leytham who is a Trustee of the present Trust, Sir George Trevelyan, and Dr Cirinei from Italy. The present Trust for the Furtherance of Psychosynthesis and Education was a re-establishment in 1980 by Lady Diana Whitmore, who had trained with Dr Assagioli, of the original foundation. In 1974 a second organization, the present Institute of Psychosynthesis, was set up in London, at Mill Hill, and is now based in Central London.

Centres were formed in the 1960s and 1970s in Padua, Italy, and in many places in the USA – California, Vermont, Kentucky, Boston, etc. Other groups have formed in most European countries, notably Holland. Both Canada and Mexico have founded groups. Assagioli was against centralization and control, and it is now difficult to know even the number of psychosynthesis centres in the world and to keep track of their opening and occasional closure. Contacts seem to be informal, personal and between particular Institutes. It is a network rather than a formal international organization. It continues to develop and evolve, and both theory and practice are modified from Assagioli's original forms in the many centres in the world. In 1980 there was an International Conference in Italy, and in 1983 a further one in Toronto.

It is similarly difficult to sum up what psychosynthesis is or may mean. One author writes:

> Neither a doctrine, nor a 'school' of psychology, nor an exclusive method of self-culture, therapy and education, it could be defined principally as a general attitude, a tendency towards, and a series of activities aiming at, integration and synthesis in every field. No one can claim to be its exclusive representative; it cannot therefore be represented by any 'superorganization'. Its external organization can be regarded not as a solar system, but rather as a constellation.[27]

In the organization, as in the theory, Assagioli refused to tie himself down, or to impose a framework.

Thus psychosynthesis, after being conceived in the intellectually exciting and buoyant period at the beginning of the twentieth century, went through a long period of gestation in Italy, being always developed by Assagioli through practice with clients. He wrote many short articles through this period, and some were published, in Italy and elsewhere. It was not until the 1960s that the theory and practice became thoroughly international again, then spreading to many countries in a network of Institutes. It was only towards the end of his life that Assagioli was persuaded to publish his two books, in 1965 and in the year of his death, 1974.

He was always in touch with a wide range of fellow philosophers and therapists, and collected books on a most catholic range of interests in a library which is still open to the public in his house at Florence. Towards the end of his life he was visited by countless people of many nationalities as a man of wisdom, humour and originality: and he is written of with great love and respect.

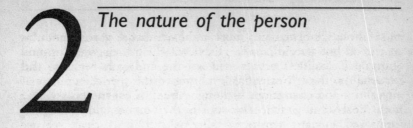

2 The nature of the person

Every social theory has an implicit view of human nature. When psychology began as a discipline at the end of the nineteenth century, it was based in an analytic, biological view of social science: interest was in the component parts of the person, and particularly in the biological 'realities' of brain, memory and so on, that could be empirically studied. When psychoanalysis emerged during the early part of the twentieth century, it produced the notion of 'personality', about the reality of someone's presence in the world. As the century has progressed, 'personality' as a notion has changed and modified with every new school. Some psychologies and psychotherapies have drawn maps of the nature of the person, a diagrammatic and necessarily static notion of a complex living reality: all have proposed conceptual statements to define what a person is.[88]

In psychosynthesis, the person is a soul and has a personality. Each personality, as in all other theories, is that complex combination of drives, defences, roles, learned adaptations and consciousness, that lives in the world and is a unique being; in some quite remarkable way each person is unlike any other being that exists, qualitatively different — and yet is subject to universal laws, social and biological causes, and learned behaviour that is common to all, and which makes for patterns of action, describable and analysable illnesses, cultures and similarities of behaviour across cultures that are discernibly 'human'.

Most psychologies and psychotherapies are interested just in the personality. It is only in recent years that a variety known as 'transpersonal psychotherapy' has emerged, which combines, or perhaps reintegrates, psychology and the personality, with theology and the soul — two disciplines and two concepts that have been firmly separated in our materialistic Western world.

In psychosynthesis I say that the person *has* a personality and *is* a soul, because that relationship is basic to the map of the person that Assagioli first published in the 1930s and used for the rest of his life. However, personalities in the world are obvious to us all: souls are only present for those with eyes to see. Assagioli's view of synthesis is of becoming more and more aware of soul, not only in oneself but also in others. His view, which is the view of most spiritual disciplines, is that soul is basic and enduring, and that personality, though essential for being in the world, is relatively superficial and changeable – though often, of course, only with a good deal of difficulty. The soul is the context, the home, the 'unmoved mover': the personality is full of content, learned responses, and is dynamic. It is easy to recognize and relate to the personality, both in oneself and in others: the soul may in many people never be recognized in any explicit way. This applies not only to the soul of the individual person, but the soul of all humanity – 'the still, sad music of humanity', as Wordsworth wrote.

The classic psychosynthesis 'egg-shaped diagram' (Figure 2.1) was first published in English translation in the *Hibbert Journal* in 1933–4.[4(4)] Assagioli describes the drawing as

> a conception of the constitution of the human being in his
> living concrete reality. . . . It is, of course, a crude and
> elementary picture that can give only a structural, static, almost
> 'anatomical' representation of our inner constitution, while it
> leaves out its dynamic aspect, which is the most important and
> essential one . . . it is important not to lose sight of the main
> lines and of the fundamental differences; otherwise the
> multiplicity of details is liable to obscure the picture as a whole
> and to prevent our realizing the respective significance,
> purpose, and value of its different parts.[1:16]

In other words, like any good map, the diagram is presented as a tool to the reader, an over-simplifier of complex reality, and good enough until something better emerges. This follows the earlier twentieth century models of the person, which also inevitably used simplifications. It is still used as a basic conceptual tool in psychosynthesis training. Piero Ferrucci describes the diagram as representing 'our total psyche'.[81:43]

In this rather complicated looking picture, there are three main parts: consciousness, which is our everyday reality, and which includes 'the field of consciousness'; unconsciousness, which is spatially speaking the greater area in most people – consciousness may be to unconsciousness the tip of the iceberg; and awareness and soul – the 'I' and the Higher Self.

Assagioli's assumption is that most people live within a relatively small field of *consciousness* – the less aware a person is, the smaller this field will be. He depicts the *unconscious* as being

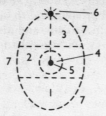

1 The Lower Unconscious
2 The Middle Unconscious
3 The Higher Unconscious or
  Superconscious
4 The Field of Consciousness
5 The Conscious Self or "I"
6 The Higher Self (or Soul)
7 The Collective Unconscious

Figure 2.1 A map of the person[1:17]

divided and hierarchical – the lower unconscious is the past, past patterns, the basic drives, and past adaptations, the higher unconscious or superconscious is potential, and the collective unconscious the history of the human race that we carry with us unconsciously, as well as consciously through historical knowledge. *The 'I'* is our personal centre of awareness, a centre which many people are hardly aware of but which is highly developed through self-awareness and self-knowledge: and *the Higher Self* is the potential which is aligned with the 'I' and of which the 'I' is a pale reflection. The conscious personality is only the field of consciousness, and it is this area that is generally dealt with by conventional psychology. Any psychology that draws on an assumption of the existence of unconsciousness would be concerned with sections 1, 2, and perhaps 7 in Figure 2.1. But it is really only transpersonal psychologies that are concerned with the superconscious and the Higher Self. The 'I' is variously dealt with in different psychological maps of the person in the different schools of psychotherapy.

In the model there is a dotted line between all the aspects of the person. This is to indicate that there is movement between them, that they can affect one another. And of course the different proportions change within a lifetime, particularly in a person concerned with spiritual growth and awareness.

The field of consciousness (4 in Figure 2.1)

This is our living, everyday reality, the part 'of which we are directly aware: the incessant flow of sensations, images, thoughts, feelings, desires, and impulses, which we can observe, analyse, and judge'.[1:18] Assagioli holds that this can be the total of which an unreflective person is aware. He writes:

the 'man in the street' and even many well-educated people do not take the trouble to observe themselves and to discriminate; they drift on the surface of the 'mindstream' and identify themselves with its successive waves, with the changing contents of their consciousness.[1:18]

Consciousness is often unreflective, determined by the many personal and social forces which have formed us.

He points out that we, in this unaware state, are largely at the mercy of these forces. 'We must realize that we are all the time possessed, even obsessed, by all the conditioning of our background and current life.'[4(27)] We seem in many ways to be almost entirely the product of our genetics, our personal environment and the society in which we live. We seem more like the creatures of our environment than the creators of it, in the grip of forces much stronger than ourselves and which we do not understand, whether these forces be biological, psychological or social. Indeed, it is often difficult for an ordinary person to see where his or her sense of freedom could originate: many people have, in fact, little or no sense of freedom in their lives.

This part of the personality could easily, without reflection, be regarded as the whole, because it is most accessible to us. But the development of depth psychology in this century has made it clearer and clearer that consciousness is only a small part of the whole. There has been an acknowledgment throughout human history that awareness beyond the conscious is possible for the individual human being, through dreams, religious experience and creativity of every kind; this is where the field of consciousness relates to unconscious material. Also it is clear that people can change and grow with awareness; this is where the field of consciousness becomes more attuned to and guided by the 'I'. It is part of psychosynthesis theory that the field of consciousness, through processes of reflection, can change and grow, and the whole of consciousness can become imbued with a different quality – no longer asleep and no longer merely determined by conditioning.

The middle unconscious (2 in Figure 2.1)

This is the most immediate layer of unconscious material and is sometimes called the preconscious. It is, in Freud's view, the anteroom of consciousness. Assagioli described it as being

formed of psychological elements similar to those of our

waking consciousness and easily accessible to it. In this inner region our various experiences are assimilated. our ordinary mental and imaginative activities are elaborated and developed in a sort of psychological gestation before their birth into the light of consciousness.[4(27)]

It is in this area that memories that are easily brought to mind are stored, that our everyday lives are routinely. processed. It is the first step into that other world beyond the mundane and the everyday.

The relationship between the field of consciousness and this first area of unconsciousness is well described by David Stafford-Clark in writing about Freud: 'consciousness is the spotlight which, sweeping the arena, lights up just that area on which it falls. Everything outside its illumination, but within its range, is preconsciousness.'[217:115] The boundary between the ordinary everyday world and this region is thin and flexible.

The lower unconscious (1 in Figure 2.1)

In the eighteenth and nineteenth centuries, before Freud, and with the values of the Enlightenment and the idea of progress, it was assumed that the human being was becoming more and more rational, and fully civilized. Dark forces were acknowledged, of course, but it was generally assumed that with the progress of science and rationality, the fully reasonable person would appear – indeed was already there in civilized society.

It was this assumption that Freud questioned, with his systematic ability to discern and get in touch with the unconscious processes in people. He saw the significance of dreams as a real communication of the unconscious to the conscious; slips of the tongue, mistakes, and illnesses manifested in ordinary living began to be acknowledged as effects of processes going on beyond our consciousness. Many hitherto unexplained phenomena came to be seen as part of the war between the strong libidinal sexual forces of the id (the drives) and the superego (the conscience). Most of Freud's work, and most of psychoanalysis, is concerned with what Assagioli came to define as the lower unconscious.

The lower unconscious is connected in all sorts of ways to childhood. In childhood all unconscious is one. As Sue Patman writes:

In the beginning, at our birth, the unconscious is both the lower and the higher unconscious. There is no division and no consciousness with which to make a division or a separation between them. As consciousness forms, however, and the differentiation is made between conscious and unconscious, so time becomes a reality and with the experience of time comes the division between the lower unconscious and the superconscious, past and future, what is and what was and what could be. What is, is consciousness; what was, is the lower unconscious; what could be, is the superconscious. The aim of synthesis is to reduce this trinity back to a fully conscious oneness.

She describes how the different parts separate through the long years of childhood in order for the person to develop his or her own personality and individuality – and separateness and isolation. She goes on:

We enter into the lower unconscious *via* childhood experiences because that is where we come from. The lower unconscious *is not our childhood*, but our childhood is the path we took from our unconscious state to our conscious state. Memories of childhood are therefore a very powerful tool we can use to return to the unconscious with our consciousness and carry our healing.[21]

It is particularly interesting to link awareness of time – indeed the very concept of time – with the division into the conscious or unconscious experience. It is these deep dark regions, usually envisaged as a sea or a cave, in which our roots seem to lie – and also from which our problems both personally and as a species seem to spring. But it is also from here that our life force springs.

Assagioli took a hierarchical view of the person and reckoned this element of the personality to be definitely 'lower'. He writes that the lower unconscious contains

the elementary psychological activities which direct the life of the body; the intelligent co-ordination of bodily functions; the fundamental drives and primitive urges; many complexes, charged with intense emotion; dreams and imaginations of an inferior kind; lower, uncontrolled parapsychological processes; various pathological manifestations such as phobias, obsessions, compulsive urges and paranoid delusions.[1:17]

Assagioli would no doubt have agreed with the description of the Freudian 'unconscious' (the 'lower unconscious' of psychosynthesis) as the cellar of the house of the personality: in other words, it is only the foundation of the whole person, and there are still the main rooms to be explored, as well as the attic with the window open to the sky. Maslow wrote in 1968, 'it is as if Freud supplied to us the sick half of psychology and we must now fill it out with the healthy half.'[163:7] In older spiritual philosophies this part of the person was seen as primeval, as 'the beast', from which strength but also evil sprang: both exist together and are intertwined.

The higher unconscious or superconscious (3 in Figure 2.1)

This is potential, an area to which many people only have occasional access. It is glimpses of 'what we might be' if we lived more from the soul and less from the personality. It is the window into the sky. Assagioli writes that it is

> from this region we receive our higher intuitions and inspirations – artistic, philosophical or scientific, ethical 'imperatives' and urges to humanitarian and heroic action. It is the source of the higher feelings, such as altruistic love; of genius and of the states of contemplation, illumination, and ecstacy. In this realm are latent the higher psychic functions and spiritual energies.[1:17-18]

In Assagioli's picture, the superconscious is a reflection from the Higher Self of all goodness, to which we can have greater and greater access with awareness. This picture assumes that human nature is basically good, which is a view diametrically opposed to the Freudian assumption, and different from the Jungian, in which the forces of good and evil are rather evenly balanced. In Assagioli's model, forces from the superconscious are available to us all our lives, but they often become distorted: for instance, sensitivity in early childhood can easily become transmuted into fear – many people carry with them a 'frightened child' for much of their lives: or a person can have a vision of greatness – it is certainly arguable that Hitler did – but it can become mixed with forces of hate and cruelty. Assagioli's view is that at the roots of all actions are good intentions: even within the worst manifestations of the human spirit, there is a superconscious force that has become distorted. Erich Fromm wrote a book on *The Anatomy of Human Destructiveness*, in which he maintained that destruction is basically 'unlived life', good instincts that have not been able to be lived in a straightforward way, and have turned sour. It is life, he maintains, that is not lived from the aware centre, the 'I', but from a place where actions emanate from unconsciousness. This is near to the fable of the angel who falls from heaven and becomes a devil.[94]

In Assagioli's view, we may become more and more aware of the superconscious, and more attuned to the forces of love, beauty, tenderness, power and true knowledge that are always present if we can discern them. As awareness of the 'I' and the Higher Self grows, the field of consciousness can enlarge to become aware of more superconscious material. But the personality has to be strong enough to cope with the power of superconscious material – one definition of madness offered in the psychosynthesis training might be of a person who has glimpses of the higher unconscious but whose personality cannot stand this experience. Knowledge and awareness of the soul can only be coped with by a strong and growing personality, which has come well enough to terms with the forces of the lower unconscious and is well centred in the strength of the 'I'.

Abraham Maslow called people in touch with superconscious material 'transcending self-actualizers'. He regarded these as people who not only had come to terms with living successfully in the world, but those who were spiritually aware and who grew in the spirit. Mystics and saints clearly fall within this category: but so do many millions of people who are aware, as the Quakers say, of 'the God within', in contact with the power and soul within themselves. Such people are more likely to follow their own inner light than to believe in outside rules and dogmas, though they may – or may not – mainly conform with them.

Superconscious material emanates from the Higher Self in Figure 2.1: it is the dynamic force, potentially in touch with all areas of the psyche. The Higher Self, like the 'I', is a still centre, the source of the power.

The conscious self, or 'I' (5 in Figure 2.1)

This is the centre of pure self-awareness, in the midst of our consciousness. The self, the 'I', is the inner still point that we experience as truly ourselves. An article in *Synthesis*, vol. 1, no. 2, states that we usually experience ourselves as a mixture between the field of consciousness and the 'I', in varying proportions. The 'I' is the organizing principle of the 'myriad contents' of the field of consciousness.[23a:94]

Most meditative techniques are an attempt to get in touch with the 'I' and, through the 'I', the Higher Self. The 'I' is the link between the field of consciousness and the potential, the personal potential and the larger potential of the collective unconsciousness. It is where we are most ourselves. We can be at rest in the 'I', like the eye of a storm. The world whirls all around, in the field of consciousness. The 'I' is both an observer and a constant centre of all the activity. Although our consciousness may change, the 'I' does not.

One assumption of psychosynthesis seems to be that many people are not aware of their 'I' in this sense as distinct from the rest of their personality. Assagioli believed that the possibility of the freedom discussed earlier is essentially related to the person's awareness of a sense of a separate and independent 'I'. It is only through this centre, dis-identifying from many of the controlling forces, that the person achieves any freedom. 'We are dominated by everything with which we become identified. We can master, direct and utilize everything from which we can dis-identify ourselves.'[23a:101]

Human beings throughout history have had different views of the significance of human consciousness and the sense of 'I'. Dostoevsky, in *Letters from the Underworld*, a study of a man who was afraid to live out and who despised the idea of fully living, wrote, 'though I stated ... that consciousness, in my opinion, is the greatest misfortune for man, yet I know man loves it and would not give it up for any other satisfaction.'[65:41] It is the blessing and the curse of individualism, that characteristic creation of Western society; the Western 'I' seems to have a different quality from the Eastern 'I'. The Western person has seen his/her individuality as isolated: in most mystical traditions the 'I' is seen as in touch with the whole. The development of consciousness, personally and collectively, is a key dynamic in psychosynthesis, and in the theories that lie behind it.

The 'I', as well as being the centre, the true experiencer, can also be seen as the observer. The journal *Synthesis* describes it as the following experience: 'it's like looking at something in the world, but calmly, serenely, from the consciousness that is supremely yours.'[23a:96] The experience is both familiar and simple, but it is also disciplined. 'Being able to take the attitude of the observer at will increases one's ability to more fully experience inner and outer events'[23a:100] and to become unafraid of living. In contrast to Dostoevsky's character, the free person can move around in his or her personality, instead of being locked into it, and in that way can be in touch with unlimited potential. This seems to be the essence of freedom.

The Higher Self (6 in Figure 2.1)

In the diagram, the Higher Self is linked directly to the 'I', and is on the edge of the superconscious and the collective unconscious.

Assagioli writes that the existence of a Higher Self has been experienced in mystic states throughout human history:

> There have been many individuals who have achieved, more or less temporarily, a conscious realization of the Self that for them has the same degree of certainty as is experienced by an explorer who has entered a previously unknown region. . . . This Self is above, and unaffected by, the flow of the mind-stream or by bodily conditions; and the personal conscious self should be considered merely as its reflection, its 'projection' in the field of the personality.[1:19]

The Higher Self is in a way the *context* of the personality.

The relationship of the Self to the 'I' seems best presented by the diagram in Figure 2.2.

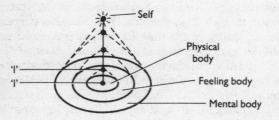

Figure 2.2 Higher Self and personality

In Figure 2.2, the 'I' is seen as the centre of body, mind and feelings, which can be assumed to make up the field of consciousness. The 'I' can be at different points in its relation to the Self. Assagioli, in a discussion meeting, said that the self at the personality level

> is a reflection of the Higher Self or the Transpersonal Self, and it reflects, however palely, the same qualities as its source. If you look at the reflection of the sun on a mirror, or on water, you see the light and quality of the sun, infinitesimal, but still the quality of the sun. So that explains why even at the personality's level the self is stable, sure and indestructible.[4(27)]

He explains that we do not usually see the sun, we only see the light from it. He sees the Self as a source of light and also of love. 'Mystical love . . . is vertical; it is the attraction or pull from above and the aspiration from below (all relative terms) which bring about a gradual approach and final unification.'[4(23)]

But there is a mystery in this relationship, in that the 'I' and the Self are seen as nearer or further away from each other, one being a pale reflection of the other, and yet they are at the same time one:

> The fact that we have spoken of the ordinary self and the profounder Self, must not be taken to mean that there are two separate and independent 'I's, two beings in us. The Self in reality is one. What we call the ordinary self is that small part of the deeper Self that the waking consciousness is able to assimilate in a given moment. It is therefore something contingent and changing, a 'variable quality'. It is a reflection of what can become ever more clear and vivid; and it can perhaps someday succeed in uniting itself with its source.[4(22)]

Assagioli presents the Higher Self also as a spectator, 'the spectator of the human tragi-comedy'.[4(26)] He also perceives the Self to be the still centre of the superconscious, just as the personal self or 'I' is the centre of 'the elements and functions of the personality'.[4(25)] Maslow gives a gloss to these descriptions in writing that the people he calls the transcenders, those, in other words, more in touch with their Selves:

> may be more prone to a kind of cosmic sadness . . . over the stupidity of people, their self-defeat, their blindness, their cruelty to each other, their short-sightedness. Perhaps this comes from the contrast between what actually is and the ideal world the transcenders can see so easily and so vividly, and which is in principle so easily attainable.[162:9]

It may be objected that this model of the person, particularly in relation to the transpersonal areas, is complete speculation. The Higher Self cannot be subjected to empirical tests in the same way that the memory can – the scientist may even doubt its existence. Assagioli, however, in presenting this model, regarded it as scientifically true, subject of course to future modification, but true according to his own view of the scientific validity of experience. He was clear that the Higher Self exists, because 'it is proven by direct experience; it is one of those primary experiences which are evidences of themselves ... and therefore have full scientific value, in the broader sense'. He added that 'one has to create the conditions for having the experience and scientists up to now have not taken the trouble to do that'.[4(27)]

The collective unconscious (7 in Figure 2.1)

Both Assagioli and Jung maintain that we carry with us not only personal unconscious material, but also, as a kind of spiritual DNA, the unconsciousness of the human race. This idea has recently been extended by Rupert Sheldrake's model of 'morpho-genetic fields'. Both these models depict the individual human being as a kind of receiver, almost like a television set, that is potentially tuned in to vast historical and geographical areas of human experience – in fact, all the experience that has ever been or is now. In this vast mass, there are archetypes, forms relevant to the human condition that have appeared in every race and time: the Mother or Father archetype, for instance, the image of the mother or father figure that seems to be carried around by every person regardless of his or her actual experience. We convey this largely unconscious human knowledge by myths and fairy-stories, by religious or sacred symbols, by depictions of forms of Good and Evil.

In this century we carry around with us unconsciously as well as consciously a great deal of knowledge, now made available to us in a way never possible before in human history, by communication through cheap printing, by radio and television, and by travel. We have to bear the massive collective guilt of two world wars, and the pain of the suffering in the world daily relayed to us.

Assagioli was anxious to convey in the diagram that the collective is automatically part of our concern and selves, whether we deny it or not. It is the collective in which we must be concerned in making the unconscious conscious, as well as the personal. And indeed the egg-shaped diagram can also be a picture of the earth as well as of the person, with the 'I' being the sense of collective awareness.

The collective unconscious is also what we carry from our own families and immediate surroundings, our countries and races. In Jung's view, it is the task of the growingly aware 'I' to face and come to terms with not only the personal unconscious, but also those collective characteristics and circumstances to which the person as a child was born: 'no matter how much parents and grandparents may have sinned against the child, the man who is really adult will accept these sins as his own condition that has to be reckoned with.'[132:117]

Thus, the nature of the person in psychosynthesis, as in other depth psychologies, assumes that the conscious is contained within the unconscious, which is both personal and collective. Self-knowledge is about being in touch with the 'I', within the context of the Higher Self, the soul. As a person takes the choice to become more and more aware, through life, he or she lives nearer to the soul, which is part of the soul of the world: but this is personal choice: probably the minority of people make that choice. A transpersonal psychotherapy offers the framework and the techniques for following a spiritual path, where the search for self-knowledge and the search for meaning are the same thing.

3 Subpersonalities and the possibility of synthesis

So far, in the description of the personality and its relation to the Self, there has seemed to be a coherence and a unity in the structure of the person. But most of us do not experience our lives like that. Rather, human beings are dynamic creatures, full of contradictions, experiencing trouble, conflict and fear as well as joy, boredom and satisfaction. This we see as our own experience and the experience of others. The traumas within the personality are clearly seen in the overwhelming emotions of the small child or in the struggles for identity of the adolescent. But the conflicts are merely particularly open to the outside observer in those age groups. Life constantly changes and brings new challenge; we often feel at the mercy of forces we only dimly perceive, and are often swayed by passions we did not know we possessed.

Assagioli used from the beginning a construct which he acknowledges as originating for him from William James, but which was an idea current from the earlier part of the nineteenth century — that of subpersonalities. This was devised as a framework to understand better these warring and constricting forces within the personality of the human being. It is the view that 'each of us is a crowd': we all contain many different selves, which are formed round the drives that are inborn and potentially creative. In the psychosynthesis view, each subpersonality, which consists of the same structure as the egg-shaped diagram in miniature, springs from a transpersonal quality. But that quality in the course of a life, particularly in the relative helplessness of childhood, may easily become distorted: for instance, sensitivity in a less than caring environment may develop into fear, and leave the person with an internal 'frightened child' who is likely to emerge at any time, long after the original vulnerability has gone. The sensitivity will have been defended by withdrawal and fear: the defence may stay for a lifetime, and then, being inappropriate, be a constant handicap in adult life.

The development of defence mechanisms was one of Freud's major interests, and Freudian theories of defence are based on concepts of the distortion of 'drives' or 'instincts', which were held to be the original life forces. Whether it is within the transpersonal framework, where the qualities of creativity are from the superconscious, or from the Freudian, where the drives are nearer his view of the 'id', these life forces are conceived as forces for creativity and fulfilment, forcing people to grow. They are always greatly modified by environment and indeed their function is a dialectical one: it is always an interaction of personal inborn qualities and the family and social environment which creates the characteristics of the personality, in the psychosynthetic view. But until the individual comes to know him- or herself, to be in touch with his or her own 'I', much of this process must be unconscious.

The cultural environment has a profound effect on the development of subpersonalities. For instance, gender conditioning is strong in most societies, so in addition to biological differences there are verbal and non-verbal messages about the proper behaviour of girls and boys. In fact, human beings learn to become the appropriate kind of baby for that society by the handling of the parents, although of course the individual will always react in an individual way to the many messages he or she is receiving.[33] From the beginning a child may be seen as 'slow' or 'intelligent' or 'good', and this message will be conveyed every time that child is handled or related to. Most of this learning is unconscious, and much is offered by the parents, so that everyone learns at this profound level roles, attitudes, conceptions of self and one's relation to the outside world which are deeply imprinted. But the baby and child in this is not a passive object, and lessons may be learned in a very different way from those intended – a deeply rebellious spirit is quite as likely to emerge from a controlling childhood as is a conforming spirit.

So from the beginning of our lives we develop many aspects, and some of these will be more conscious than others. Some subpersonalities will be very useful – being a 'quick learner' or having an easy sociability; other parts will be less conscious – a deeply hidden fear of sexual experience for instance – or distinctly difficult to handle – an automatic resentment of authority of *any* kind would be an example. But lives change, and once useful attributes become redundant, the unconscious may become more conscious and the awkward characteristics within oneself may become the most valuable. The concept of subpersonalities is essentially a dynamic one, assuming that new attributes emerge in us all our lives, if we allow them to, and that people can change and go on changing until the moment they die.

The concept of subpersonalities is to do with the struggle of good and evil, of constructive tendencies and those which are destructive, of multiplicity and unity, being driven and having control from a conscious centre, being more or less aware of the forces that move people. William James in his *The Varieties of Religious Experience*, based on lectures given in 1901–2, was concerned – as were all psychologists around the turn of the century – with the difference between 'healthy' and 'sick' ways of living. He devoted one of his lectures to 'the religion of healthy-mindedness', where he postulated the belief that in some people there was a unity, emanating from a centre that is naturally happy and optimistic and always striving towards growth, 'whose soul is of this sky-blue tint, whose affinities are rather with flowers and birds and all enchanting innocencies than with dark human passions, who can think no ill of man or God'.[124:94] This was the person in touch with the immanent spirituality inside herself or himself, who is naturally centred, and whose subpersonalities are also relatively known and understood. He contrasts this with a lecture on 'the sick soul' and another on 'the divided self'. He writes:

> The sanguine and the healthy-minded live habitually on the sunny side of the misery line, the depressed and the melancholy live beyond it, in darkness and apprehension. There are men who seem to have started life with a bottle or two of champagne inscribed to their credit; whilst others seem to have been born close to the pain-threshold, which the slightest irritants fatally send them over.[124:144]

These are the people who relate more to the transcendent view of spirituality, to a split, a duality, between spirit and matter, where the conscious self and the shadow are far apart, and the subpersonalities may be seen as conflicts and impediments, with many being only vaguely known.

James, in examining these states, puts forward the nineteenth century view of heterogeneous personalities, which in that pre-Freudian time had 'been explained as the results of inheritance – the traits of character of incompatible and antagonistic ancestors [who] are supposed to be preserved alongside each other'.[124:175] But he was writing at the time that Freudian work was just appearing, and James used this in giving an early description of what is still the basis of subpersonality work in psychosynthesis:

> Now in all of us, however constituted, but to a degree the greater in proportion as we are intense and sensitive and subject to diversified temptations, and to the greatest possible

degree if we are decidedly psychopathic, does the normal evolution of character chiefly consist in straightening out and unifying the inner self. The higher and lower feelings, the useful and the erring impulses, begin by being a comparative chaos within us — they must end by forming a stable system of functions in right subordination. Unhappiness is apt to characterize the period of order-making and struggle . . . wrong living, impotent aspirations; 'what I would do, that I do not; but what I hate, that I do', as Saint Paul says; self-loathing, self-despair; an unintelligible and intolerable burden to which one is mysteriously the heir.[124:175-6]

In working with subpersonalities we are indeed working with unconscious forces that trouble people, often to do with the profound things learned in childhood, always with 'unfinished business' with parents and other significant figures of that time. Depression may present itself as a melancholy character, the 'oughts' people have learned will be seen as a 'critic' often stern and judging, fear will be perceived in various childhood shapes. Often people carry many repressed and unacknowledged characteristics that may emerge in illnesses or other physical manifestations. Natural aggression may have been suppressed and come through in a variety of ways, as repression of oneself or others, as insensitivity, or as timorousness. And it is part of the assumptions of psychosynthesis that each characteristic somewhere has its opposite, that we all carry all the aspects of the human inheritance in some shape, though this shape may be hidden and denied.

The image often used in psychosynthesis is that of an orchestra. The subpersonalities are all the instruments, the potential of music. But they may be playing chaotically. Some sections may be completely out of tune. Some may not be prepared to play at all. It is only as we become aware of the centrality of the conductor, the 'I', that we can begin to see the parts as a coherent whole and to choose the music that seems the right score. And as we recognize and bring in more instruments to assist the ones presently carrying the whole burden, then we can pay attention to those that need that attention, that have been neglected; and, as we get to know what we have, we may decide to change the tune and play a different kind of music, constantly modifying it throughout our lives.

Working with the unconscious is always about more awareness, of bringing the unconscious that troubles us, that loads our life with weight and rubbish, into awareness. This question of 'knowing what we do', knowing the implications and significance of what we do and are, is, Assagioli and Jung believed, part of the human task. The state of ourselves and the world as it is presently run is a result of not consciously knowing what we are doing from an aware centre. So long as we are driven by unconscious forces, or deny large parts of ourselves, that unlived life and ignorance will plague us individually and collectively. The concept of subpersonality is a means of approaching these hidden and often seemingly forbidden areas.

Stephen Kull wrote an unpublished paper in 1972 called 'Evolution and Personality', in which he discusses the development of subpersonalities. He indicates the usual picture of subpersonalities in an ordinary person as shown in Figure 2.3:

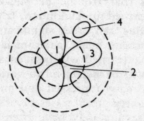

Figure 2.3   Central and peripheral subpersonalities and their relationship to the 'I'

In Figure 2.3, 1 is equal to the 'I', the centre. 2 is the core personality, the immediate field of consciousness, whose extent is related to the awareness of the person. The subpersonalities named as 3 are central to the person, recognized and related to by her or him, and with whom the person easily identifies. Some of these exist almost entirely in the conscious, but may have roots in less accessible parts of the personality. For instance, a woman with children may be very conscious of and identified with her role as a mother, which is a significant subpersonality – sometimes so much so that it might at times feel like her 'I'. Such a significant subpersonality may suppress other parts of herself that remain latent. She may have little chance to express her more light-hearted and frivolous nature or her professionalism.

The subpersonalities not in touch with the centre, marked 4, may be hardly known and not identified with the person's view of self. Some of these peripheral and repressed parts may be in direct opposition to the more central, more conscious parts. These hidden parts may be particularly personal and/or represent hidden aspects of the culture – the sexuality of a respectable Victorian man, or more particularly woman, for instance. Piero Ferrucci calls these more peripheral subpersonalities 'exiled gods – caricatures, degraded specimens of the original, luminous archetypes'.[81:55]

Work on unconscious material this century has induced many writers to echo the conviction of mystics in the past that the inner world of the person is as extensive, potentially, as the external world of the universe. Hermann Keyserling, the twentieth century philosopher whose work Assagioli greatly respected, puts this conviction in a short passage that Assagioli quotes:

> Each fundamental personality tendency is actually an autonomous entity, and their combination, conditions and transmutations produce . . . an inner fauna, an animal kingdom the richness of which is comparable to the external one. It can truly be said that in each of us can be found, developed and active in various proportions, all instincts, all passions, all vices and virtues, all tendencies and aspirations, all faculties and endowments of mankind.[23a]

This is a vital point in any consideration of the relationship of the self to society as it is increasingly clear that the one lives out the other: the clear distinction between a person's inner life and external environment can no longer be routinely maintained. And looking at the make-up of a person in this way, it is increasingly clear how much people project on to the external world, particularly material that they repress in themselves. This does not mean that people do not choose their path, consciously or unconsciously, or that people are not different from each other: but the concept of subpersonalities, like the rest of psycho-synthesis, indicates how much common material we have, personally and collectively, however we each choose to organize it.

A framework for the classification of subpersonalities

As subpersonalities spring from the need of the person to grow, some will clearly represent the forces of change. But as change occurs, people may become nervous of 'losing themselves' and their sense of who they are, so other subpersonalities may strive to maintain the status quo, the sense of order and identity. This same tension occurs in every system and is part of systems theory. Every unity, whether it is an individual, a biological organ in the individual, a society, or a universe, is always facing the same tensions of growth and change on the one hand, and order and maintenance on the other.

On another scale, subpersonalities seem to fall on another dimension, that of love and will: the urge to will or power is the urge to control the environment and to modify it; the need to love is related to the need for acceptance and benign relationships. So the simple graph is as shown in Figure 2.4. On this graph is indicated the sort of subpersonality that can fall in each category.

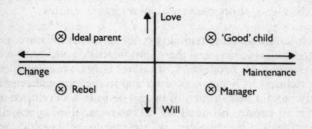

Figure 2.4

In this framework, as in the rest of the theory about subpersonalities, the assumption is that the pattern could either serve, or control, the 'I'. The function of the *change* agents is to enable the person to live his or her life flexibly, being able to let go, not over-identifying with the past, having energy, vitality and enthusiasm. On the other hand, the forces towards change could get distorted, so that change is being forced for its own sake, the person is never able to stay quiet and still, limits are feared and forced, egoism takes over without thought for the people or natural things around. Life can begin to be a series of tasks, and the person feels driven and never tranquil.

So the need for *maintenance* can also be seen. In maintaining a position one can structure, stabilize, form. There is a sense of 'being' rather than 'doing', a connectedness with the earth and with a sense of purpose and timelessness. Patience, rhythm and containment are all positive forces that accompany maintenance. At its best, there is stillness, serenity, contentment, regeneration and rest. However, the distortions of maintenance are cowardliness, a refusal to move whatever the circumstances; closed-mindedness, inertia and an over-identification with the status quo, rigidity and dependence on structure.

So we live all the time in the tension of change and maintenance

– the fear of being bored versus the fear of being exposed, put in the negative way, or, the possibility of living fully and flexibly from a still centre, the positive. Subpersonalities abound on both sides of the line.

Equally, we live all the time balanced between love and will. Assagioli asserts that 'love and will are generally present in individuals in inverse proportion',[2:95] though he does not give any evidence for such a statement. But it is clear that many subpersonalities are short on love, while others lack any willpower. The teaching within psychosynthesis is that both love and will are needed to live out to the full.

Assagioli spent the whole of his final book writing about *the will*, which is the force for action in the world, and which has been missed out of much of the thinking in humanistic psychology and in the growth movements. He gives seven qualities of the will in his book: energy, mastery, concentration, determination, persistence, initiative and organization: all good, old-fashioned virtues. He agrees with Toynbee that there is in the modern world a 'wide gulf between man's external and inner powers', between the West's considerable technological powers and the quality of life for most people, and he recommends 'the simplification of his outer life, and the development of his inner powers'.[2:4]

Psychosynthesis is unusual among the therapeutic systems in looking constantly for an application of learning back into the world, and of course the will is vital to taking action in the world. Assagioli puts emphasis on using a conscious will in all situations:

> All with whom we are associated can become our co-operators (without their knowing it!). For instance, a domineering superior or an exacting partner becomes, as it were, the mental parallel bars on which our will – the will to right human relations – can develop its force and proficiency. . . . So the Buddhist saying goes: 'An enemy is as useful as a Buddha'.[2:444–5]

He advocates the skilful will – that is the will that takes into account psychological understanding, understanding of how the social world works, so that the use of the will can be economic and effective. This also goes along with the recognition that the transpersonal will and the universal will, both levels of the will that we may experience, do not have the characteristic of striving. The true use of will is in a sense letting go and yet being fully present. It is cooperating with the benign forces of the world, which is where love and will are fully consistent and almost one. So once again the subpersonalities in the 'will' section of the graph can be a problem — figures representing greed and envy; or they can be using will with the full recognition of love. Both a Christ and a Hitler are men fully in touch with the strong use of the will, but in a Hitler the shadow dominates the transpersonal.

Love is the fourth quality in the graph. Assagioli saw love, like will, as being truly present only when it takes understanding and insight into account. It is not only sympathy, the pleasure in another person's existence, the affirmation of oneself and others, but the true quality of love implies also understanding and empathy:

> There are fathers and mothers who love dearly their sons and daughters and make ungrudgingly great sacrifices for them, yet fail to understand what is going on in their children's minds and hearts, what are their true and vital needs. . . . This blind love has such bad and sometimes terrible consequences that their unconscious originators would be appalled if they realized them. I mean maimed lives, cramped and spoiled characters. . . . We must realize that blind love, however well-meaning and self-sacrificing, does not prevent mistakes or harmfulness. We must realize that love, in order to truly fulfil its mission of being helpful and satisfying to the beloved, must be allied to insight; even more, permeated and blended with wisdom; without understanding there cannot be harmlessness.[4(16)]

So love, like the other three qualities, has its negative side. Any subpersonality representing jealousy, possessiveness or strong needs attempts to draw in love and approval from others as a primary goal — the good child, the jealous lover, the clinger. Ferrucci sees love as being the profound impulse to unity which lies at the root of real self-love, sexual love, altruistic love or 'agape':

> Perhaps because it [unity] is a principle so intrinsic to organic life and so much embedded in our primeval roots, a harmonious unfolding of this trend seems to generate immense benefits for the mental health and well-being of a person. On the other hand, a disturbance in this area — when this need for union is warped, repressed, or frustrated — causes major difficulties to arise in the psychological life of an individual. Indeed, love is what we live by. And yet it is also what we blind ourselves by, what we suffer by, and what we torture each

other by. Probably Dante was right when he said that love – its presence, its lack, its distortions – is the single cause explaining all the joys and sorrows of humanity.[81:17]

It is love that is nearer need that brings about the distortions – when the need to receive love is far greater than the willingness to give it and to recognize the 'love that moves the sun and the other stars'.[61c:33.145] That is not to say, of course, that we do not all need love, acceptance and approval, but those needs alone do not make a loving person. Ferrucci has the notion of 'conscious love' which is close to loving understanding, and which is derived from A. R. Orage's book *On Love*. Conscious love is 'the wish that the object should arrive at its own native perfection, regardless of the consequences to the lover', and this kind of giving love involves will. It is delight that something or someone actually exists in their own right.

So it is clear when we begin to examine the four qualities in the system that make up the graph on which our subpersonalities can be plotted, that this graph should actually be three-dimensional. We can on the horizontal level see an array of subpersonalities in different relationship to change, maintenance, love and will. But we can also see that subpersonalities appear at different 'vertical' places in the egg-shaped diagram, some representing very primitive need, or repressed material, others nearer to the transpersonal qualities themselves, particularly those of love and will. The significance of this vertical dimension is in awareness and the quality of consciousness. The more transpersonal, the more inclusive the person can be of all the different parts of him- or herself, the more centred, and the more free to move around and mobilize different parts of him or herself. The essential and freeing thing in therapy with subpersonalities is that the more that part of oneself can be recognized, the more a person can grow and mature, the more centred it is possible to become.

The possibility of synthesis in relation to subpersonalities

So the promise of work with subpersonalities is that we are now fragmented and can become whole. This does not promise a stasis, as clearly each person's nature is so potentially rich and varied that a lifetime can probably only allow each person to develop a limited proportion of the potential. Neither does unity and centredness in psychosynthesis mean homogeneity: the concept is that the more each subpersonality is recognized and accepted, the more it can make its own unique contribution to the whole. The idea of synthesis is that both the whole and the parts retain their own integrity without rigidity.

Synthesis is 'brought about by a higher element or principle which transforms, sublimates and reabsorbs the two poles into a higher reality'.[4(1)] The map for the classifying of subpersonalities is based on the tension of opposites – love and will, change and maintenance. Vargiu quotes the case of a person who has both a mystic and a businessman in his make-up, where each finds it hard to accommodate the other. Such tensions of subpersonalities at the personal level (or international tensions at the world level, as it is quite possible to see the nations as the subpersonalities on a world scale), cannot usually be resolved on the same 'level' as they occur. If two are in conflict, or one is repressed and under-developed, the solution may be found in the 'I' and the Self, which are able to see the warring parts from a different place which is nearer the soul than the personality.

Assagioli developed many triangle-shaped diagrams to express this relationship in different situations. On the bottom line of the triangle are the two opposing qualities, and at the midpoint between them is the ordinary common-sense accommodation between the two. For instance, the only way the sympathy and antipathy might be resolved towards the same person or object is indifference: a person can feel drawn to living and to the pleasures of the world but may also experience a strong sense of nausea and shock about many of the things that take place in it. A common way to reconcile the two feelings is by withdrawing, not being able to cope with the contradictions. But a real alternative, once glimpsed, is bringing another reality to bear on the issues, whereby the two original qualities become transformed into a quality that can contain them both – in this example it could be 'benevolent understanding' and tolerance, compassion. So Assagioli sets it out as shown in Figure 2.5:[4(1):6-8]

It was Assagioli's view that if a person could learn to live in a more centred way, nearer the soul, then the tensions between the unconscious material expressed by the subpersonalities could be resolved more satisfactorily and more creatively. His view was that any life situation could be used by a person who was centred and living from a state of spiritual awareness: that such a person did not have to carry so much rubbish from the past, or use up massive energy in constantly holding down unresolved problems. Suffering, pain, crisis and conflict could be situations for growth, leading, if lived through consciously, to greater growth and awareness.

In therapeutic work with the subpersonalities, there are five

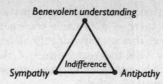

Figure 2.5

Another two similar diagrams are shown in Figure 2.6:

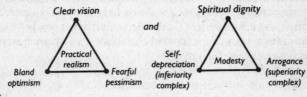

Figure 2.6

stages – recognition, acceptance, coordination, integration and synthesis.

In beginning therapeutic work, some troublesome subpersonalities are likely to be outstanding and not difficult to recognize. As work progresses, a person is likely to see new facets of her- or himself developing, and to be able to help them emerge and grow. Many subpersonalities will be of no concern and many will be positively helpful. Vargiu, in his article on subpersonalities in the journal *Synthesis*, vol. 1, advises a light touch in this work and recommends working with only half a dozen at any one time, at the most. Work is often done through the techniques of an 'evening review', a meditation on one's daily life, and through guided imagery. In accepting a subpersonality it is important to recognize and know the negative sides in order to be able to modify them: but it is also often difficult to accept and acknowledge really positive qualities in oneself – partly because with acceptance comes the necessity to use that positive energy, which is likely to lead to change. 'In general, the subpersonalities that are consistent with our self-image are easily accepted. Those who do not fit it are usually rejected.'[23a:79] But it is possible for one's self-image to gradually change: it is generally another opposing subpersonality, more deeply entrenched, which is doing the rejection. Then there is a need to work with the two subpersonalities together from the centre. This technique is used in Gestalt with the 'top dog/under dog' technique, or in Transactional Analysis with the relationship of the Adult to the warring factions of the person.

Because it is the psychosynthesis assumption that at the root of all subpersonalities there is a positive transpersonal quality, it is important to discover that quality and the defences that have been built up around it. With the recognition of this, it is possible to begin to coordinate the qualities and the subpersonalities that are likely to be changing with work.

> The process of integration leads from a general state of isolation, competition, and repression of the weaker elements by the stronger ones, to a state of harmonious cooperation in which the effectiveness of the personality is greatly enhanced, and its emerging aspects find the space and nourishment they need to develop fully.[23a:84]

This does not make for homogeneity, however. It is possible to hold many contradictory elements in one's own personality, in the short or long run, and be prepared to live with them with some understanding: it is perfectly possible for a socialist to be a lover of fine and esoteric art, or a Christian to enjoy detective fiction. The concept of subpersonalities makes it more possible for one to accept the inconsistency within oneself with tolerance – and maybe that is the lesson that could be applied again to the variety in the external world. It is multiplicity within unity which is the aim, not standardization.

The aim of synthesis is a person basically in harmony with her- or himself, able to live with her own multiplicity and the variety of the world around from a still place: and able to contribute from that same place to others and the greater integration of the world. The aim of psychosynthesis is ambitious and on many levels.

4

The search for meaning: the Self, the superconscious and the collective unconscious

'Souls are not in fashion,' wrote William James at the beginning of this century, and psychosynthesis is even now one of the few psychologies that contain the notion of the Higher Self or soul. Assagioli, from his earlier writing onwards, seems to have moved freely between the different 'levels' of the personality. He assumes that many people, at some time in their lives, will search for the transpersonal. In his 'Spiritual development and its attendant maladies', published in the *Hibbert Journal* in 1937, he writes of the possibility of 'the awakening of religious aspirations and new spiritual interests' at some point in a person's life: thus this person, instead of merely 'letting himself live', can begin to search for meaning through himself or herself in the context of the soul.

In the version of this article reprinted in his book *Psychosynthesis*, published in 1965, he was able to call on Maslow's work. Maslow made a firm distinction, in looking at creative and fully alive people, between those he called 'self-actualizers' and those to whom he gave the pretentious name of 'transcending self-actualizers'.

The self-actualizer, *tout court*, is the person who, in psychosynthesis terms, has come to know the different parts of him- or herself from a secure centre. This self-actualizing person can live out freely, without fear, and do what he or she intends to in the world in a reasonably well-harmonized way. Such people live fully in the world and come to fulfilment within it. 'They master it, lead it, use it for good purposes, as (healthy) politicians or practical people do. That is, these people tend to be 'doers' rather than meditators or contemplators.'[162]

These are the people who have followed through, in whatever way is known to them, the process examined in the third chapter. In this chapter, however, we are concerned with the next, larger process – that of living from a place nearer the soul rather than from the personality: of seeing the personality in the light of the personal and collective soul.

Maslow in his paper lists twenty-four differences, perceived or expected, between non-transcending and transcending self-actualizers. The latter group are at ease, as Maslow points out, with what he calls the Language of Being, under the aspect of eternity. They see the sacred, the beautiful, the eternal in all things, and will find this recognition just as 'real' as the practical world. They may also find the world more painful as they are more in touch with how things could be. They will be aware of themselves as subjects within a larger whole, prefer simplicity and respect the mystery of being and all the creatures within the world: they live 'sub specie aeternatatis', though they may be just as active in the world. *IN ETERNAL HOPE*

This vision has been written of in both Eastern and Western religions, and this I will discuss more fully later. But I will give two examples of this awareness here. The first example is from Meister Eckhart:

> The Scriptures say of human beings that there is an outward man and along with him an inner man.
>
> To the outward man belong those things that depend on the soul, but are connected with the flesh and are blended with it, and the co-operative functions of the several members, such as the eye, the ear, the tongue, the hand and so on.
>
> The Scripture speaks of all this as the old man, the earthy man, the outward person, the enemy, the servant.
>
> Within us all is the other person, the inner man, whom the Scripture calls the new man, the heavenly man, the young person, the friend, the aristocrat.[119:49]

The second example is by S. Radhakrishnan, in his commentary on the *Bhagavadgita*:

> The Supreme is within us. It is the consciousness underlying the ordinary individualised consciousness of everyday life but incommensurable with it. The two are different in kind, though the Supreme is realisable by one who is prepared to lose his life in order to save it. For the most part we are unaware of the Self in us because our attention is engaged by objects which we like or dislike. We must get away from them, to become aware of the Divine in us. If we do not realise the pointlessness, the squalor and the irrelevance of our everyday life, the true self becomes the enemy of our ordinary life. The Universal Self and the personal self are not antagonistic to each other. The Universal Self can be the friend or foe of the personal self. If we subdue our petty cravings and desires, if we do not exert our selfish will, we become the channel of the Universal Self. If our

impulses are under control, and if our personal self offers itself to the Universal Self, then the latter becomes our guide and teacher. Every one of us has the freedom to rise or fall and our future is in our own hands.[195:189-90]

It is clearly difficult to write about such ineffable subjects. In thinking of such matters we are considering the mystery of human life, and going far beyond the realm of the human mind's capacity. But it is living from this clarity, with this sure sense of meaning in relation to the whole, to which the spiritual way is leading. Assagioli based this on his own mystical experience and knowledge.

The superconscious, or the higher unconscious

In his article on 'The superconscious and the Self', Assagioli wrote that:

strictly speaking, 'superconscious' is just a term to designate the higher spiritual, or transpersonal aspects of the psyche. In it various psychological functions, processes, and energies are to be found, just as in the personality, although in the superconscious they can display much greater activity and diversity. So the difference between the superconscious and the personality is one of level, not of nature. And superconscious experiences consist fundamentally in becoming aware of the activity which is going on in the higher levels of the human consciousness. For example, states of ecstasy, of joy, of love for all living creatures, reported by many mystics, . . . creative flashes of the artist, all belong to the higher levels of the superconscious.

He goes on to write in the same article that

the Self is to the superconscious as the 'I', or personal self, is to the elements and functions of the personality, with the difference that the 'I' is often identified with the personality elements, while the Self is not identified with the superconscious.

The superconscious is what Assagioli calls a 'vehicle of expression' for the Self.

The superconscious expresses the energy from the unchanging Self and from the collective unconscious. It transmits a knowledge of the archetypes and of archetypal qualities to the personality. It is these qualities that are either developed clearly and serenely through the personality, and/or which become distorted through a person's life experience. It is in trying to live out these qualities, to which we have access all our lives, that we develop our subpersonalities and our more or less self-actualizing personality.

For Keyserling, the unconscious, particularly the superconscious, is the source of all real knowledge. He thinks and writes directly, he says, from the unconscious: his 'whole mentality is opposed to ratiocination, to reflection and to scholasticism. . . . I have never gained anything by mere thinking. What I know is all brought out from the Unconscious and emerges in my conscious as a revelation.'[183:275]

The superconscious acts as a constant force in the person's life if she or he will allow it to. The superconscious provides the key to real liberation: 'liberation is a key to inward being, to subjectivity; bondage is enslavement to the object world, to necessity, to dependence.'[196:49] If a person is not in touch with the superconscious, at some time in their lives there is then 'the sense of insufficiency, of barrenness and dust, [which] is due to the working of the Perfection, the mystery that lurks at the heart of creation'.[196:51] The superconscious is the source of inward knowledge, transmitting the wisdom of the Self: if it is ignored, it is a source of unsettlement and a goad for that person, a restriction of the potentiality of life.

Many writers are conscious of the functions of the superconscious in creativity of any kind. One of the Eastern mystics, Sri Aurobindo (1872–1950), speaks of the 'creative power in the spirit of the higher consciousness which is capable of actually transforming this apparent "burden" of body and world into a more perfect image of the Divine';[23a] this is achieved for him in his practice of Integral Yoga. But for this process of inspiration to be possible, the willingness to search for oneself must be there. This willingness must be present in any creative act. Assagioli quotes Murray in his essay 'Vicissitudes of creativity':

> there must be sufficient permeability (flexibility) of boundaries, boundaries between categories as well as boundaries between different spheres of interest and – most important for certain classes of creation – sufficient permeability between conscious and unconscious processes . . . too much permeability is insanity, too little is ultraconventional rationality.[1.49]

The superconscious is a particular source of inspiration and enlightenment, but must be in appropriate relationship to the personality, neither excluded nor overwhelming.

Psychosynthesis is the only theory of the personality produced in the West which not only has a theory of the unconscious, but also makes a distinction between these different levels of lower unconscious, middle unconscious and superconscious, together with the concept of the collective unconscious. Assagioli points out the difference between Jungian and psychosynthetic theory in his lectures on Jung and psychosynthesis, given in 1966.[4(14)] Jung does not make a distinction between 'archaic' and 'higher' qualities in the unconscious including the collective unconscious, whereas for Assagioli this distinction is fundamental. Assagioli essentially sees the world as benign, with the higher qualities predominating: this is not at all so clearly the case in Jungian thinking.

The collective unconscious and the archetypes

In the 'egg-diagram' there is a dotted line drawn between the superconscious and the collective unconscious, with the Self being placed astride the two. The collective unconscious also circles the middle unconscious and the lower unconscious, as it is seen as the sphere in which the person lives. The collective unconscious consists of qualities, concepts, and fundamental forms which are known as archetypes.

It is worth quoting Assagioli's paper on Jung at some length as it gives us clearly his own view of the issues around this very important area:

Jung's most important contribution to the psychology of the unconscious is presented by his extensive studies of the collective unconscious. Before him, psychoanalysis had concerned itself almost exclusively with the study of the personal unconscious. Jung then showed the great extent of collective psychic elements and forces, which exercise a powerful effect on the human personality. In my diagram of the constitution of the psyche, the collective unconscious is represented as lying outside the individual psyche. The demarcation line is dotted, to suggest the continuous exchanges going on between the collective and the personal unconscious. The unconscious exists at all levels, in both the personality and the collective psyche.

The collective unconscious is a vast world stretching from the biological to the spiritual level, in which therefore distinctions of origin, nature, quality and value must be made. It should be noted that Jung often disregards these distinctions: he speaks of the collective unconscious en bloc and is inclined to confuse what he calls 'archaic', that is, what originates in the ancient collective human experience, with what is higher (we would say superconscious) and in the spiritual sphere. Thus Jung speaks of 'archetypes' as 'images'; but at times he describes them as archaic, racial images, charged with strong emotional tone accumulated during the centuries, and on other occasions he treats them as principles, as 'ideas'; and he himself suggests their affinity with Platonic ideas. In reality, there exists not only a difference but an actual antagonism between these two conceptions of 'archetypes' and from this confusion between them arise various debatable consequences, debatable at the theoretical level and liable to be harmful in therapy, as I shall have occasion to mention in writing of Jungian therapy. In my opinion, it can be said without disrespect that Jung himself has been dominated by the potent fascination of the collective unconscious, against which he puts his patients on guard.[4(14):8]

The origin of the term 'archetype' as used by Jung can be traced to his earliest publication, 'On the psychology and pathology of so-called occult phenomena', published in 1902. Jung comments in his *Archetypes of the Collective Unconscious*, originally written in 1934:

At first the concept of the unconscious was limited to denoting the state of repressed or forgotten contents. Even with Freud, who makes the unconscious – at least metaphorically – take the stage as the acting subject, it is really nothing but the gathering place of forgotten and repressed contents, and has a functional significance thanks only to these. For Freud, accordingly, the unconscious is of an exclusively personal nature, although he was aware of its archaic and mythological thought-forms. A more or less superficial layer of the unconscious is undoubtedly personal. I call it the personal unconscious. But this personal unconscious rests upon a deeper layer, which does not derive from personal experience and is not a personal acquisition but is inborn. This deeper level I call the collective unconscious. I have chosen the term 'collective' because this part of the unconscious is not personal but universal; in contrast to the personal psyche, it has contents and modes of behaviour that are more or less the same everywhere and in all individuals. It is, in other words, identical in all men and thus constitutes a common psychic substrate of a suprapersonal nature which is present in every one of us.[129.9.1:3-4]

Stevens traces back the definition of the word 'archetype' to that of 'prime imprinter'; the term referred to the *original manuscript* from which copies were made.[220:47] Two further definitions from Jung make the concept more complex. He writes, 'the collective unconscious contains the whole spiritual heritage of mankind's evolution, born anew in the brain structure of every individual';[129.8:342] the archetype 'is not meant to denote an inherited idea, but rather an inherited mode of functioning, corresponding to the inborn way in which the chick emerges from the egg, the bird builds its nest.'[129.18:1228]

Stevens states that 'the archetypes which order our perceptions and ideas are themselves the product of an objective order which transcends the human mind and the external world'.[220:74] In this view, becoming yourself, the process which Jung calls individuation, means that you become what you were meant to be from the beginning. In this view also, the Self becomes 'the archetype of archetypes', a concept that Assagioli took issue with and which will be discussed later.

It is easy to see why Assagioli commented that a whole world of ideas are tied up in the Jungian view of archetypes and the collective unconscious. It would be helpful at this point to try to separate some of these concepts.

(i) An archetype is a primary form: it is basic to the whole scheme of human consciousness.

(ii) There are many archetypes, which together are synonymous with the collective unconscious of the human race.

(iii) All human babies are born with a pre-existing experience of these forms; rather as DNA is the prototype of the biological make-up of each human being, so the sum of archetypes is the prototype of the psychological make-up of the person: we are born already pre-patterned. The difference is that either we can choose to become what we were meant to be, or our experience of life can entirely or partially divert us from that path. This is spelt out clearly in the Hindu tradition:

> Karma is the hand dealt to him at birth from a celestial pack of cards – his fixed destiny. Dharma is his religious and moral duty to play the hand in the best possible way – his free will. The point of the card game is salvation – to free the Atman from the bondage of the body, or mother, through a cycle of death and reincarnation, and to reunite it with God.[169:94]

(iv) The nature of the archetypes is in some dispute. They may be qualities, perfect forms, in the Platonic sense of the word. In the psychosynthetic framework, these would exert a positive draw on the personality through the superconscious and the Self.

If, however, they are patterned on the whole history and experience of the human race, they would be less than benign, and in fact may be positively destructive. Each baby in the West in the late twentieth century would be born with some unconscious experience, for example, of the two world wars. The problem of good and evil of course comes in here, though neither Jung nor Assagioli thought much in those terms.

(v) Archetypes are essentially related to human action – they are activators, not simply ideas. They are not only qualities but also express deep patterns of human action – there is, for instance, a concept of the Mother or the Father archetype. Jung, in his book on four archetypes, also analyses the Trickster archetype. It is likely that Assagioli would call all of these, at least partially, subpersonalities, and this would be where the different interpretations would really matter.

Thus, in Jungian terms and to some psychosynthesis thinkers, the archetypes can be destructive. In discussing the Mother archetype, Stevens comments, 'while, on the one hand, the Great Mother is creative and loving, on the other, she is destructive and hateful.'[220:90] The archetypes are also curiously impersonal, though they are expressed through a human being. Stevens quotes Neumann as saying, 'it is not the personal individual, but the generically maternal that is the indispensable foundation of the child's life. . . . In this sense, she is anonymous and transpersonal, in other words, archetypal.'[220:95] In this sense, it is the expectation of being mothered, not only the individual mother herself, that matters to the child.

In Jungian theory as in psychosynthesis, the opposites are always present. Jung has the concept of the Shadow, which is present in each person, an archetype for the qualities that are not expressed and which lie deeply embedded in the unconscious. Stevens writes, 'awareness of the Shadow means suffering the tension between good and evil in full consciousness, and through that suffering they can be transcended.'[220:241] This is an old gnostic idea, one of the key themes of this book, to be taken up later.

The potentially destructive nature of the collective unconscious and the archetypes as envisaged by Jung can be seen most clearly in some of his political comments. In 1936 he gave a lecture at St Bartholomew's in London on contemporary events and the collective unconscious. He said:

If thirty years ago anyone had dared to predict that our psychological development was tending towards a revival of the medieval persecutions of the Jews, that Europe would again tremble before the Roman fasces and the tramp of legions, that people would once more give the Roman salute, as 2000 years ago, and that instead of the Christian cross an archaic swastika would lure on millions of warriors ready for death – why, that man would have been hooted at as a mystical fool.[129.9.1:48]

Jung thought of archetypes as 'primordial images',[135:102] 'the hidden treasure upon which mankind ever and anon has drawn, and from which it has raised its gods and demons, and all those portents and mighty thoughts without which man ceases to be man'.[135:105]

The whole problem of good and evil lurks here. A significant issue is, however, that both Jung and Assagioli were anxious that their work should be seen as scientific, and indeed be scientific. They did not conceive of themselves as creating religions, though clearly a lot of the work they used was deeply religious. They differed in that Jung seemed to see the constructive and destructive forces on every level, from the personality to the collective unconscious, whereas Assagioli had a strong concept of 'higher' and 'lower' forces, with the higher forces being paramount and positive. Assagioli saw the world as basically and in the end good, creative, tending to the infinite: it is not at all certain that Jung did. Assagioli has a hierarchy of values that seem to me not present in Jung. The question here is again whether Assagioli was simplistic, over-sanguine. Clearly, both attempts to visualize the infinite, the unseen, can only be elaborated metaphors. The differences can at this point only be stated; they can hardly be judged from any 'objective' standpoint, because there is not one.

The issue about whether psychosynthesis, or for that matter Jungian or Freudian theory, is 'scientific', or whether each framework is a metaphor or an alternative reality to the everyday world, is a fundamental question in this book. In the nineteenth century, religion and science were quite frankly split. Susan Budd, in her fascinating book *Varieties of Unbelief*, a study of the growth of unbelief in nineteenth and twentieth century England, writes that in this period 'science is presented . . . as a sort of knowledge which is created by a uniquely powerful method of reasoning; positivist, experimental, in short, rationalist, which is destroying emotive, intuitive, unsystematic, in short, mystical approaches to truth'.[52:144] In my view, although both Jung and Assagioli were using in large measure the second, mystical approach, they were both convinced they were rationalist and scientific. Assagioli was working within psychology and developing the idea of the personality: he was not a moralist concerned with the origins of good and evil, and he was not a religious leader, in his own eyes. Psychosynthesis is a psychotherapy based on a scientific view of human nature, in his definition: it is not a religion. This fundamental issue will be further discussed in the general analysis of psychosynthesis and in reflecting on the ideas and the bases of knowledge in which psychosynthesis is embedded.

The Self, or the Higher Self

To make a very simple analogy, the Self is like the pivot point, or hinge of a door; the door swings, but the hinge remains steady. Yet, the Self is not only the focal point around which many of the superconscious processes occur; it is also the *cause* of those processes and the *source* of the energy that makes them possible. So the Self is the unchanging, enduring reality; a stable centre of life on its own level, which has functions but is not a function.[4(25)]

The Self links up and is the key to the whole psychic system of the human being.
It is astride the collective unconscious and the superconscious. It is also in a direct line to the 'I' and can become, in a person in touch with the transcendent, almost synonymous with the 'I'. So here is the direct line from our knowledge of archetypal qualities, of the wholeness of the universe, of transcendence and immanence, to everyday life. But this knowledge depends on awareness, on preparedness for that source of knowledge to be available.

This source has been known in most of the major religions, and various terms have been used, including Atman, Tao, Suchness, God. The idea of the soul is equivalent to the idea of the Higher Self.

The experience of the Self has a quality of perfect peace, serenity, calm, stillness, purity, and in it there is a paradoxical blending of individuality and universality. The Self experiences universality but without 'losing' itself within the vast Universal Self. It remains at the centre, immovable. One way we can begin to realize this is by opening ourselves to the experience of infinity. For we can have the awareness of infinity, the perception of infinite space, without losing our sense of individuality. That is, it is the conscious 'I' who has the perception and the experience of infinity. Infinity IS . . . and man gropes to a feeble but increasingly profound realization of its existence.[4(25)]

'That which is deeper, more substantial than the individual is never the "general", but the "universal": and the "universal" expresses itself precisely through the individual, and the latter becomes more universal in the measure in which he becomes deeper'[4(25)] — that substantiating statement from Keyserling indicates something of the effect on the human being when she or he is in touch with the Self.

In psychosynthesis, the Self is seen as a reality, and can be directly experienced. Assagioli quotes Gratry, from *La Connaissance de l'Ame*:

> We possess an 'inner sense' which at special times when we succeed in interrupting the habitual flow of distractions and passions gives us direct and clear knowledge of our Soul. . . . I used to experience an inner form, full of strength, beauty and joy, a form of light and fire which sustained my entire being; stable, always the same, often recaptured during my life; forgotten at intervals, but always recognized with infinite delight and the explanation, 'Here is my real Being'.[4(14)]

Again here Assagioli parts company with Jung, because Assagioli regards the Self as a part of the person, even though it is also astride the Infinite. For Jung, however, it is an archetype, 'without possibility of scientific proof'.[4(14)] Again the problem of 'what is the truth' and 'how can we know things?' arises. We can know from scientific study and we can know from experience, but they are different kinds of knowledge. In this realm of the transpersonal, in the end it is experience rather than reason that is the true basis of knowledge.

Yogi Ramacharaka in *Raja Yoga* writes that when the consciousness of the Real Self is an everyday experience, a person can know a oneness with the universe and a sense of being at home in the world. The Self can be experienced as a familiar 'otherness', a being to be communicated with and consulted, as Stuart Miller's article 'Dialogue with the Higher Self' implies. He writes of:

> the common practice among creative people of wrestling with a problem, reaching a point of frustration, letting go, and then simply waiting for a solution . . . it is enough that there are in

us positive human potentials for more wisdom, love, strength, compassion and growth, than we have yet discovered.[23a]

Many people envisage this otherness as a wise person, always available to be consulted – in other words, the wisdom is there in ourselves, if we will only listen. The vision is wider than we could otherwise have: 'the work of art is the object seen sub specie aeternis; and the good life is the world seen sub specie aeternis'.

This doctrine is of course very old, particularly in Eastern religions. Radhakrishna in his introductory essay to the *Bhagavadgita* writes, 'God's light dwells in the Self and nowhere else. It shines alike in every living being and one can see it with one's mind steadied.' The *Gita* was one of the Upanishads, which probably date from the fifth century BC. In Hinduism, as in other major religions, the sense that the transcendent and the everyday world are close is very old. You can live in the Higher Self and yet remain in the world.

> The entire world of manifestation and multiplicity is not real in itself and only seems to be real for those who live in ignorance . . . only the wisdom that the universal reality and the individual self are identical can bring about redemption.

But in the religions the difference is that the fight is between good and evil; 'for the Gita the world is the scene of an active struggle between Good and Evil in which God is deeply interested.' 'The whole teaching of the Gita requires man to choose the good and realise it by conscious effort.' In psychosynthesis, which was based in science, good and evil are less overtly the issue: but covertly the whole theory of psychosynthesis is based in notions of the good, and the 'higher' significance of the good.

The journey and the goal

In psychosynthesis, seven paths are specified on the journey to the Higher Self. The first is the heroic way or way of the will – people who dedicate their lives to a cause outside themselves, who live altruistically in the true sense of that tricky word, who lose themselves in service to all, will come within that category.

The second way is the way of love or inner illumination – probably through a process of meditation and increasing concentration and enlightenment. The light shed on life through this process enables the person to love other beings, constantly being aware of the other person's Higher Self.

The third way is similar to the first – it is the way of action and involvement in the world. The person following such a path becomes entirely disinterested, prepared to sacrifice and not wish for any personal rewards from such a sacrifice. Such a person, on this path, is dedicated specifically to God.

The fourth way is the aesthetic way.

> It can be called the realization of divine immanence through beauty. . . . This way has been expounded best by Plato. He speaks of 'The Ladder of Beauty'; first one admires the beauty of physical forms; then one rises to the realization and admiration of inner beauty, of the higher, inner qualities or virtues. From that one reaches towards the idea of beauty, the source of all beauty in its essence, to what we call the archetype of beauty, which in itself is independent of all forms. . . .[4(23)]

The scientific way is the fifth way – that is, the sincere and disciplined investigation of our physical universe. This study is leading to a conviction that there is a cosmic order, and that the energy that is the source of life in the universe is God. Einstein himself wrote, in a much quoted sentence:

> Everyone who is seriously involved in the pursuit of science becomes convinced that a spirit is manifest in the Laws of the Universe – a Spirit vastly superior to that of man, and one in the face of which we, with our modest powers, must feel humble.[66:33]

The devotional way is the sixth – this is very well known, and would be the path that would spring to mind for most people, as this is the path of most of the religious saints and mystics: the aim is a mystical union with God through love.

The final way is through ritual or ceremony, through rites of initiation which can awaken the spiritual consciousness.

Any individual person may follow any way or combination of ways to awaken and unite with the transcendent sense in life. This is done through the therapeutic techniques described later, and through spiritual disciplines and awareness. The way each person follows is necessarily unique, varying greatly from one person to another.

This kind of thinking about the nature of life is natural for a religious person – to consider life as a journey, having a purpose. The assumption is deep in Bunyan's *Pilgrim's Progress* and in Christian philosophy quite as much as in the *Bhagavadgita* and Hinduism. But it is of course antithetical to much Western materialistic thinking, and certainly far from the usual way of thinking in our society. It is this problem that Frank Haronian addresses in 'The repression of the sublime' and with which Maslow is concerned in much of his writing.

Haronian comes out very strongly against the Freudian view of the person – the person who aims at adjustment rather than at growth and giving. He writes of 'the self-image of the well-psychoanalysed man; he has undergone a sort of psychoanalytical lobotomy of the spirit, a deadening of his normal sensitivity to the higher unconscious and to the possibility of spiritual growth.'[15] Because the sublime and the spiritual are not common currency in our present society, especially among the academic community, they are not part of what is regarded as knowledge – except in so far as such qualities are hived off into 'religious' areas of life. People can be committed and devoted to many of the paths described earlier, but refuse to see any ultimate meaning in what they are working at and making the centre of their lives. Haronian holds that we can fear our highest impulses quite as much, perhaps more, than we fear our lowest. We may fear the greatness and the strength which is in us all. We certainly may fail to recognize the strength and the courage with which many people, in all areas of society, live their lives.

Maslow has written of the envy which is aroused by people who do attempt to follow a spiritual journey, and to see others 'sub specie aeternatatis', as though each person has a soul, a Higher Self. He delineates the qualities of 'transcenders' in his well-known 'Theory Z'.

The goal of this whole process is synthesis, which means, in psychosynthesis:

(i) being in touch with the centre, 'I', and allowing oneself to be in touch with the Higher Self. This is done by being constantly aware of the strength within oneself, and of the spirit constantly at work in the world. Being able to see the transcendent and the immanent qualities in other people, in animals, in all creation;

(ii) working on the subpersonalities, and on the impulses from the lower unconscious, so as to be freer to be oneself in the world;

(iii) recognizing that a spiritually aware person is on a journey towards becoming aware of what he or she can be;

(iv) being able to live and share with other people in a more humble and accepting way;

(v) being able to work well and give to the world from a centred place; being committed to the causes one sees as important;

(vi) being aware of the creative forces which have occurred throughout human history and upon which we can all draw.

Jung, in *Psychology and Alchemy*, writes of

> the treasure hard to find . . . [which] lies in the ocean of the unconscious, and only the brave can reach it. I conjecture that the treasure is also the 'companion', the one who goes through life at our side – in all probability a close analogy to the lonely ego who finds a mate in the Self, for at first the Self is the strange non-ego. This is the theme of the magical travelling companion.

In transpersonal psychotherapy terms, the search for spiritual meaning is also the search for the Self, the 'God within', which is linked to the soul of the world.

5

Psychosynthesis therapeutic work with the unconscious: dreams, symbols, myths, and fairy-tales

The theory of the unconscious

In the egg-shaped diagram (Figure 2.1), Assagioli described several kinds of unconsciousness – the lower, middle and higher unconscious, and the collective unconscious. The conscious part of the personality is 'the sphere of consciousness' organized around the 'I'. Subpersonalities live mostly in the unconscious area of the personality. So much of the therapeutic work in psychosynthesis, as in most other twentieth century therapies, relates to the unconscious, in an attempt to contact those 'energies and feelings that mysteriously motivate our lives'.[81:37] But Assagioli, unlike some other therapists, is cautious about his contact with the unconscious, both because he values the conscious parts of the person, as psychosynthesis is aiming at more and more conscious awareness of the whole personality, and also because he sees dangers in becoming too intrigued with the unconscious.

It is instructive to reflect on these dangers as Assagioli lists them, because his comments give something of the unique flavour of psychosynthesis. Assagioli accepts, and refers to Adler as his authority, that the present structure of each person's personality has a history and a purpose – defences are there for a good reason, for instance, though that original reason may have become outdated. Therefore, to delve into the unconscious forces at present largely controlled by part of these defences may be playing with fire: he warns against 'the premature and uncontrolled release of explosive drives and emotions from the unconscious'.[1:98] He also fears that instead of the tendency for multiplicity to become more unified, which is part of the process of psychosynthesis, unconscious forces released may overwhelm the Self. Assagioli's theme, then, even when dealing with the unconscious, is still will and rationality, and the use of those forces in the development of the Self. He states quite clearly that 'we do not aim at a thorough, complete, exhaustive exploration of the unconscious' and 'when the unconscious disturbs, it has to be dealt with; if it keeps quiet, we do not make a systematic offensive against it'.[1:100] In these comments, Assagioli seems mainly to be referring to the unconscious as first defined by Freud and designated by Assagioli as the 'lower unconscious'.

The main point, however, is that discipline and caution are required in working with unconscious material. Assagioli's other reservation concerns the self-absorption that can come out of constant self-analysis, and also what he refers to as 'psychic inflation'.[1:99] This is not just becoming 'high' on therapy, but also refers to mania and other neurotic and psychotic conditions. These dangers relate to the strong sense that Assagioli has that therapy is for use. The point of therapy is not only that the person should be able to be more fully himself or herself, but that the energy released and the sense of purpose achieved should be grounded by action, positive action, in the world. If it were to be a choice between extensive examination of unconscious material and the possibility of someone being quickly able to contribute more coherently and effectively towards other people and society, Assagioli would probably go for the latter. He shows little interest in therapy lasting intensively and extensively for many years, but more in techniques which are immediate, direct, understandable and always tending towards conscious understanding.

At this point it is necessary to discuss briefly the nature of the unconscious, particularly as it is seen in psychosynthesis.

Adler states succinctly the idea of the unconscious in the phrase 'man knows more than he understands'.[194:20] In the fascinating book *The Unconscious before Freud*, L. L. Whyte traces references to an understanding of a force beyond the rational and the conscious that a few people have always been aware of; throughout history it has usually been commented on by poets and philosophers. Freud, in fact, acknowledged this on his seventieth birthday celebrations when he said, 'the poets and philosophers before me discovered the unconscious. What I discovered was the scientific method by which the unconscious can be studied.'

Koestler, in his introduction to Whyte's work, refers to Plotinus in the second century AD writing:

> There is a mirror in the mind which, when correctly aimed, reflects the process going on inside that mind, and when displaced or broken fails to do so — yet the processes continue all the same, and thus that thought is present without an inner image of itself.

The implication here is that the mind is deep and that we need a vehicle to be in touch with its processes – a mirror. This gives the therapeutic idea of communication with the unconscious very well – it is not easy, it requires awareness and skill, but it is possible; on the other hand, the conscious being may lose touch with his or her own mind – may 'displace' the mirror. The relationship of the conscious to the unconscious has been compared many times to an iceberg, where the part showing, the conscious, is greatly inferior in volume to the part hidden below the water, though the material is similar and there is no absolute dividing line.

Whyte gives many examples of a definition and recognition of the unconscious before the eighteenth century and the Enlightenment. St Augustine, who lived between 354 and 430, wrote:

> Great is the power of memory, exceedingly great. O my God, a spreading limitless room is within me. Who can reach its uttermost depth? Yet it is a faculty of soul and belongs to my nature. In fact, I cannot totally grasp all that I am.[239:79]

Ralph Cudworth, the English philosopher who lived from 1617 to 1688 and who had the idea of a plastic power pervading nature, which is similar to the idea of the unconscious, wrote:

> There is a more interior kind of plastic power in the soul (if we may so call it), whereby it is formative of its own cognitions, which itself it is not always conscious of; as when, in sleep and dreams, it forms interlocutory discourses betwixt itself and other persons, in a long series, with coherent sense and apt connections, in which often times it seems to be surprised with unexpected wiseness and repartee, though itself were all the while the poet and inventor of the whole fable.[239:95]

These writers and philosophers see the unconscious much as Jung seems to have seen it – as the source of wisdom in man. What has happened over the last three hundred years in Western thinking is that the values of individualism and conscious rationalism have become predominant, and materialist science the overriding form of knowledge. This form of thinking and invention has of course been spectacularly successful and has changed the world and the daily experience of living for people in the West, but we have paid a large price for this success. Whyte writes that the European and Western ideal 'of the self-aware individual confronting destiny with his own indomitable will and sceptical reason as the only factors on which he can rely is perhaps the noblest aim which has yet been accepted by any community'.[239:98] But the loneliness of the individual in such a position is very great, because the sense of being part of a much larger and unknown whole has been denied. And this isolated rational man (typically man) has invented the means of destroying the world without the corresponding humility and sense of awe which could hold that destructive power in check. The unconscious, the feminine and the whole have been largely lost sight of in this process.

Throughout those three hundred years, however, there have been writers and thinkers who have acknowledged the unknown forces in the person as well as those in the universe, and have seen these linked together. Whyte writes:

> The general conception of unconscious mental processes was conceivable (in post Cartesian Europe) around 1700, topical around 1800 and fashionable around 1870–80. . . . It cannot be disputed that by 1870–80 the general conception of the unconscious mind was a European commonplace and that many special applications of this general idea had been vigorously discussed for several decades.

In 1868 von Hartmann published a popular book, *Philosophy of the Unconscious*, which tuned in to much of the thinking of the time. This thinking, however, was cut off from religious established thinking as such. Science and religion existed in two different worlds. When Freud started his work, he investigated the unconscious as a doctor and a scientist. He investigated, first through hypnosis and then through techniques of free association, people who were ill. His interest was initially in hysterical personalities. And he regarded the religious sense as an aberration, as a sickness.

By 1896 he had already made the seminal discoveries that were to divide man's understanding of himself into ante-Freud and post-Freud: that human actions were more governed by unconscious motives than had previously been thought possible by more than a small number of men through the centuries; that repressed tendencies, pushed from the conscious mind and battened down in the unconscious, played a great and unsuspected role in human life; that neuroses were not the result of small so-called functional changes in brain tissue but the outcome of complicated mental processes and of strong emotional conflicts; and that knowledge of these facts could enable a doctor to understand mental disease and in suitable cases even cure it.[57:141]

It is ironic that Freud, working in the scientific, rational, medical tradition, concerned with illness and with pathology, should have been the means of bringing the conscious and the unconscious, the rational and the subjective/irrational, together into one framework which eventually became accepted in Western thinking. Freud remained to the end of his life interested in pathology and treatment; he saw the unconscious as largely to do with repression, particularly of sexual material. Jung – and Assagioli – split with him on this particular view of unconscious material. Jung linked the idea of the unconscious to the religious instinct of the period, to Eastern thinking, to the wisdom and language of myths, and an ancient knowledge. In the Hindu religion, indeed, there are three planes of consciousness – the subconscious (instinctive and affective thought): the conscious (ideological and reflexive thought) and the superconscious (intuitive thought and the higher truth).

The massive work and speculation on the scientific study of the unconscious has meant that in the twentieth century we have the means of uniting the split in Western thinking, of subject and object, mind and matter, reason and feeling, conscious and unconscious. Whyte writes:

> The most profound aspect of Freud's hold over many minds may have little to do with his scientific discoveries, with sex, or libido, or any special aspect of the unconscious, except as an opportunity for the conscious subject to escape his isolation, for the individual to relax his lonely self-awareness in a surrender to what is organic and universal.[239:28]

Assagioli does not intend that in psychosynthesis people 'surrender' to the unconscious, but rather that they should be in communication with those deep forces enough to be able to use them rather than to be used by them. He acknowledges the Freudian concept of what he calls the lower unconscious, but also sees the unconscious as potential and as wisdom in the older and more classic sense.

Dreams

Freud published his *Interpretation of Dreams* in November 1899. In it he asserted that 'we are justified in assuming the existence of systems (which are not in any way psychical entities themselves and can never be accessible to our psychical perception) like the lenses of the telescope, which catch the image'.[93:611] He writes:

The unconscious must be assumed to be the general basis of psychical life. The unconscious is the larger sphere, which includes within it the smaller sphere of the conscious . . . the unconscious is the true psychical reality; in its innermost nature it is as much unknown to us as the reality of the external world, and it is as incompletely presented by the data of consciousness as is the external world by the communications of our sense organs.[93:612-13]

He postulated a preconscious, which is like a screen between the conscious and the unconscious, which he thought at the time was inadmissible to consciousness. He also accepted at this time that 'we are probably inclined greatly to over-estimate the conscious character of intellectual and artistic production. . .'.[93:613]

Freud saw dreams as a route to the unconscious and therefore of concern to physicians. His first bold statement in the book is:

In the pages that follow I shall bring forward proof that there is a psychological technique which makes it possible to interpret dreams, and that, if the procedure is employed, every dream reveals itself as a psychical structure which has a meaning and which can be inserted at an assignable point in the mental activities of waking life.

Freud saw dreams basically as wish-fulfilments. Later on, he developed a complex sexual interpretation of dream material, laying emphasis on the repressive nature of the conscious mind. As Fromm explains:

We dream of hating people we believe we are fond of, of loving someone we thought we had no interest in. We dream of being ambitious, when we are convinced of being modest; we dream of bowing down and submitting, when we are so proud of our independence.[96:8]

Since Freud, dreams have been widely used as a way into the unconscious by therapists, particularly in psychoanalysis. Assagioli is, however, far more cautious about the use of dreams.

In our practice we ask patients to recount their dreams, and we give them the needed instructions for the analysis of them, but we definitely point out the fact that dream-interpretation is only *one* of the techniques and not the chief one.[1:94]

He points out later in the book *Psychosynthesis* that Freud had developed the analysis of dreams so extensively because they avoid the 'therapeutically superficial circular thinking characteristic during Free Association',[1:288] which was one of the original techniques used by Freud to tap the unconscious. But Assagioli felt strongly that interpretation of dreams introduced a passive element into the therapeutic relationship which is undesirable, particularly as the appearance of dreams is uncontrollable. He also felt strongly that it is probably impossible to convert the experience of dreams into conscious language without using classical analysis and interpretation, of which he was very suspicious because of its reductive nature. The comparable technique used in psychosynthesis is, therefore, guided imagery, guided daydreams or initiated symbol projection, similar techniques which allow the 'patient' to mediate himself or herself between conscious and unconscious material: these techniques will be described fully in the next chapter.

Fromm brings out the contrasting theories of Freud and Jung on dreaming and on the whole nature of the unconscious. Perhaps his distinction is rather crude when he writes that the Freudian view 'says that all dreams are expressions of the irrational and a-social nature of man', and that Jung's interpretation 'says that dreams are revelations of unconscious wisdom, transcending the individual'.[96:109] Both Fromm's view and Assagioli's (and it is clear that Assagioli had read Fromm's *The Forgotten Language*[1:288]) seem to indicate that dreams can give us access to any aspect of our unconscious being – and that presumably would apply to the use of guided daydreams.

To sum up the relationship between dreams, the conscious and the unconscious, perhaps it would be helpful to quote from Henri Bergson's classic *Dreams*:

> You ask me what it is I do when I dream? I will tell you what you do when you are awake. You take me, the me of the dreams, me the totality of your past, and you force me, by making me smaller and smaller, to fit into the little circle that you trace around your present action. That is what it is to be awake. That is what it is to live the normal psychical life. It is to battle. It is to will. As for the dream, have you really any need that I should explain it? It is the state into which you naturally fall when you let yourself go, when you no longer have the power to concentrate yourself upon a single point, when you have ceased to will. What needs much more to be explained is the marvellous mechanism by which at any

moment your will obtains instantly, and almost unconsciously, the concentration of all that you have within you upon one and the same point, the point that interests you. But to explain this is the task of normal psychology, of the psychology of waking, for willing and waking are one and the same thing.[34:33-5]

Symbolism

Personal dreams draw on all the areas of the unconscious. Myths and fairy-stories, in the hypothesis of the unconscious, draw on the collective. In Jung's view, they express a deeper reality than can be perceived by our rational everyday existence. These stories express something about the whole human unconscious, put in symbolic form. From the psychotherapeutic view, particularly the therapy of Jung and Assagioli, they are important because they are available to people in their work in relation to the unconscious.

Both the communication in dreams and that in myths and fairy-tales is symbolic. Symbolism has been studied throughout this century by anthropologists, such as Raymond Firth with his work on symbols; by students of religious history, such as Mircea Eliade who has written many fascinating and significant books on myth over the last thirty years or so; by psychologists and therapists, particularly of course Carl Jung but also some of the more recent humanistic and transpersonal writers like Ira Progoff, as well as Erich Fromm, the prolific writer from the Frankfurt Critical Sociological School where psychological and sociological material is related; and by art historians such as the Spanish J. E. Cirlot. As in psychosynthesis itself, many disciplines have contributed to the creation of an area of knowledge and activity in an immensely productive way.

Firth gives a straightforward definition of 'symbol' – 'the essence of symbolism lies in the recognition of one thing as standing for (representing) another, the relation between them being normally that of concrete to abstract, particular to general'.[83:15] In this sense, as several writers point out, all words are symbols. We think symbolically because we think abstractly. Assagioli points out that the relationship between the symbol and the 'reality' it represents is based on analogy – 'analogy, we might say is an important psychological link or connection between outer and inner realities'.[1:178] And a basic part of psychosynthesis, a key concept, is that we can work therapeutically with deep and often inaccessible areas of the unconscious by working through the more accessible symbols.

Several writers refer to the idea that symbols can have a

transcendental element. Jung wrote in his *Symbols of Transformation*, 'symbols are not allegories and not signs: they are the images of contents which for the most part transcend consciousness'.[129.5:77] And Eliade has argued in *Images and Symbols* that 'the symbol reveals certain aspects of reality, the deepest aspects, which defy any other means of knowledge'. A symbol of course can be any object, which still stays as an object in its own right; a rose, or a lion, seen as representing an aspect of reality for someone still exists in its own right. So a symbol is both itself and a personal or collective representation of some other meaning on a different plane of reality. Some symbols are so universal that Jung referred to them as archetypes – the Mother, the Cross. These carry enormous universal symbolic meanings. But they, or indeed any other object, may carry personal meaning – one of the most famous examples is Proust's association with the madeleine cake and all the memories and representations that object held for him. Fromm, in fact, distinguishes between conventional symbols, like words or a flag, accidental symbols which have a personal meaning and connection, and universal symbols like fire, water, the sun – and like many myths and fairy-stories.

Juan Cirlot gives a very good introduction to his *Dictionary of Symbols*. His book consists of a list of symbols used frequently about the world and something of their origin and meaning. He writes that 'symbols link the instrumental with the spiritual, the human with the cosmic, the casual with the causal, disorder with order',[56] and they point to the transcendental. He, like Fromm, speaks of a universal symbolic language which links internal conception to external reality:

> This language of images and emotions is based . . . upon a
> precise and crystallized means of expression, revealing
> transcendent truths, external to Man (cosmic order) as well as
> within him (thought, the moral order of things, psychic
> evolution, the destiny of the soul) . . . . the essence of the
> symbol, is its ability to express simultaneously the various
> aspects (thesis and antithesis) of the idea it represents.

These writers stress the great significance of perceiving the symbolic nature of so much that takes place. Their descriptions of the importance of symbolism have much in common with the idea of immanence – perceiving the universal in the particular, whilst it still remains particular and entirely unique.

There is an 'esoteric' and to some extent magic world on which symbolism always borders. Eliade put something of this idea in a more 'psychosynthetic' form in his *Images and Symbols*:

> It must not be thought that a symbolic connotation annuls the material and specific validity of an object or action. Symbolism *adds* a new value to an object or act, without thereby violating its immediate or 'historical' validity. Once it is brought to bear, it turns the object or action into an 'open' event: symbolic thought opens the door on to immediate reality for us, but without weakening or invalidating it; seen in this light the universe is no longer sealed off, nothing is isolated inside its own existence; everything is linked by a system of correspondence or assimilations. Man in early society became aware of himself in a world wide open and rich in meaning. It remains to be seen whether these 'openings' are just another means of escape or whether, on the other hand, they offer the only possible way of accepting the true reality of the world.[72:xiv]

Symbolism can be seen from a specifically transcendental view. Jung contrasts 'archaic man', who lived easily with myths and symbols, with 'modern man', who is resistant to religion and the unconscious. He writes:

> The naive man of antiquity saw the sun as the great Father of heaven and earth, and the moon as the fruitful Mother. Everything had its demon, was animated like a human being, or like his brothers the animals.[129.5:21]

That this experience has occurred throughout the ages is illustrated by a passage he quotes from Seneca:

> When you enter a grove peopled with ancient trees, higher than the ordinary, and shutting out the sky with their thickly intertwining branches, do not the stately shadows of the wood, the stillness of the place, and the awful gloom of this domed cavern then strike you as the presence of a deity? Or when you see a cave penetrating into the rock at the foot of the over-hanging mountain, made not with human hands, but hollowed out to a great depth by nature, is not your soul suffused with a religious fear? We worship the sources of the great rivers, we erect altars at the place where a sudden rush of water bursts from the bowels of the earth, warm springs we adore, and certain pools we hold sacred on account of their sombre darkness and their immeasurable depth.[129.5:73]

Many people have lived with two realities throughout the ages; they express the more inaccessible and deeper reality through symbol, myths and fairy-tales, among other means.

Assagioli directly uses symbols in many of his therapeutic techniques. He discusses several assessment tests where symbols are seen as a bridge between the conscious and the unconscious; and more particularly Assagioli uses symbols in therapeutic methods such as guided daydream and 'techniques of symbol utilization'. Symbols are also used very directly in words, music and art, free drawing, imaginative work, visualization, and some kinds of meditation.

He sees symbols as 'containers' of meaning, as transformers through playing out a problem or situation on another level, and as 'conductors or channels of psychological energies'. Through playing with ideas, feelings, attitudes, on this other level, it is often easy to bring in factors, other experiences and other symbols not usually seen in relation to the original issue before, and to find new ways of looking at things.

Myths and fairy-stories

Often in working with the unconscious, myths and fairy-stories appear in the material, as these are a cultural stock to which we all have access. They are a particularly available form of symbolism.

Both myths and fairy-stories represent eternal truths in a way that is easy to understand. Bettelheim, in his Freudian book *The Uses of Enchantment*, writes that both attempt to answer the eternal questions: 'What is the world really like? How am I to live my life in it? How can I be truly myself?'[42:45] The stories externalize inner issues. Both Fromm and Bettelheim in their investigation of fairy-stories consider the messages that may be conveyed by, say, 'Red Riding Hood' or 'Cinderella', though some of the hazards of interpretation emerge as each has a different framework for his interpretation. The personal meaning, the symbolic differences, come out quite clearly and can be an important piece of learning for a psychotherapist – that each person's understanding of even familiar symbols may have very particular connotations.

Both myths and fairy-stories are timeless. In fact, Eliade maintains that their very essence is that they are outside history; they are repeated truths, not linear events.

Both also, as all symbols, may have a transcendental element. Many myths are very old and may spring from a less conscious, certainly less self-conscious period in human history. Susanne Langer, writing of the philosophy of Ernest Cassirer, one of the great experts on the subject of myths, wrote:

> The earliest products of mythic thinking are not permanent, self-identical, and clearly distinguished 'gods'; neither are they immaterial spirits. They are like dream elements – objects endowed with demonic import, haunted places, accidental shapes in nature representing something ominous – all manner of shifting, fantastic images which speak of Good and Evil, of Life and Death, to the impressionable and creative mind of man. Their common trait is . . . the quality of holiness.[149:387]

ESKIMO STORIES.

Myths and fairy-stories draw on unconscious material rather than rationality to make sense out of living in the world. Some of the basic experience of mankind has been passed on through the tales. Malinowski, one of the great anthropologists of the twentieth century, expressed it thus:

> Myth warranting the belief in immortality, in eternal youth, in a life beyond the grave, is not an intellectual reaction upon a puzzle, but an explicit act of faith born from an innermost instinctive and emotional reaction to a most formidable and haunting idea.[156:43]

They represent, according to Eliade, the essential human condition.

In psychosynthesis it is very common to find subpersonalities founded directly on fairy-stories (the wicked witch, Cinderella, the big bad wolf) or on myth (St George, the beautiful victim, the archetypal mother). And in the sequences of the guided daydreams, myths such as the ascent of the mountain, the pursuit of the holy grail, the symbolism of the centre,[75:17] are basic to the work. The richer the symbolism known to the workers, the wider the knowledge of the culture in which they live, the more creative the imagination, the more extensive can be the access to the collective imagery in both personal and group work. The potential of this work is limitless.

6 Techniques in psychosynthesis work with the unconscious

It is not possible or appropriate in this chapter to attempt to encapsulate the complex and delicate guiding work which is the action of psychosynthesis. This work has clearly changed a good deal over the century, from the earliest use of hypnosis to the Gestalt and guided imagery of the present day. What has remained constant is the spiritual context of the work, the assumption that the client contains his or her own wisdom, and the relatively equal relationship of client and guide.

Psychosynthesis is known for its large number of techniques. In his book *Psychosynthesis*, which is clearly the fruits of his lifetime of therapeutic work, Assagioli lists and comments on many skills, some dating from the beginning of the century, like free association, and others devised by him in the course of therapy, like his dis-identification exercise. Since the book's publication in 1965, many more skills have been incorporated – the development of theories of loss and change as applied to psychosynthesis, particularly through attention being paid to the creative as well as the destructive possibilities of pain, crisis and failure; incorporation of more knowledge about the place of mourning and catharsis in relation to past traumatic events; the greater use of group skills and increased knowledge of group unconscious processes; more material about social factors in psychological processes, about the use of systems theory; and the moderation of the heterosexual assumptions of the original psychotherapeutic mode, and some use of feminist theory.

Also in the last twenty years or so, psychosynthesis has incorporated many of the humanistic techniques, particularly those which concentrate on the messages given by the body: body/posture, physical sensations which may be symbolic of emotional states, and the deepening of experiences through physical acting out. Techniques to ground and integrate the material have also been refined and developed: clients and trainees are encouraged to work on their own through active self-observation, meditation, drawing, writing, and the regular and repeated use of exercises, over shorter or longer periods, that might actively support the next step in their growth process.

All that can be done here is to trace historically some of the symbolic techniques that have been used in relation to therapeutic work with the unconscious. These are the techniques most relevant to this particular study, but any person actively training within psychosynthesis will learn a far greater range of methods than those which can be incorporated here. Different schools have developed independently throughout the world from this original base.

The original techniques of psychosynthesis

Assagioli initially categorized four functions of work with unconscious/conscious material. These are: (i) assessment and diagnosis; (ii) personality work – 'neuroses' and 'complexes' in his original language; (iii) physical level work – work with illness, combined with psychological work; and (iv) transpersonal work, as described in his section on spiritual psychosynthesis. These are not discrete pieces of work, but run into each other.

At the beginning Assagioli, who was of course a psychiatrist, accepted that most of his work would be done with patients who presented themselves as sick, either in body or in mind. His writing, therefore, tends to assume a pathological diagnosis. From the beginning, however, Assagioli assumed that this would be seen in a transpersonal context, dealing with superconscious as well as lower unconscious material directly.

Freud, at the beginning of the century, experimented with various techniques for use in both diagnosis and treatment: hypnosis, that is, putting the patient into a sleep-like state in which he or she was more likely to have access to unconscious material, was used in the earliest psychoanalytic work. The repeating of painful material was practised as catharsis, often under hypnosis, as it was discovered that re-living the original traumatic events could help the client both recognize them and re-experience them with a different quality of insight and with support. Catharsis is still used, inevitably, but with the client's active and aware consent.

According to Leuner and Kornadt, 'Freud discarded Hypno-Catharsis because he was unable to hypnotise all patients, at least as deeply as he believed was required. Later he decided that hypnosis conceals transference and resistance, the analysis of which was essential to his treatment.'[1:287] In experiencing this technique, the patient 'was asked to recall when the symptom first appeared and, in as much detail as possible, the circumstances in which it had appeared.'[57:99] It was in the development of his use of the dialogue between patient and doctor that Freud began the technique of 'free association'. This he derived partly from the early nineteenth century writer Ludwig Borne and from the British anthropologist Francis Galton; Galton published an article on a 'word association test' in 1879, after writing rather endearingly that the mind is 'apparently always engaged in mumbling over its old stores'.[57:120]

Word association tests were routinely used by most therapists at that time, including Freud, Jung and Assagioli. This technique helped to build up a picture of the client's unconscious processes of thought, the linking of concepts and feelings at a deep level. Free association, not only of words but also of connections on a wider scale, was also developed. In connection with both these techniques, Assagioli used Jung's 'Hundred Words'. He wrote that 'with some additions they have proved to be a very fruitful survey of the field of the unconscious, using "survey" in a similar sense as in the systematic drilling of territory for oil'.[1:92]

It is worthwhile looking back at Freud's original instructions to his patients about free association, as it gives some of the flavour of therapeutic work at that time:

> One thing more, before you begin. Your talk with me must differ in one respect from an ordinary conversation. Whereas usually you rightly try to keep the threads of your story together and to exclude all intruding associations and side issues, so as not to wander too far from the point, here you must proceed differently. You will notice that as you relate things various ideas will occur to you which you will feel inclined to put aside with certain criticisms and objections. You will be tempted to say to yourself: 'This has no connection here or it is quite unimportant, or it is nonsensical, so it cannot be necessary to mention it'. Never give in to these objections, but mention it even if you feel a disinclination against it, or indeed just because of this. Later on you will perceive and learn to understand the reason for this injunction, which is really the only one which you have to follow. So say whatever goes through your mind. Act as if you were sitting at the window of a railway train and describing to someone the changing views you see outside. Finally never forget that you have promised absolute honesty, and never leave anything unsaid because for any reason it is unpleasant to say it.[57:122-3]

These instructions still make great sense in all the techniques discussed here – visualization, dreams and guided imagery, as well as word association and free association.

Assagioli, like both Freud and Jung, approached therapy as a doctor – he assumed there was something wrong with the 'patient' (a word he still uses in his book *Psychosynthesis*): he was looking initially for 'complexes'; 'the first and most telling symptom (of a complex) is the prolongation of the time of reaction (to words), i.e., hesitation or even failure to answer. In Jung's studies he carefully recorded the length of the reaction time'.[1:92] Psychosynthesis has, however, developed in a much more democratic way than the above quotation would suggest, and – as far as I know – tests such as word associations are rarely if ever used for assessment, which is now a far more mutual process. But certainly words, slips of the tongue, and body movements are noticed and used in psychosynthesis by client and guide alike or by all members of a group, although the interpretation would generally be left to the person making the statement, verbal or physical.

Dreams, of course, have been the classic entry into the unconscious ever since Freud published his *Interpretation of Dreams* at the turn of the century. Assagioli sees dream analysis and understanding as being only one of many techniques, because of the passive nature of the dream experience, and also because dreams tend to give access to only one part of the unconscious – the lower unconscious (although transpersonal dreams are some of the most famous in history, especially in the Bible).

Dreams, free association, and word association can all be used in both assessment and therapy; in the medical profession there is a clear distinction between assessment of pathology (diagnosis) and treatment. Psychotherapists and more particularly psychologists have in the main kept this distinction, though it is accepted that reassessment must constantly take place, in emotional experience even more than in bodily illness. Assagioli throughout his early years also kept this distinction and was therefore particularly interested in the psychological development of projective tests which gave access to the unconscious. These he saw as useful tools in beginning to work with a patient, along with 'free drawing, free movement, clay modelling etc.'[1:94] which are some of the more active tools still used in psychosynthesis today.

Projective tests have changed their form over time, though the concept itself is still of immense and indeed basic value. In projection we assume that outside events, objects and people have properties which are actually unrecognized inner properties: it is therefore impossible to perceive clearly or to tackle the inner unconscious material. The actual tests make it possible to contact the material which is not easily available in everyday life or on the conscious level. Assagioli built up his own set of standard pictures, based on an idea of Murray, which related more to transpersonal as well as personality themes. And the material was used not so much in a test form; people were asked more about what the picture meant to them and encouraged to let their imagination have free play.

The spirit of this comment leads naturally on to the use of *free drawing and writing*, which are both assessment and therapeutic tools in work with the unconscious. Drawing is more likely to be using unconscious material, as it is difficult for many people to go much beyond the rational and the controlled in writing. Body movement, particularly dance, and music, also touch on areas beyond the conscious, and Assagioli advocates their use in therapy.

Both Assagioli and Ferrucci discuss free drawing, whose history is as old as mankind. The technique is simple in that the client is asked to draw whatever comes to mind, either on a particular theme or more open-endedly. Assagioli advocates ' "letting it happen" in a free, relaxed, playful mood, seeing with eager curiosity what will happen'.[1:97] Ferrucci says:

> We should greet our drawing as if it were a person coming from a distant land whose customs are very different from those of our own country. . . . We seek to resonate with it and intuitively capture the message it gives us about ourselves.[81:37]

He emphasizes the use of insight rather than intellect in interpreting the drawing, and the assumption is that the person making the drawing will be most familiar with the meaning in interpreting it. Drawing and writing are encouraged as therapeutic techniques in the client's own time. People are encouraged to explore the unconscious drives within themselves, to get used to those unseen forces and not to be surprised by them. In the same way that the women's movement advocates getting to know your own body, Assagioli encourages us to get to recognize some of the unconscious forces which move us. In both cases, knowledge is de-mystified and shared.

Symbols and visualization in personal and transpersonal psychosynthesis

Visualization in psychosynthesis is mainly a conscious tool. But Assagioli fully recognizes the imaginative function of the use of all the senses – sight, touch, hearing, smell, taste – and the possibility of using these to get in touch with unconscious and maybe very creative material. This can be done individually and in a relatively unstructured way. But throughout the twentieth century, techniques of guided imagery, guided daydreams and the use of myths and stories have been brought into the therapeutic field and used with great effect, enjoyment and power.

All these methods use symbols, and can employ the myths and fairy-stories to which we all have access, which have been discussed in the last chapter. Ferrucci devotes the eleventh chapter of his book to visualization and the use of symbols to get in touch with the unconscious as part of his therapeutic work. He points out that visualizing symbols for a particular state of mind can:

> connect us with regions of our being which are completely unavailable to our analytical mind. Thus they train us to understand by seeing directly, jumping the intermediary stage of discursive thinking, which is sometimes more of an obstacle than an aid to understanding. This deeper kind of understanding awakens a faculty whose importance is almost universally neglected: *the intuition*.[81:118]

Piero Ferrucci gives a series of visualizations which can be practised alongside more personal and individual material. Most of these relate to the superconscious, and include exercises on 'the lighthouse', 'the butterfly', 'the sun', 'the flame', 'the arrow'. Each exercise involves *becoming* in imagination the symbol envisaged and allowing its qualities to become more like one's own. These are really spiritual exercises, always drawing on unconscious, usually superconscious, material.

To illustrate this use of visualization and symbolism, the exercise on the sun will now be given, together with one client's response and use of the technique.

The sun

Visualize yourself on the beach at dawn. The sea is almost motionless as the last bright stars fade away.

Feel the freshness and the purity of the air. Watch the water, the stars, the dark sky.

Take some time to experience the silence before sunrise, the stillness filled with all possibilities.

Slowly, the darkness melts and colors change. The sky over the horizon becomes red, then golden. Then the sun's first rays reach you, and you watch it emerging slowly from the water.

With half the sun's disc visible and the rest still below the horizon, you see that its reflection in the water is creating a path of golden, shimmering light leading from you all the way to its very heart.

The temperature of the water is pleasant, and you decide to go in. Slowly, with joy, you start to swim in the golden radiance. You feel the light-filled water touching your body. You experience yourself floating effortlessly and moving pleasurably in the sea.

The more you swim towards the sun, the less aware you are of the water, and the more the light around you increases. You feel enveloped in a beneficient, golden light which permeates you completely.

Your body is bathing now in the vitality of the sun. Your feelings are pervaded by its warmth. Your mind is illumined by its light.[81:122]

Ferrucci gives the response to this by one client, who was feeling rejected and resentful over events and relationships in her life:

I am on the beach at dawn. A few stars of an incomparable delicacy twinkle in the clear sky; the air is fresh and the sea almost motionless. Suddenly a golden ray, warm and radiant, reaches my face, and I surrender to its light and warmth. The sun rises slowly from the sea like a golden diamond and opens a luminous path on the water towards me. Completely naked, I move towards this path.

The limpid water caresses my body and is almost cold. The sun's radiance envelops me completely, and I walk until the water comes above my waist; then I start swimming in this path of light towards the sun. At a certain point I become aware I am no longer swimming in the water, but in the light, and I enter the sun.

I surrender to its immense warmth and brilliant light; the solar energy acts on me, caressing my whole body, my hair, my face, and enters me through my vagina. It rises slowly, pervading all my organs, transforming them into light. When it reaches my heart, I feel my whole chest expand. For a moment I cannot breathe; the energy penetrates my throat and my brain. I feel my head almost opening up, and suddenly my body starts emitting this luminosity within it. At last, my whole being blends with the sun and becomes the light of the sun. It is hard to describe this sense of expansion and the ecstacy that derives from it. After a while my body rebuilds itself little by little, but now it is all made of light.[81:117-18]

The clearly sexual nature of this experience is acknowledged by the client in her comments about the meaning of this experience for her. But there is a larger comment behind this – that sexual experience involving a sense of unity is only *one* of many ways of achieving this sense of wholeness, oneness and meaning. The client, Veronica, comments:

> That visualization helped save the feminine in me. I didn't want it to die, even if for the time being it was not being reinforced. It was a part of me that had remained latent for too long, and now I did not want to lose it. Doing this exercise made everything seem transformed. The light reached the darkest parts of my unconscious, transmuting my passions. I succeeded in transferring them to another level of my being.
>
> Of course, the relief I felt after doing the exercise did not last long at first. Soon I was back where I had been before, and the crisis repeated itself several times. But I kept performing the exercise until all of a sudden a big change happened. Some sort of illumination and renewal occurred; the forces of life were coming back again.[81:118]

Symbols are used in this transpersonal work as goals and models for qualities trying to emerge in the person's life. Visualization and the use of symbols is characteristic of the psychosynthesis approach. Assagioli points out that only therapists at peace with their own unconscious material should work with that of others. The material of the unconscious, the archetypes, the myths, the destructive as well as the transpersonal forces, are powerful and need to be treated with great caution and respect.

The history and development of guided imagery

An alternative name for guided imagery is initiated symbol projection or ISP, developed by Hanscarl Leuner. This technique uses all the ideas already discussed in visualization and symbol work, but develops the form, so that a 'story' can be developed on structured lines. The work can run close to the myths and fairy-stories discussed at the end of the last chapter.

The technique developed in the 1930s and 1940s. Carl Happich, who as a 'Darmstadt internist' was a follower of Hermann Keyserling, developed the idea out of his 'literary and practical knowledge of Oriental techniques', together with his familiarity with depth psychology.

> Happich took the level of consciousness he called 'symbolic consciousness', which seems to lie between consciousness and unconsciousness, as the point of departure for all creative production and, therefore, also for the healing process. On this level the 'collective unconscious' can express itself through symbolism.[1:305]

Leuner dates his work from 1948.[151]

In the Eastern tradition, great attention is paid to breathing in these exercises; the subject attempts an increasingly passive respiration. There are then four exercises: (i) the meadow meditation; the meditator leaves the room he is sitting in and, in his imagination, goes to a pleasant meadow covered with fresh grass and flowers, stays and rests there with pleasure, and then in imagination returns to his room; (ii) the mountain meditation, in which the meditator climbs a high mountain, reaches the peak, and looks out on an expanse of the surrounding countryside; (iii) the chapel meditation, in which the meditator 'passes through a grove and reaches a chapel which he enters and where he remains for a long time'; (iv) the meditator goes in imagination to an old fountain and sits on a bench listening to the murmur of the water.[1:305]

Kretschmer writes:

> when a certain depth of meditation is attained, such symbols lose their ordinary meaning and their symbolic value is slowly revealed. As the meditator returns to the meadow, he does not experience things as he would in the ordinary world. . . . The meadow represents the blossoming of life which the meditator seeks. It also represents the world of the child . . . he returns to the positive, creative basis of his life. . . . In climbing the mountain, the meditator will generally symbolize some obstacle in his way so he must prove himself. Climbing in this psychic sphere always implies 'sublimation', in the Jungian rather than the Freudian use of the term. The words transformation, spiritualization, or humanization might convey the idea better than the word 'sublimation'. In any case, the climbing is a symbol of the movement during which man demonstrates his capacity to develop towards the goal of psychic freedom, the peak of human being. The passage through the forest on the

way to the mountain gives the meditator the opportunity to reconcile himself with the dark fearful side of his nature.[1:308-9]

The chapel represents the place where a person faces the existential questions of human life – death, meaning, integration and synthesis. Kretschmer comments on the religious basis of Happich's work, the combination of psychological and religious concerns which is also the basis of psychosynthesis. Happich, in addition to these four frameworks for meditation, also uses a mandala meditation, and a meditation on significant words – which Assagioli regularly employed.

Robert Desoille, who was French, was a significant contributor in the work of developing guided imagery (or directed daydreams, as he called the technique). He first published his description of the psychotherapeutic method he called 'rêve éveillé dirigé' in 1938. Frank Haronian translated some lectures he subsequently gave in 1965, and it is from this material that English-speaking readers generally know this work.

Desoille was originally an engineer, and was greatly influenced by Pavlovian theories of the personality – particularly those on human learning taking place through the mechanism of the conditioned reflex. He believed the structure of the guided daydream to be the condition under which unconscious material could be tapped and consequently used:

> The directed daydream, an intermediate hypnoidal state which shades between wakefulness and sleep, is essentially a device for tapping the inexhaustible reservoir in which one accumulates, during the course of one's life, anxieties, fears, desires, and hopes. These factors maintain their determining influences over ongoing behaviour whenever one is coping with the external world.[64]

Desoille's assumption is that in any person exhibiting problems there was unhealthy original conditioning. It is the function of the work with the unconscious to expose that conditioning and to encourage the person to build up another, better suited pattern in order to meet the demands of his life.

Although Desoille approaches his theory and technique from this mechanistic framework, the method and its results are very similar to those of Happich. This is in spite of the fact that he had no time for ideas of the Self. He writes, 'as for Jung's individuation processes' (similar to the idea of psychosynthesis for the individual), 'they pre-suppose the existence of a "Self" to which Jung attributes almost superhuman qualities. This transition from psychology to metaphysics is inimical to scientific research'.[64:30]

Desoille however believes that in directed daydreams the person can see images of reality and of nocturnal dreams, images from fables and myths, witches, dragons, demons in the lower unconscious, and for the transpersonal wise people, angels, winged horses, and religious imagery, and finally mystical images, expressing a quality, and similar to visions seen by mystics. Desoille uses the fairy-tales and myths very directly – he is very fond of Sleeping Beauty, the wicked witch, the dragon, and the sorcerer. He sees different symbols for men and women as being relevant for the particular work he is doing – for example, the symbol for confronting one's more obvious characteristics is, for men, a sword, and for women, a vessel or a container.

According to Kretschmer, Desoille believed that the patient must come to terms with the 'archetypes of the collective unconscious' within himself. 'He can then comprehend and resolve his personal conflicts within the larger context of man's inherent problems. Thus the patient experiences his personal conflicts as having an impersonal and collective background.'[1:310] This is a most interesting idea, which I believe could be developed much further.

The final piece of European work that must be mentioned in this field is that of Leuner,[152] who is referred to by Assagioli, and who has produced a textbook on guided imagery.

Most of the original work on guided imagery was done in Europe, and was familiar to Assagioli and increasingly incorporated into psychosynthesis. It is used to help a person become clearer about vague and painful parts of unconscious material, to get in touch with shadowy sides of the personality, to help people sort out alternative possibilities in their lives at a symbolic and relatively safe, and yet at the same time vivid, level, and to take immense personal steps in their lives and to practise doing so. It is a vehicle for watching oneself as a client, yet being fully involved. A major theme in guided imagery is the transformation of material through symbolism, so the technique can be used at every level of the work.

The latest development of the idea, which is beginning to be used in psychosynthesis, is the use of guided imagery in helping people use their own body resources to fight illness. Carl and Stephanie Simonton in their book *Getting Well Again*[211] and Brenda Kidman in *A Gentle Way with Cancer* on the Bristol Cancer Help Centre[141] both describe guided imagery as visualizing the cancer cells as being attacked by the natural defences of the body. Using the techniques for imagining the interior of the body – much as in the film *Fantastic Voyage* – and meditating on the dissolution of the illness seems to be a most positive and creative use of the technique, once again converting the 'client' into an active initiator rather than a passive victim. The use of will has remained a prime factor in the process of growth and the manifestation of potential.

The development of psychosynthesis techniques

Through the twentieth century, many other techniques have been incorporated into psychosynthesis work, to create the rich variety there is today. Some, like the dis-identification exercise, are related to the recognition of the 'I': others bring into relationship transpersonal, lower and collective unconscious material and consciousness. Yet others incorporate Gestalt insights and methods. These techniques were mentioned at the beginning of this chapter and this discussion is developed in Chapter 18. They are the subject of several books and articles in my bibliography (4–27: 48: 81: 251). New techniques are incorporated year by year; they are in a constant state of change.

7 The possibility of synthesis

This account of psychosynthesis is necessarily selective. It is not a therapist's account, though it pays attention to the ideas and experience behind therapy. It is close to the account given by Assagioli who died over a decade ago, and psychosynthesis has moved on since then in the many centres founded around the world. The models I have given were presented by him, but he always insisted they were 'not true': they have been reworked and modified in the different psychosynthesis centres in the world. My interest here, however, is in the ideas and experience behind the original conception of the system: these ideas are referred to by Assagioli, but are not fully spelt out or discussed by him.

The major psychosynthesis concepts considered here are the nature of the person, and particularly the relationship of the conscious to the unconscious, the personality to the soul, and the therapeutic methods of working with this material. But Assagioli's prime concept, spelt out in the name of the psychotherapeutic system, is that of synthesis. This is the understanding that at the individual level, at the level of the group, society and the world as a whole, we are fragmented socially and spiritually. His view was that every manifestation in the world, however destructive, represents a creative possibility, both in the individual or in society: that this destruction springs from unconscious material by which people are driven and which they are not in touch with: that the fragmentation can be healed by people becoming aware of the force of this unconscious material from a centred place, the 'I', and allowing spiritual forces to work towards a new and qualitatively different reconciliation of opposites: and that personal, social and spiritual knowledge of the inner world is a direct counterpart to true knowledge of the external world. It is not possible for the outer world to become more whole without a comparable understanding of conscious and unconscious processes in the inner life of individuals. The unconscious offers all the creative possibilities as well as the destructive ones, and for a truly whole individual or world to emerge there must be awareness, constant awareness, of those possibilities that are trying to be born. Therefore there must be an attitude of mind in relation to experience and knowledge which is receptive as well as active: a preparedness to work through and transform the accretions and rubbish gathered not just through a personal lifetime, but carried through from past generations in family dynamics and historical processes. This he saw as the task of the person prepared to become aware and to search for self-fulfilment as an intrinsic part of a search for a less fragmented and more whole world. In this he drew on many mystic traditions as well as on the newer psychotherapeutic insights made possible by the scientific approach of the twentieth century.

He did not regard himself as being either religiously or politically specific. He considered that every strong belief system had some part of the whole truth. In his personal notes he lists the strengths and weaknesses of all the political parties as he saw them – the creativity of the radical parties but the danger among them of violence and hatred; the preservative instincts of the conservatives but the blindness in relation to new ideas and the excessive adherence to known forms and institutions; and the integrity of the liberal and moderate parties but the danger of indecision, self-righteousness and lack of direction. He was widely read in the mystical traditions of the world, and knowledgeable about the nature of orthodox religions, but he did not wish to adhere to any one particularly, seeing all search as being a search for wholeness, for what people perceive is the spiritual nature of the world expressed in many specific forms. He saw difference as being valuable, if it could be contained within a wider context, and believed that greater wholeness contained the possibility of a greater variety of separate and different unique parts. As Huston Smith wrote in *The Religions of Man*,

> The various religions are but the different languages through which God has spoken to the human heart. 'Truth is one: sages call it by different names.' It is possible to climb life's mountain from any side, but when the top is reached, the pathways merge. As long as religions remain in the foothills of theology, ritual or church organisation, they may be far apart. Differences in culture, history, geography, and group temperament make for different starting points. . . . But the goal beyond these differences is the same goal.[214/235]

For the individual, psychosynthesis can work at several levels. For many people who come for therapy, the problem is one that may be an acute crisis, mainly dealing with lower unconscious material – people come to seek help because of some issue that is impeding, maybe destroying, their ordinary capacity to live fully in the world: it may be an issue involving despair, depression, isolation, sexual difficulties, fear. However, the work is always done within a transpersonal dimension, though this may not be very explicit. Here a psychosynthesist helps his or her client, out of that client's own strength, to live more fully. This is the level of Maslow's 'self-actualization'.

For many people, however, the problem is partly or wholly one of meaning and purpose and is therefore explicitly a spiritual one. Jung believed that most of his clients over 35 were deeply concerned with death and the meaning of life, and it is here that a transpersonal therapy really comes into its own, with the possibility of exploring personal and social meaning within this broader context. Some people may be attracted to psychosynthesis not because of any definite personal problem – their lives on all ordinary criteria are fulfilling and acceptable – but entirely because of lacking a sense of meaning.

It is generally the experience of psychosynthesis therapy that the more the person contacts transpersonal material, the more lower unconscious material will be stirred up in response, and the more capacity for both depths and heights there will be. Evelyn Underhill, in her book *Mysticism*, relates the mystical journey and includes it in the description of the 'dark night of the soul'. Assagioli was clear that the exploration of the unconscious, urgent as it sometimes may be, is a process to be treated with respect and with knowledge. This is, of course, one of the major functions of the therapist or guide in the process, acting sometimes as an unobtrusive helper and sometimes in the position of an external 'I' to whom the client has temporarily handed over their centred position. The power of this position is dangerous, of course, and a warning about the intrinsic problem of synthesis is cited by Freud in a passage that Assagioli contains in his notes:

> The neurotic human being brings us his mind racked and rent by resistances: whilst we are working at analysis of it and removing the resistances, this mind of his begins to grow together; that great unity which we call his Ego fuses into one all the instinctual trends which before had been split off and barred away from it. The psychosynthesis is thus achieved through analytic treatment without our intervention, automatically and inevitably. . . . There is no truth in the idea that when the patient's mind is dissolved into its elements it then quietly waits until somebody puts it together again. We

reject most emphatically the view that we should convert into our own property the patient who puts himself into our hands in search of help, should carve his destiny for him, force our own ideas upon him, and with the arrogance of a Creator form him in our own image and see that it is good.[26:1:14]

This is, of course, a major area in the process of therapy where there was disagreement between Freud and Assagioli, though there is no indication in Assagioli's notes whether Freud wrote the article directly in relationship to psychosynthesis as a system. The reply could be that in psychosynthesis the client could be seen at almost all times to be in control of the process. There is little, if any, direct interpretation of material by the therapist – the client is assumed to know at a deep level the meaning of his or her own unconscious material, and it is the function of the guide to help the client make his own sense of his experience in therapy. There would be agreement between Assagioli and Freud that the client carries his own strength and capacity for growth and that this is always working, as knots are untied and unconscious material uncovered. There is less emphasis on transference as a primary tool in psychosynthesis, and more on the relationship of adult to adult, especially at the beginning and end of each session. And the element of the transpersonal gives a context to the whole interaction which is not there in psychoanalysis, where the therapist holds the process together more directly.

Assagioli, as indicated throughout his last book, saw the use of personal will as being the primary directing agent in synthesis: 'will is a synthetic power. It dominates multiplicity and welds it into unity.' Synthesis, for him, is about living with a 'dynamic creative balance of tensions' from a still centre.[26:1:4] He quotes Montefiore in saying, 'the more perfect a man is, the more he can reconcile in his action and in his character opposing tendencies and claims.'[26:1:12] The paradoxical question seems to be: how can we become who we really are? The theory is that our potential self is already available to us if we could become aware of it, just as Assagioli believed that the world as a whole is perfectly there if we could become aware enough. But to reach it involves a long way through the unconscious – through Dante's Hell and Purgatory – because negative qualities (the lustful Leopard, the violent and proud Lion, and the avaricious Wolf) bar the way.

The goal of the transcendental journey seems to be that new recognition: to be at a place where it is not necessary to project inner material from the personal and collective past on to the present world, and being able to live more from the Higher Self than from the personality, being with the current and power of what is happening in life rather than struggling hopelessly against it. T. S. Eliot in the *Four Quartets* gives four lines that seem to encapsulate this view:

> We shall not cease from exploration
> And the end of all our exploring
> Will be to arrive where we started
> And to know the place for the first time.

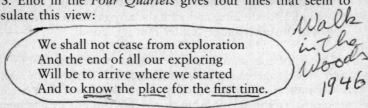

Walk in the Woods 1946.

It was Assagioli's view that the development of the individual is not only an end in itself, but also a means to an end. Otherwise the process of psychosynthesis can become self-indulgent and inward-looking. His view was closer to that of the Boddhisattva in the Buddhist tradition – the person who takes on not only his or her own personal suffering but also the suffering of the whole of humanity, and indeed of all creatures. The Boddhisattva vows to return to earth again and again until all suffering is worked through: in psychodynamic terms, until all unconscious material has become conscious and aware, and the inner world is not projected on to the outer.

In this view, all living things are linked with all others – in Francis Thompson's words:

> All things to each other, hiddenly linked are,
> That thou canst not stir a flower without troubling of a star.

This is why in the egg-shaped diagram (Figure 2.1) the divisions between the personal and the collective unconscious are broken.

Assagioli's view was that there is a natural progression towards synthesis: that as people live nearer to the soul than to the personality, there is automatically a move to the 'next larger whole', which might be a personal relationship, a committed group, an awareness of a national or international concern, a different commitment to the universal. There is likely to be a development of service, a service that is not 'driven' by unconscious needs, but springs from a clearer and more conscious place.

Both Assagioli and other psychosynthesis writers have spoken about psychosynthesis work with the couple, the family, the group, the institution. In all their work the basic principles are similar to those of work with the individual – the working out together of unconscious material, and the development of awareness that a greater context is already present. The number of factors involved in the work changes as the size of the group grows larger and more complex, though the nature of the work involved is not necessarily more testing. The process of synthesis in any of these larger entities also involves recognizing the part we play in this process – as Jung so graphically wrote, 'we have seen the enemy and it is us.' It is difficult for all these social organizations to see the parts the members play in producing their own hells – and to acknowledge sometimes their own heavens.

Assagioli was particularly concerned with education as a process – in a move away from the achievement-oriented and technical education which is the basis of our present system, towards a process that would take equally into account intellect and feeling, and the development of awareness of service and commitment to the whole of humanity. For it was to the whole that Assagioli was committed himself. To this end he believed that all great people went on learning and growing until the day they died – he quotes with approval Michelangelo, Goethe, Tagore and Keyserling, who continued to change with energy and a child's enthusiasm to the end of their lives.

He was aware of the chaos that one generation passes on to the next – that each generation starts off not only with a background of achievement through civilization, but of massive problems through the history of mankind. It was this awareness that made him quote Paul Tournier's dedication to his book *Les Desharmonies de la Moderne*: 'To our two children and to the younger generation, whose forgiveness our generation must beg for bequeathing to them so sick a world.' He was also most conscious of the visions of unity offered by great writers of the past and present – Dante's view of the universal world, Emerson's and Mazzini's attempts to envisage the interdependence of the nations, the images of Vico, Spengler and Toynbee in tracing the sense of history and attempting to see that history from a wider perspective, from the context rather than the content. He had clearly been most influenced by a paper given at an international philosophy conference in 1911 by the Polish writer W. Lutoslawski, 'Nations as metaphysical entities', which described the national consciousness as adolescent, being driven to search for identity and pride.

This picture of the nations as developing beings has been carried forward in recent psychosynthesis writings: both Astrid Koch[145] and Michael Gigante[99] have seen nations as being the superpersonalities of the world, warring, projecting unconscious material, seeking recognition, with great destructive potential, yet seeking cooperation and a greater vision. Donald Keys, with his campaign on a new planetary initiative for a world we actually choose, is in line with this analysis in his powerful writing. Mark Horowitz, in his *Psychology in the Global Area*,[24(3)] writing within a psychosynthesis framework, puts forward that the soul, the Higher Self of the world, is already there, and once again the message is the same as it was for the individual, that we must work through the Shadow, and also contact and recognize the transpersonal, to glimpse that place, Dante's 'Paradise'.

In Assagioli's papers there is a quotation by Martin Buber from his *Israel and the World*:

> We can know and accept the fact that unity, not division and separation, is the purpose of creation, and that the purpose is not an everlasting struggle to the death between sects or classes or nations. Our purpose is the great upbuilding of peace. And when the nations are all bound together in one association, to borrow a phrase from our sages, they atone for each other. In other words: the world of humanity is meant to become a single body; but it is as yet nothing more than a heap of limbs each of which is of the opinion that it constitutes an entire body. Furthermore the human world is meant to become a single body through the action of men themselves. We men are charged to perfect our own portion of the universe – the human world.[50:185-6]

Buber saw this in relation to the history of the Jews and Israel, but clearly this vision of unity for both Buber and Assagioli was one which, by its very nature, applies to all nations. It is a picture of all individuals and groups being related to all others, in space and in time, and of each person being responsible for the whole. It could be summed up in U Thant's words, which Assagioli also quotes: 'we cannot end the war between nations unless we end the war in the hearts of man.'

II

The Split between Scientific and Religious Knowledge

Introduction

In the first part of this study we saw some of the themes that spring from an account of key areas of psychosynthesis theory. There is the idea that fragmentation of conscious and more particularly unconscious material can dominate an individual's development, and that such a fragmentation may dominate the development of the human race as a whole. It is in first recognizing and then working through the most disabling aspects of the person, in the light of a spiritual context, that the negative and destructive may become more related to an integrating centre, the 'I'. The unconscious may become more known: the spiritual unconscious may become more available.

Much of this unconscious material is known, not only through observations and empirical study, but also through myths and symbols which have long traditions in many societies. There are several kinds of subjective and objective knowledge, which both a therapist and a client may use. And it may be that the destruction in the individual, and in the world, is based in unlived potential, in the fragmentation and accretion which is the sign of a lack of awareness and of not yet being able to cope with this potential. In Assagioli's view, these unconscious forces can be recognized and worked with, in the light of both spiritual consciousness and scientific methods and techniques becoming newly available. But at the present time the outward split between the disciplines of scientific knowledge and religious experience is a reflection of an inward split between these two kinds of 'knowing' in the individual. Fragmentation is present at many levels.

In Part Two, I trace the split development of scientific and religious/mystical thinking as it comes to be experienced and perceived in our present society. This is taken back to the relationship of these two modes of knowing in the sixteenth and seventeenth centuries in Europe, which is described in Chapter 8. But to trace the religious and spiritual influences on Assagioli, it is necessary to go back much further; Chapter 9 examines the nature of mysticism through twenty centuries, and Chapters 10 to 14 examine the particular Western schools most relevant to this search. Plato and Dante were life-long influences on Assagioli: the gnostic, neoplatonic and Jewish mystical schools, combined with Eastern mysticism, were the foundation of Theosophy and of Jung's framework of knowledge – one that was close to psychosynthesis. Also, it is clear from his library and from his writing, both published and unpublished, that Assagioli had an extensive knowledge of and interest in world spiritual thought. Much of this material came together around the turn of the nineteenth/twentieth centuries in an upsurge of interest in both Eastern and Western religious wisdom and knowledge, and this is examined in Chapter 15.

When psychology, psychiatry and psychotherapy began to develop in the late nineteenth century, it sprang largely from the scientific tradition and from clinical practice. In psychotherapy in particular, the interest was in the study of unconscious material, which for the first time in history was studied scientifically and systematically. These movements are the subjects of Chapters 16 and 17.

Thus in the second Part of the book I am tracing the roots of what originally seemed to me the extraordinary ideas of psychosynthesis. I had wondered where these ideas came from: what were the sources of Assagioli's certainty? Why was his psychology so different from that taught in universities today?

Part II contains my guesses in answer to these questions.

8
The split development of scientific and mystical thinking over the last four hundred years

In the following section, the development of mystical thought particularly relevant to psychosynthesis will be traced over many centuries, up to the time that Assagioli started writing at the beginning of the twentieth century. Assagioli was also a doctor and a psychiatrist, based in the scientific tradition. In asking about the origin of the ideas contained in psychosynthesis, and the nature of the knowledge that it embraces, it is necessary to examine the relationship of mystical to scientific knowledge, because that is the tension within psychosynthesis and indeed within any transpersonal psychotherapy.

It is not possible to do this without going back again into historical material. The roots of this tension lie in what has been seen as 'knowledge' in the last four hundred years in the West, and the massive change not only in the nature of our knowledge but also in how we think of it.

Science and the scientific method have been seen in this period in the West as the way to truly objective knowledge. The science that is the basis of modern Western culture is inductive – in other words, it is based on observation and experimentation and is sceptical: from the observations made, generalizations and laws are created but are always subject to query. This method was first used in relation to the natural sciences, particularly astronomy, physics and chemistry, and has developed through the great technological discoveries that have transformed our lives. It assumes that the observer, the scientist, is objective and value-free: anyone performing the same process would come up with the same results. It is also based on a premise of growth and of control – the more we can find out, the more power and control we can have over the nature of things, and the more the human race can develop. This assumption has been carried over from the natural sciences to the social sciences, into the study of the individual in psychology, developed in the late nineteenth century, and of society through sociology, first developed in the nineteenth century by Comte.

The part of the scientific observer in this process has, however, been pondered over by many philosophers of science: what any scientist perceives depends on the questions he or she asks and the structure of thought that that scientist takes to a particular problem. This point was made by Giambattista Vico (1668–1744) in opposition to the eighteenth century conviction of the validity of rationality. Scientific knowledge, he maintained, is not about a system of rules that governs reality, but a man-made artefact, useful as far as it goes but no further. In science we are not so much discovering 'truth' as constructing pictures of reality from the human brain – a picture that is *created* by the *structure* of the brain. We can understand the 'world' because we ourselves have created it.

This has remained a counter-idea to the widespread belief in the ultimate truth of science through the centuries since then, particularly by phenomenologists. Modern science can be seen not only as a continuous accretion of new knowledge about the nature of things, but also as a huge metaphor or myth – perhaps the myth of our age and of the last four hundred years. It works within its own framework and boundaries, just as any myth does: but science may also be a restriction on our knowledge if we think it can account for all our reality. Vico maintained that it was:

> a perverse kind of self-denial to apply the rules and laws of physics or of any other natural sciences to the world of mind and will and feeling; for by doing this we would be gratuitously debarring ourselves from much that we could know.[35:96]

The idea of science as a creation of human reality has been taken further by a contemporary historian of ideas, Thomas Kuhn, in his well-known book *The Structure of Scientific Revolutions*, which was first published in 1962. Kuhn maintains that at any one time there is an accepted picture of scientific reality which he calls a paradigm – for instance, Ptolemaic astronomy. This is the pattern of 'conventional routinized practice' upon which all scientists of the time work, and is related to a set of models about the nature of the world which all the practitioners can accept and develop. Eventually, the practitioners will begin to discover more and more anomalies and exceptions, and gradually the paradigm will be questioned – often against the considerable opposition not only of the scientific community but of the society at large: this occurred, for instance, in relation to Copernicus's astronomy in the sixteenth century and to Darwin's theories of evolution in the nineteenth, both of which questioned contemporary religious and spiritual as well as scientific pictures of the nature of the universe and of the human race within it. This bursting of the paradigm and creation of a new one is the scientific revolution referred to in the title of the book. And then, as Kuhn states, 'though the world does not change with a change of paradigm, the scientist afterward works in a different world.'[147:121] He maintains, as Vico also did, that the assumptions of a particular paradigm are likely to be incompatible with those of another: knowledge does not simply build up incrementally bit by bit, but is in competition with other kinds of knowledge in other paradigms. As Vico wrote, each society creates its own unique vision: it was not that the rationality of the scientific society in his own day was superior to other societies in some absolute way, it was simply governed by a different set of values, and the world was seen through different eyes. The Western world may have lost much as well as gained much by the predominance of the scientific and technological mode of thinking.

Science in our culture is the pre-eminent mode of 'knowing'. The validity of knowledge in universities is governed by the test of objectivity, of evidence, of the quoting of authorities, of openness. Mystical and religious knowledge, on the other hand, is presently regarded with a good deal of suspicion. Science in general assumes that the nature of reality is material – and in any case that is science's only true domain because it is not possible to test mystery and spirituality. Religion in its personal form is the experience of the spiritual. Jung maintains that religion is about the transcendental. But the difficulty here is that not only is the knowledge personal, not open, it is also interior, untestable. It is likely to relate to a conviction about the nature of the universe that is taken to be absolutely true, but untestable. It deals in belief and conviction, and in subjective knowledge: and from this belief, ways of action are deduced. The assumption is that the universe is not basically material but spiritual, and that is the greater reality. And an assumption of the importance of spirituality may impose restrictions of human curiosity that the scientist as such is unwilling to abide by. On the whole, spiritual knowledge, such as that traced in this earlier section of Part Two, is based on completely different assumptions from those of science and technology. The two live in the modern world uneasily together. Science is the more powerful mode by far, though it is recognized by most people that the great hope for human progress held so fervently in the nineteenth century through science has met with disillusion. Religion, and particularly mysticism, is generally suspect and marginal.

Both science and conventional religions have built up strong institutions. The different churches can be seen to represent the religious impulse, but as Jung indicates, <u>churches are 'codified and dogmatised forms of religious experience.</u> The contents of the experience have become sanctified and usually congealed in a rigid, often elaborate structure'.[133:6] Similarly, scientific interest groups have developed, heavily financially backed by powerful elites in society (<u>as is also the case among established religion).</u> Science in particular is buttressed and supported by national and international companies, universities, professions, and the developed expectations of the population. Knowledge held to be 'real' is by no means a neutral matter, but involves the power of definition of how the society ought to be run, and what values should underlie it.

To look at the origin of the scientific world we know now, we need to go back to the sixteenth century, at the time of a major scientific revolution which changed the way people saw the nature of things.

> In 1500 educated people in Western Europe believed
> themselves living in the centre of a finite cosmos, at the mercy
> of supernatural forces beyond their control, and certainly
> continually menaced by Satan and all his allies. By 1700
> educated people in Western Europe for the most part believed
> themselves living in an infinite universe on a tiny planet in
> (elliptical) orbit round the sun, no longer menaced by Satan,
> and confident that power over the natural world lay within
> their grasp.[67:1]

This latter picture is not so different, with modifications, from the picture most people have of the nature of reality today. This quotation indicates the power and relativity of the basic assumptions with which people at different historical periods lead their lives.

The earlier religious world view was Christian and was encapsulated in the picture of the Great Chain of Being, described on page 112 – a spiritual, hierarchical image of reality which related matter to spirit throughout the world, from rocks and worms to the highest God, and seeing Good and Evil as separate, powerful forces at work in the world. The only attempt that could then be made in such circumstances to control the world was through magic, including alchemy; magic was arguably the forerunner of our modern science – Francis Bacon called his own science 'natural magic'. The differences in the practices of religion and magic were brought out in relation to this earlier period by Keith Thomas:

> The essential difference between the prayers of a churchman and the spells of a magician was that only the latter claimed to work automatically; a prayer had no certainty of success and would not be granted if God chose not to concede it. A spell, on the other hand, need never go wrong, unless some detail of ritual observation had been omitted or a rival magician had been practising stronger counter-magic. A prayer, in other words, was a form of supplication: a spell was a mechanical means of manipulation.[225:46]

The power sought in magic was similar to the power based in science today.

But in the sixteenth century the two were not yet divided. Robert Fludd, for instance, who lived in England from 1574 to 1637, could attempt to write down the whole of human knowledge. He first wrote of the macrocosm, the external world of nature: then of the microcosm, the internal world, the world of prophecy, knowledge of higher worlds, the body, palmistry, and invention. He was a medical man, a doctor, an inventor, an engineer, a scholar of the Kabbalah and other Western esoteric writings, an astronomer, a classicist, a Biblical scholar, a geometrist, a man with a particular interest in the weather and the winds, a musician, a surveyor, a military tactician, and an illustrator. The great figures of the Renaissance – Leonardo, Michelangelo – often had a similar range of interests and skills and saw the spiritual and the material as one great vision. What is more, apart from the rather small-scale attempts at control through magic, there was a respect for the earth and the creatures of the earth, combined with fear of retribution from supernatural forces if mankind went beyond its natural limits. The spirit of this time in England is beautifully portrayed in Tillyard's classic *The Elizabethan World Picture*. He describes the order of that world, and the sense of all things being in their place, encapsulated in the Great Chain, with the possibility both of great optimism because of the goodness of the world and the skills and intelligence of the human being, and of terrible pessimism because of the imperfection and evil of things. But the view was explicitly a world view, a view of the universe, in contrast to the material and mundane view routinely taken today. There was a sense of the abundance of things and the respect due to them. Tillyard instances Spencer's 'Hymn of Heavenly Beauty':

> Then, look, who list thy gazeful eye to feed
> With sight of that is fair, look on the frame
> Of this wide universe and therein read
> The endless kind of creatures which by name
> Thou canst not count, much less their natures' aim;
> All which are made with wondrous wide respect
> And all with admirable beauty deckt.[226]

The investigations of science into the creatures of the earth were to change that attitude for many people, in the scientists' wish to investigate and change living creatures rather than marvel at them: though of course the possibility of wonder as well as control is still present in the world.

Mankind was seen at this period as half-way between God and beast, spirit and matter, but always within a cosmic setting. The sense of mankind's potential through God, and of imperfection and sin, was paramount. A French writer of the period put it thus:

> If we well consider man in the first estate that God created him, it is the chief and principal of God's work, to the end that in him he might be glorified as in the most noblest and excellentest of all his creatures. But if we consider him in the estate of the general corruption spread all over the posterity of Adam, we shall see him nuzzled in sin, monstrous fearful deformed, subject to a thousand incommodities, void of beatitude, unable ignorant variable and hypocrite. . . . But if we will consider afterward as being made all new by the immortal seed of God's word ye shall see him restored not only in all his first honours and goods but much greater; for there whereas sin is poured out for to let and hinder him, the grace of God is more abundantly poured out for to succour him, making him a new creature.[226:87]

But the fundamentally spiritual view of the universe was changing by the seventeenth century. In 1593, Richard Hooker wrote, in line with all the foregoing, 'see we not plainly that obedience of creatures unto the law of nature is the stay of the whole world.'[170:6] Only twelve years later, in 1605, the scientist Kepler, who had been a Rosicrucian, wrote to a friend, 'my aim is to show that the celestial machine is to be likened not to a divine organism but to a clockwork.'[170:128-9] Francis Bacon (1561–1626) was clear that man wished to know about nature so that he could control her – the pronouns here are very significant. Nature could be used, and there was no limit to the possibilities and little morality involved.

> The new man of science must not think that the 'inquisition of nature is in any part interdicted or forbidden'. Nature must be 'bound into service' and made a 'slave', put 'in constraint' and 'moulded' by the mechanical arts. The 'searchers and the spies of nature' are to discover her plots and secrets.[170:169]

The transcendental God was still believed in by such scientists of the seventeenth century, but the immanent God present in all things had vanished. Instead, natural things were seen as being legitimately subjectable to the forces and language of the Inquisition.

Bacon's utopian *New Atlantis* foresees the control of biology:

> The New Atlantis had parks and enclosures for beasts and birds where just such experiments were performed: 'By art likewise we make them greater or taller than their kind is, and contrariwise dwarf them, and stay their growth; we make them more fruitful and bearing than their kind is, and contrariwise barren and not generative. Also we make them differ in colour, shape, activity, many ways.'[170:183]

The future development of test-tube babies is almost foreseen. As Merchant comments, 'rational control over nature, society and the self was achieved by defining reality itself through the new machine metaphor.'[170:193]

Merchant, a historian of the changing attitude of the seventeenth century, sees the process as one much to be regretted, as it brought a controlling, non-respectful, male attitude to bear on the way people live their lives, which has continued to this day.

> The process of mechanising the world picture removed the controls over environmental exploitation that were an inherent part of the organic view that nature was alive, sensitive, and responsive to human action. Mechanism took over from the magical tradition the conception of the manipulation of matter but divested it of life and vital action. The passivity of matter, externality of motion, and elimination of the female world-soul altered the character of cosmology and its associated normative constraints. In the mechanical philosophy, the manipulation of nature ceased to be a matter of individual efforts and became associated with general collaborative social interests that

sanctioned the expansion of commercial capitalism.
Increasingly it benefited those persons and social classes in
control of its development, rather than promoting universal
progress for all. It was intimately connected to an empirical
philosophy of science and a concept of the human being as a
designer of experiments who by wresting secrets from nature
gained mastery over its operations.[170:111]

Throughout the seventeenth century there were bitter conflicts
between the religious and the scientific views of the world. In
1650 Jacob Bauthumley, who was a member of the seventeenth
century religious sect the Ranters, wrote:

> God is in everyone and in every living thing, man and beast,
> fish and fowl, and every green thing, from the highest cedar to
> the ivy on the wall. . . . God is in this dog, this tobacco pipe, he
> is me and I am him.[170:124]

By way of contrast, René Descartes in the same period had a
vision of the certainty of the new science:

> All science is certain, evident knowledge. We reject all
> knowledge which is merely probably and judge that only those
> things should be believed which are perfectly known and about
> which there can be no doubts.[54:42]

His view that scientific knowledge is really true on some objective
basis is the one that prevails in much of society today: after
Kuhn's work, we could now say that the Western scientific view
can be seen as objectively true only within its own paradigm, and
no more than that. But Descartes believed in the ultimate truth of
analytic, rational thinking – 'the belief', according to Fritjof
Capra, 'that all aspects of complex phenomena can be understood
by reducing them to their constituent parts'.[54:44] He rejected the
idea of the unconscious. He believed in a complete split between
mind and body: 'there is nothing included in the concept of body
that belongs to the mind; and nothing in that of the mind that
belongs to the body.'[54:45] Again Descartes uses the analogy of a
clock in thinking about the whole world, including animals and
human beings, and he believed, with Bacon, that the purpose of
science was to gain control over nature. This split between mind
and body was of radical significance to subsequent thought, and
one that broke from the picture of the body as a symbol of the
soul.

Isaac Newton (1642–1717) synthesized the work of Bacon and Descartes: 'going beyond Bacon in his systematic experimentation and beyond Descartes in his mathematical analysis, Newton unified the two trends and developed the methodology upon which natural science has been based ever since.'[54:50] It is interesting, however, that even by the eighteenth century Newton the scientist was still interested in occult, alchemical and esoteric knowledge, and was also particularly interested in the meaning of the Book of Revelation. He conceived of himself as only on the outskirts of knowledge – picking up a pretty shell or pebble on the beach whilst the whole ocean of truth lay before him, untouched. But many lesser scientists took his discoveries as the ultimate laws.

In fact, the widespread assumption of the religious basis of knowledge was probably not finally eroded until the nineteenth century, and then particularly through the work of Darwin. Lovejoy maintains that the assumption of the Great Chain of Being as the basis of reality in the universe was still widely accepted until the end of the eighteenth or even the early nineteenth century. In fact, eight major scientific works were sponsored under the will of the Earl of Bridgwater in 1829, under the stipulation that the works should illustrate 'the Power, Wisdom and Goodness of God, as manifested in the Creation; illustrating such works by all reasonable argument'. The works produced emphasized the supremacy of man – one was called 'On the adaptation of External Nature to the Physical Condition of Man'. As J. W. Burrow, in his introduction to the Penguin edition to Darwin's *The Origin of Species*, comments, 'the Bridgwater Treatises were the last great monument of an intellectual tradition which had provided assurance that man and nature were linked in an almighty purpose, that the world was not soulless, indifferent or malign. . . .'

Darwin's theory of natural selection was seen as undermining the fundamentalist views of the Bible. Darwin himself wrote in his autobiography about the effect of his researches on himself:

Formerly I was led by feelings . . . to the firm conviction of the existence of God, and of the immortality of the soul. In my Journal I wrote that whilst standing in the grandeur of a Brazilian forest, 'it is not possible to give an adequate picture of the higher feelings of wonder, admiration and devotion which fill and elevate the mind'. I well remember my conviction that there is more in man than the mere breath of his body. But now the grandest scenes would not cause any such convictions and feelings to rise to my mind. It may be truly said that I am like a man who has become colour blind.[52:1]

The statement is perhaps one of the most significant ones of the modern world, describing in a few words the change from the spiritual to the mundane view of reality when many people have lost the sense of wonder Darwin describes. Interestingly, and by way of contrast, Alfred Russel Wallace, the co-discoverer of the theory of natural selection, developed interests in mysticism and spiritualism.[58] The overall effect of Darwinism was, however, to question religious orthodoxy and the authority of the established church. Susan Budd, in her study of atheists and agnostics in Victorian society, comments that the new science lay outside the established order, and that the belief in a wholly rational scientific basis of knowledge was strongest at the end of the nineteenth century.

T. H. Huxley in the nineteenth century repeats some of the optimism about the potentiality of scientific knowledge that could be found in the earlier seventeenth and eighteenth century scientists. He writes in 1870:

The whole of modern thought is steeped in science; it has made its way into the works of our best poets, and even the mere man of letters, who affects to ignore and despise science, is unconsciously impregnated with her spirit, and indebted for his best products to her methods. I believe that the greatest intellectual revolution mankind has yet seen is now taking place by her agency. She is teaching the world that the ultimate court of appeal is observation and experiment and not authority; she is teaching it to estimate the value of evidence; she is creating a firm and living faith in the existence of immutable moral and physical laws, perfect obedience to which is the highest possible aim of an intelligent being.[52:147]

Susan Budd traces in England a process that was occurring throughout the Western world, of a growing secularization of knowledge, which has continued to this day. Christianity still obviously exists as a force in the Western world, but it is possible for millions of people to live in this world without any but a most superficial link to it. The development of science, technology and industry profoundly affects us all.

The spiritual versus the scientific issue in the twentieth century is the context of psychosynthesis, and this will be discussed later. Work on what is now called the 'transpersonal' is clearly an interesting phenomenon of this century. This development is not within any of the orthodox centres of learning, either scientific or religious, though some individuals within these institutions are beginning to take an interest in this new form of relating mysticism to science. The religious sense has clearly never died throughout the time of the prominence of science. The scientific attitude *per se* has throughout the period been questioned as being the only source of truth. There are now many groups who believe that a new reconciliation, or even a drastic shift in perspective is about to take place because of the clear inability of science on its own to deal with the dangerous moral questions of the twentieth century. But this can only be seen in any form of perspective against the backcloth of the last four hundred years.

In this section, I am drawing both on the perspective of the sociology of knowledge, and the emphasis on the institutional basis of knowledge – the deep roots of both science and religion in the major institutions of the time, and the history of ideas, particularly scientific ideas which have won so great a preponderance in the Western world. The battle between the two has looked mainly like a battle of ideas, but the link into the industrial, economic, political and educational institutions and the scientific basis of most of our assumptions is quite obvious in the modern world. It is interesting and extraordinary that the modern scientific world view sprang from the mystical:

> It is one of the more profound ironies of the history of thought that the growth of mechanical science through which arose the idea of mechanism as a possible philosophy of nature, was itself an outcome of the Renaissance mystical tradition.[250:150]

9 The nature of mysticism, particularly as applied to psychosynthesis

Some scholars and mystics have claimed that there is a common base to all mystical experience: 'all mystics, said Saint-Martin, speak the same language and come from the same country.'[222][9:xiii] Throughout recorded history men and women known as mystics have experienced a certainty about the nature of reality, about the place of human beings and other sentient creatures in that reality, and a perspective on everyday mundane life, that seems to bear a remarkable similarity from culture to culture, from one century to another. It is as though they experience that the soul, the Higher Self, in communion with the Absolute, God, Divinity, can be a greater, higher, more inward reality than the personality living in the visible world. The greater reality suffuses the lesser and alters it beyond recognition. 'The infinite shines through the finite and makes it more and not less real.'[206:28] This is not a doctrine, a dogma learned through a church or established religion, but a personal experience, an inner knowing, which lies at the root of all religious doctrines and is prior to them.

It is by common consent difficult to define mysticism. A helpful list of salient characteristics is however given by Roberto Gimello in his article on 'Mysticism and meditation'.[100] These include a feeling of oneness, of unity, with the universe; a conviction that the experience has an objective validity, that it is about the nature of reality; a conviction that the experience cannot be explained or even described in human language; an understanding that the experience is not just a rational or an emotional one – it is a superior kind of knowing not generally available to people; an understanding that opposites meet, synchronize, are one – that paradox is basic; and a strong affective tone – a feeling of completion, of joy, of incomparable pleasure. There does seem to be a remarkable similarity about many descriptions which conform with this picture. Many writers, particularly Aldous Huxley in his *Perennial Philosophy* and W. T. Stace in his *Mysticism and Philosophy*, argue that indeed the experiences indicate a common reality of the human condition for those sensitive enough to experience it: and because of the ineffability of the subject it is difficult to disagree with these statements with any competence. But there are also some indications that, though much may be experienced in common, there may also be cultural differences and religious specificities which are of significance to our understanding of the nature of mysticism.

In most cultures, the basic view of the world, the cosmology of the society, is spiritual. From the beginning of thought, human beings have been concerned to build up a picture of the whole of reality, and to see people within that wider meaningful setting. The universe has been seen as the place of all-mighty God, or Oneness, or Gods, or spirits: human experience has been perceived within this wider framework. Human nature has been understood as part of a whole. All societies have myths, their own construction of the nature of reality, usually in the form of stories, though sometimes worked out more philosophically or rationally.

This cosmology is likely to structure the nature of the mystical experience. Carl Keller argues that 'in reality, when we compare mystical texts, we are comparing doctrinal systems or, in other words, total myth-dreams of societies, communities and individuals'.[138] Modern students of mysticism tend to maintain that it is impossible to have a pure 'experience': that to every experience, however deep, we bring a set of concepts already learned in the societies in which we live: that 'there is a clear causal connection between the religious and social structure one brings to experience and the nature of one's religious experience'.[136:40] For instance, in cultures that stress the objectiveness and 'otherness' of God, and the puniness of the human condition, this image is likely to affect the way in which the whole mystical experience is perceived: for a Buddhist, with no picture of a 'God' as such, the imagery is entirely different because the basic cosmology is so dissimilar. 'The mystic brings to his experience a world of concepts, images and symbols, and values, which shape as well as colour the experience he eventually and actually has.'[136:46] It is only likely to be a Catholic who will see a vision of the Virgin Mary.

This speculation is very interesting because it reflects another two somewhat opposed views of the nature of this experience. Most older cultures have tended to see the world as being separate from the individual. However, some modern psychology and philosophy has led us to understand how much we create our own worlds because of the structure of our brains, our eyes, and the relationship between them; this has led in turn to an interest in different states of consciousness, an experience of course always recognized by mystics, but now perceived more explicitly as being part of the creation of human beings. There is in modern literature a 'psychological' as well as a 'cosmological' view of reality – or perhaps our psychological view is part of modern 'scientific' cosmology.

So modern writers have raised questions as to whether the mystical experience really has something basically in common for every person sensitive to its potentiality, in whatever culture or time: we are left in doubt (as we basically always were, on an intellectual level), about whether mystical awareness does really signify a common reality for all sentient beings – even though it is a reality that most people only fleetingly experience, if at all.

As a source of knowledge, mysticism is of course in opposition to the scientific mode – the empirical, testable, provable knowledge which is the currency of the modern Western world. Freud, Jung and Assagioli, all medical doctors, trained in the scientific method, had to maintain the validity of their work against such opposition as that of Karl Popper and his criticism of 'closed systems' theory, and still are hardly regarded as respectable in the university system. Jung and Assagioli had the added 'disadvantage' of drawing on a personal spiritual awareness which they regarded as fundamental to their work.

To indicate that there might be some possibility of the reconciliation of these two systems of knowledge in this century, it is salutary and encouraging to quote the great twentieth century scientist Einstein. He wrote:

> The most beautiful emotion we can experience is the mystical.
> It is the sower of all true art and science. He to whom this
> emotion is a stranger . . . is as good as dead. To know that
> what is impenetrable to us really exists, manifesting itself as the
> highest wisdom and the most radiant beauty, which our dull
> faculties can comprehend only in their most primitive forms –
> this knowledge, this feeling, is at the centre to true
> religiousness. In this sense, and in this sense only, I belong to
> the ranks of devoutly religious men.[242:4]

The great Jewish scholar of Jewish mysticism Gershom Scholem considers that the phenomenon of mysticism occurs under specific historical conditions in the history of the human race. There was no need for the search for unity and meaning before human beings became self-conscious, when humans (just as other animals still seem to be) were at one with their universe. He maintains that:

> Religion's supreme function is to destroy the dream-harmony
> of Man, Universe and God, to isolate man from the other

elements of the dream stage of his mythical and primitive consciousness. For in its classical form, religion signifies the creation of a vast abyss, conceived as absolute, between God, the infinite and transcendental Being and Man, the finite creature.[206:7]

This is the issue of duality, which we still struggle with today – the sense of being strangers in a strange world, of alienation, of yearning for something which would make life on earth meaningful, a greater context than the common-sense world, a reality once known and forgotten.

Mysticism does not deny or overlook the abyss; on the contrary, it begins by realising its existence, but from there it proceeds to a quest for the secret that will close it in, the hidden path that will span it. It strives to piece together the fragments broken by the religious cataclysm, to bring back the old unity which religion has destroyed, but on a new plane, where the world of mythology and that of revelation meet in the soul of man.[206:8]

In this view, mysticism, through the realization of immanent spirituality, heals the transcendent split between God and man.

The picture of God as 'the other', out there, of a different nature from corrupt matter, outside ordinary experience, is fundamental to many Western and some Eastern religions. People pray to and worship the infinite and all-mighty God, and expect to be judged by Him (as Scholem points out, this is a masculine God, all-powerful). God is perceived as perfect and self-sufficient, and man as imperfect and needy. Plato writes in the *Philebus*, 'the Good differs in its nature from everything else in that the being who possesses it always and in all respects has the most perfect sufficiency and is never in need of any other thing'.[154:42] Similarly, the Christian God is perfect, and to be worshipped: He *sent* His only son, Christ, to earth to redeem people, but He stays separate and transcendental. Though the mystery in Christianity is that Jesus said, 'The Father and I are one.'

Evelyn Underhill, in her brilliant study of mysticism published in 1910 and highly regarded by Assagioli, writes that transcendental theories, where spirituality emanates from the divine source, are the language of pilgrimage, of exile, of rejection of the world. 'Never forget', says St John of the Cross, 'that God is inaccessible. Ask not therefore, how far your powers may comprehend Him, your feelings penetrate Him.'[229:98] This, says

Underhill, portrays the kind of mind that William James called 'the sick soul', the soul of the penitent and the humble, 'appalled by the sharp contrast between itself and the Perfect which it contemplates', struggling like the salmon working upstream to find the home it once knew. It is the complete separation of the human and all living creatures from the Creator, the Divine. But in Christian thought this separation is redeemed by *God's* love for man.

This duality is at the root of most gnostic thought, where the supreme God is seen as different from the Demiurge, the creative force that allows the existence of evil as well as good. The separation of spirituality from matter is the classic attempt to explain evil, where the good, all-powerful God is seen as completely distinct from His creation, which is debased in matter.

The Great Chain of Being, the perception of the world which originated in classical Greece and lasted till the middle of the eighteenth century, falls largely within the transcendental vision, as all good is seen as coming 'downward' from the supreme Being and as being dependent on Him. It starts in the conviction, as Lovejoy indicates in his powerful lectures given in the 1930s, that 'true being, the world in which the soul can find itself at home, must be *somehow* other than "all this" '.[154:29] The Great Chain of Being is rooted in Platonic and neoplatonic thinking, though adopted by Christians for most of their history in order to relate perfect spirit to imperfect matter. Macrobius, the fifth century philosopher, describes the justification for and basis of the theory succinctly:

> Since, from the Supreme God Mind arises, and from Mind, Soul, and since this in turn creates all subsequent things and fills them all with life, and since this single radiance illuminates all and is reflected in each, as a single face might be reflected in many mirrors placed in a series; and since all things follow in continuous succession, degenerating in sequence to the very bottom of the series, the attentive observer will discover a connection of parts, from the supreme God down to the last dreg of things, mutually linked together and without a break. And this is Homer's golden chain, which God, he says, bade hang down from heaven to earth.[154:63]

The picture of the Chain of Being is of God at the apex of the universe, suffusing the whole, purely spirit: at the base is matter – the most primitive matter that can exist, rocks, earth, the most simple forms of the universe – these are purely matter and not spirit. In between is the hierarchy of all living things. Mankind is midway between the depth of matter and the heights of spirituality. Below the human race come all animal forms, in descending order of complexity to simplicity. Above mankind are the angels and other spiritual beings.

This picture is like that of Dante's *Divine Comedy* with God in the Heavens, in Paradise, and a long harsh way for the soul to travel, through Hell and Purgatory, in order to reach the spiritual goal.

The mystic in relation to the transcendent God, then, is the searcher for that which was lost, the seer of visions, the humble penitent seeking the great 'other'. But mysticism has also another conception of God, that of immanence – the God within. In this view, every living moment contains the possibility of the spiritual; we always can be what we may be, we can always cooperate with the spiritual and with our inner vision. The mystic does not have a long hard road to travel to an immanent God: all he or she needs to do is to remember, to realize the presence in the soul and in the universe; it is the mysticism of James's healthy-minded souls: 'an opening of the eyes of the soul in which Reality is bathed. For them the earth is literally "crammed with heaven".'[229:99] 'In Him we live and move and have our being.' This experience of immanence, writes Underhill, 'provides the basis of the New Testament doctrine of the in-dwelling spirit. It is variously interpreted, the "spark of the soul" of Eckhart, the "ground" of Tauler, the Inward Light of the Quakers. . . .'[229:100] 'If', says Boehme, 'thou conceivest a small minute circle, as small as a grain of mustard seed, yet the Heart of God is wholly and perfectly therein: and if thou are born in God, then there is in thyself (in the circle of thy life) the whole Heart of God undivided.'[229:100-1]

In Anya Seton's *The Winthrop Woman* is a beautiful vision of immanence, of the spiritual nature of all existence which is open to those who can see:

A ray of sunlight started down between the tree trunks. It touched the pool with liquid gold. The pool became transparent to its green depths and her self was plunged in those depths and yet upraised with joy upon the rushing wind. The light grew stronger and turned white. In this crystal whiteness there was ecstasy. Against this light she saw a wren fly by; the wren was made of rhythm, it flew with meaning, with a radiant meaning. There was the same meaning in the caterpillar as it inched along the rock, and the moss, and the little nuts which had rolled across the leaves.

> And still the apperception grew, and the significance. The
> significance was bliss, it made a created whole of everything she
> watched and touched and heard – and the essence of this
> created whole was love. She felt love pouring from the light, it
> bathed her with music and with perfume: the love was far off
> at the source of the light, and yet it drenched her through. And
> the source and she were one.[106:90-1]

In psychosynthesis, immanence is contained in the notion of the 'I'
being in direct line with the Higher Self, which is a spark of the
spiritual reality: but the assumption is that not everyone is in
touch with their own centre or their own soul: in fact, few may
realize their own potential in the world.

The danger of the concept of immanence is a vague pantheism,
a somewhat removed spiritual sense, but its strength is the
conviction of power from within, a radiance that is always
available, a sense of unity with all living beings. The danger of the
transcendent reality is divorce from the world and a conviction of
hopelessness and lack of worth, but its strength is in the energy it
can create in the search for truth. It is difficult for most people to
contact their own sense of unity through the mystic awareness to
which Einstein refers at the beginning of the chapter. 'At the very
base of men and women's consciousness, then lies the ultimate
Wholeness,' writes Ken Wilber in his *Up from Eden*.

> But – and here's the rub – it is not, in the vast majority,
> consciously realised. Thus, the ultimate whole is, for most
> souls, an Other. It is not, like Jehovah, an ontological Other –
> it is not set apart, divorced, or separated from men and women.
> Rather, it is a psychological Other – it is ever-present, but
> unrealised; it is given, but rarely discovered; it is the nature of
> human beings, but lies, as it were, deep in the depths of the
> soul.[242:11]

It is precisely to the possibility of this awakening that psychosynthesis addresses itself.

Evelyn Underhill, throughout her book on mysticism, paints a
graphic picture of the unrealized self, the equivalent of Plato's
prisoners in their cave, the prisoners of the psychological and
social conditioning to which we are all subject. We as the
prisoners believe that the material world we see is the whole truth;
a tree is simply a tree, a social institution is something to be
believed in without question, relationship with a person is just an
everyday event; we are born and we die and that is all there is to

it. The person only in touch with consciousness, the senses and the socialization learned through childhood, takes the world for granted; reality is what is given; 'sanity consists in sharing the hallucinations of our neighbours.'229:10

For the mystic the 'ordinary' world is but a pale shadow of the reality he or she has glimpsed. The limitation is not only to believe that the world as perceived by human senses is *the* world as it is, but also to believe that consciousness (the area defined by Assagioli in his egg-diagram) and personality are the entire self. Again, for transpersonal therapists and for mystics alike, each person has the possibility of going beyond the personality and being in touch with the soul, the Higher Self. This is a world of becoming, the 'what we may be' of Piero Ferrucci's book. The pearl lies in the oyster, but must be found.

The journey from an unawakened state to a different reality is the theme of all the subsequent chapters in this section. Plato's well-known images of the cave and the harp depict the relationship of mundane to mystical reality in this great philosopher of ancient Greece; the prisoners' journey to the sun is a description of the travel towards the transcendental, the image of the harp and its music is more within the immanent tradition. Dante's is the classical transcendental journey, accompanied by Reason (Vergil) only so far, but finally being guided by the power of Love (Beatrice). This was a vision conceived within and accepted by the orthodox Catholic church in the Middle Ages. Jewish mysticism and the Kabbalah, a transcendental picture of reality with emphasis on the seeker, was also part of Assagioli's inheritance. The neoplatonic, gnostic and hermetic streams of mysticism have often remained underground through the last fifteen hundred years, but have a direct bearing on Assagioli through Theosophy. Neoplatonic thinking, based on Plotinus, is largely conscious of immanent reality, and has been an inspiration for artists, philosophers and poets all over Europe throughout the centuries – particularly influencing the Renaissance (and Florence was the Renaissance city *par excellence*) and mystical and Romantic work. Gnostic thinking in its classic sense is predominantly aware of mystical reality as 'the other', which is inaccessible, remote, far from the degradation of matter; however, writing in the Gnostic Gospels of the first and second centuries AD is softer, more optimistic, closer to immanence. Many of these writings came to be accessible at the turn of this century, at which time there was also a considerable interest in Eastern mysticism and religion, and this was the atmosphere in which Assagioli formed his ideas. But the strength of his belief in what later came to be known as transpersonal psychotherapy was not just derived culturally from the environment. Mystical knowledge was a fundamental part of his own experience and conviction. Psycho-synthesis was based purely on experience, not just on tradition: 'spiritual traditions may have been an inspiring factor for him, never a source of proof' (letter from Piero Ferrucci to the author).

Oriental writing which particularly influenced Assagioli included the *Bhagavadgita*, Aurobindo, and Sri Shankara's *The Jewel of Discrimination*, and his library contains mystical and spiritual writing from all religions and all periods of time. In picking out and describing the particular writers and schools that I have, I have been aware of the early influences on Assagioli – his classical and Italian education, the philosophy adopted by his mother and later his wife, and his Jewishness. Later parts of the book will comment on other influences in the twentieth century.

10 The influence of Plato

At the beginning of *The Act of Will* Assagioli comments on the contrast between modern external achievements and the lack of inner vision, knowledge and control that would be perceived by a classical Greek visitor to the twentieth century:

> Were he a Plato or a Marcus Aurelius and refused to be dazzled by the material wonders created by advanced technology, and were he to examine the human condition more carefully, his first impressions would give place to great dismay . . . this supposed demigod (modern man), controlling great electrical forces with a movement of the finger and flooding the air with sound and pictures for the entertainment of millions, would seem to be incapable of coping with his own emotions, impulses and desires.[2:3-4]

We seem to have advanced little in fundamental spiritual and moral ways in the last two thousand years – in fact, we may have regressed.

Assagioli received a full classical education, and the influence of classical striving for goodness, knowledge and reality was basic to all his work. In the *Republic*, Book VII, Plato (through Socrates) put forward his view that personally and politically most people live in a dream. It is the task of the philosopher to wake up and live both fully and with awareness, and to take part in social and political affairs wide awake.

The understanding that most human beings are asleep is linked to Plato's view of the nature of reality: that the world we see around us is an imperfect copy of the truly real world, the perfect Form or Archetype. The 'Platonic view of the material world as an image of its ideal archetype'[233:9] is central to much later mystical thinking and experience. Reality itself is perfect, in this view; within it are Forms which are the original blueprint (the archetype) for the world we see around us. These Forms are of physical objects such as tables or plants, but they also hold the perfect vision of Beauty, Goodness and Love. The world we perceive is a pale reflection of this reality, if we are unawakened: it is only the soul who can see things as they really are. 'Knowledge – true knowledge – is remembering what the soul once knew.'[153:1] Plato in *Phaedo* asks whether we were born knowing many things; and whether, when we learn true things, we actually recollect what we knew before birth; whether 'our souls existed long ago, before they were in human shape, apart from bodies, and then had wisdom';[189:522] and whether 'there are two kinds of existing things, one visible, one unseen . . . and the unseen is always in the same state, but the visible constantly changing'.[189:555] This concept also applies to the relationship between soul and mortal being – that the body and earthly state changes, but the soul, if contacted, is always there, 'pure and everlasting and immortal and unchanging'.[189:556] The point of a philosopher's life is to 'pursue the real'.[189:541]

True knowledge is 'the colourless, formless, intangible essence, visible only to the mind, the pilot of the soul'.[106:181] The realm of Forms is the divine world and the search for it is the experience of the aware person: to find it is the true homecoming.

This sense that most people live their lives asleep is illustrated by Plato's most famous image, that of the cave, which is given as a metaphor for human nature:

> Imagine mankind as dwelling in an underground cave with a long entrance open to the light across the whole width of the cave; in this they have been since childhood, with necks and legs fettered, so they have to stay where they are. They cannot move their heads because of the fetters, and they can only look forward, but light comes to them from a fire burning behind them higher up at a distance. Between the fire and the prisoners is a road above their level, and along it imagine a low wall has been built, as puppet showmen have screens in front of them over which they work their puppets. . . . See, then, bearers carrying along this wall all sorts of articles which they hold projected above the wall. . . .
>
> What do you think such people would have seen of themselves and each other except their shadows, which the fire cast on the opposite wall of the cave? . . . suppose the prisoners were able to talk together, don't you think that when they named the shadows which they saw passing they would believe they were naming things. . . .
>
> One might be released, and compelled to stand up, and turn his neck round, and to walk and look toward the firelight; all this would hurt him, and he would be too much dazzled to see

distinctly those things whose shadows he had seen before . . . then, supposing he was compelled to look toward the real light, it would hurt his eyes, and he would escape by turning them away to the things he was able to look at, and these he would believe to be clearer than what was being shown to him. . . .

Suppose, now, someone were to drag him hence by force . . . when he came into the light, the brilliance would fill his eyes and he would not be able to see one of the things now called real? . . .

He would have to get used to it, surely, I think, if he is to see the things above. First, he would more easily look at the shadows, after that images of mankind and the rest in water, lastly the things themselves. After this he would find it easier to survey by night the heavens themselves and all that is in them. . . .

Last of all the sun itself, by itself, in its own place, and see what it is like, not reflections of it in water or as it appears in some alien setting. . . .

Then we must apply this image. . . . The world of our sight is like the habitation in prison, the firelight there would be like the sunlight here, the ascent and the world view is the rising of the soul into the world of the mind . . . our reasoning indicates . . . that this power is already in the soul of each, and is the instrument by which one learns.[189:371-7]

Plato regarded the world of the mind, that of Forms, as the highest reality. Many mystics, both Eastern and Western, have named this highest reality as the Higher Self or simply the Self, in touch, however, in both concepts with the universal reality. Plato, along with many later mystics, believed that through socialization and culture, through the routine and offered banality of much everyday living, people learn to live in a false reality, an alienation, a fundamental unawareness of the truth of things. Evelyn Underhill writes of the different states of consciousness in which people live:

By false desires and false thoughts man has built up for himself a false universe: as a mollusc, by the deliberate and persistent absorption of lime and rejection of all else, can build up for itself a hard shell which shuts it from the external world, and only represents in a distorted and unrecognizable form the ocean from which it was obtained. This hard and wholly unnutritious shell, this onesided secretion of the surface consciousness, makes as it were a little cave of illusion for each separate soul. A literal and deliberate getting out of the cave must be for every mystic, as it was for Plato's prisoners, the first step in the individual hunt for reality. . . . We see a sham world because we live a sham life.[229:198-9]

The powerful image of the cave is basic to psychosynthesis. We live in our personalities driven by powerful and often unconscious forces, seeing only what we can bear to see, carrying many defensive accretions, until such a time as we begin to wake up, to relate to transpersonal elements, and to the Higher Self. It is the task of the psychosynthesis therapist to act as guide to the person, the client, on his or her journey. Assagioli in *Psychosynthesis* refers to Plato's image of the cave, and to the task of the therapist in helping his or her client to greater awareness.[1:47-8] The first step is the awakening which is the recognition of the false self, the many defences and fragmentations, the skewed perceptions. Plato, in what has been called 'the Magna Charta of Western Mysticism', writes in *Phaedo*:

When the mind returns into itself from the confusion of sense (that is, of cave life), as it does when it reflects, it passes into another region of that which is pure and everlasting, immortal and unchanging, and feels itself kindred thereto, and its welfare under its own control and at rest from its wanderings, being in communion with the unchanging.[229:556]

Plato brings out the relationship of transience to the eternal once more in the analogy of the harp in *Phaedo*:

The harmony is invisible and bodiless and all-beautiful and divine on the tuned harp; but the harp itself and the strings are bodies and bodily and composite and earthy and akin to the mortal . . . we conceive the soul to be something like this – that our body being tuned and held together by hot and cold and dry and wet and suchlike, our soul is a kind of mixture and harmony of these very things, when they are well and harmoniously mixed together. . . .
    . . . . if, then, our soul is a kind of harmony, it is plain that when the body is slackened inharmoniously or too highly strung, by diseases or other evils, the soul must necessarily perish, although it is most divine, just as other harmonies do, those in sounds and those in all the works of craftsmen. . . . [189:563]

The search for reality and awareness which he expressed so

clearly in *Phaedo*, in the *Republic* and the *Symposium* is about the 'final attainment of knowledge in terms of clear vision',[102:122] which relates both to the analogies described, of the cave and the harp, ideas of both reason and insight, and the relationship of the body and the personality to the soul. As Gosling puts it, the final stage:

is grasped as a result of ever wider synoptic considerations, in the Symposium of 'the vast ocean of the beautiful', in the Republic of the solar system of Forms. The vision is of why the beautiful things are to be called beautiful, in the Republic of what makes all good things good.[102:123]

But final knowledge 'is not attained or discovered: it *comes upon the soul, it is revealed* to the soul. It is outside the soul's capacity; it is something given and received'.[153:13] A similar theme emerges in the Paradiso of Dante's *Divine Comedy*.

These themes are all basic to psychosynthesis. Assagioli is most aware of the symbolic nature of beauty, and uses visualization as a familiar technique. He writes on music and its significance, the search for knowledge, the several ways to the Self. The notion of pure qualities is present in the concept of the superconscious, and these are directly related to ideal Forms.

Plato holds that everyone, even the most misguided or evil person, pursues the good according to his or her own vision.[102:26] The difficulty is attuning to a true vision of what is real! In this all the faculties and dualities are needed – logos (the reasoned proposition and the active basis of thought) and eros (the power of heart and feeling), the body and the soul, pathos (sensitivity and receptivity) and ethos (dynamism)[2:104] are directed to perceiving what is truth, what is real and therefore what is good.

He places a strong emphasis on self-discipline (the will in psychosynthesis) as a means to freedom. Gosling stated that in the *Republic*:

Plato aims to show that a really undisciplined man least of all does what he wants. This claim takes two forms; first that he is dominated by a subset of his desires, so that not all his desires are satisfied, and second that like all men he wants the best out of life, but lacking knowledge pursues something else.[102:82]

Plato sees virtue as being the health of the personality and vice as a form of disease. Doing ill is related to lack of awareness – this comes even more strongly in subsequent neoplatonic thought. The tyrannic man, like the tyrannic state, is slave to fear, want, every sort of misery and every sort of wickedness. The philosopher, by way of contrast, lives his or her own life, because of the truth of his or her own vision. The pursuit of reality is also the pursuit of freedom.

Plato was concerned with the development of the inner life and the strength this offers: 'the bravest and wisest souls would be least disturbed and altered by any experience from without.'[189:229] In the *Symposium* he postulated several kinds of love – common love, heavenly love, and right loving, and he discusses the people who are 'pregnant in soul', searching for the potential of love and truth and their birth in their own lives.

He developed the analogy between the state and the person – the need for order, cohesion and wholeness, of a somewhat hierarchic nature. Plato constantly moved between the individual and society in his consideration – for instance in thinking about the nature of justice in the *Republic*: 'we will examine justice in the single man, looking for the likeness of the larger in the shape of the smaller':[189:214] the microcosm and the macrocosm. He perceived warring forces in society just as in the individual, but each of these forces symbolized a valuable quality.

> The Greeks declared that two world spirits dwell in the fabric of cosmic and human life and they stand in mortal combat with one another. This combat is of such power and magnitude that we can by no means foretell its outcome. The growing spirit is the spirit of civilisation; it ever seeks to create forms wherein life may expand, may build, and make itself more secure. The burning one on the other hand, seeks life in movement, change, adventure, battle, and at times even in conflict and violence. The growing one is peaceful, the burning one is warlike; civilisation is conserving and often conservative, while the opposing dynamism is revolutionary.[113:107]

Just as different qualities clash in the individual, each however containing something of worth, so they do in the state.

As in the individual, the only wise place to take a decision is from the calm centre. It is up to the people who are on the path of awareness and who are philosophers to make their contribution to public life, and it is really only those who have attained wisdom who are fit to rule:

> The truth is more or less that the city where those who rule are least anxious to be rulers is of necessity best managed, and has

least faction in it; while the city who gets rulers who want it most, is worst managed.[189:379]

In the true form of the city state the rulers would be those who had attained contemplation and were thus able to discern principles concerning human life . . . the contemplation of the Good is something to be used for the benefit of others.[153:16]

This principle is certainly not applied to the political scene today. Assagioli was anxious to develop psychosynthesis from a concern with personal therapy to an application to groups and societies, but this, so far, is largely implicit and undeveloped.

Thus we can trace a similarity of ideas from the greatness of Plato to a particular application in psychosynthesis. We know from the first quotation in this chapter and from other references that Assagioli was aware of and built on Platonic ideas, among many others. The themes of awakening, realization of another reality, the context of the soul, the simplicity and perfection of the Real, the possibility of harmony in the individual and the world, are all basic to the psychosynthesis framework. Assagioli had learned of these values early in his life, at school, and he often acknowledged their inspiration.

11 The gnostic and the neoplatonic traditions

Assagioli's mother and wife were both Theosophists. So originally was Alice Bailey, an English mystical writer with whom he later worked. Assagioli was very particular about keeping psychosynthesis and his professional work separate from his interest in the esoteric tradition: and also he was widely read in all the mystical traditions. But the direct descent of Theosophy from the gnostic tradition is significant in the whole of his thinking and affects the basic assumptions upon which psychosynthesis was founded.

The pervasive influence of gnosticism on our culture is not widely recognized. Ahern in his introduction to gnosticism and the esoteric tradition underlying Anthroposophy calls it 'probably the most profound imaginative tradition of the West, influencing Shakespeare, Goethe and W. B. Yeats among many others; also, unless some recent scholarly doubts are well-founded, it was the matrix from which modern science emerged.'[28:135] Poets, artists and philosophers have at many key times been greatly involved in this tradition, particularly at the time of the Renaissance, in the Romantic period in the early nineteenth century, and around the turn of this century. And, most significantly for this study, it is the view of at least one Jungian scholar, Stephen Hoeller, that Jungian psychology is gnosticism in twentieth century dress, and the same could be said of Assagioli and psychosynthesis.

What then were the roots of these doctrines, which have remained as an undercurrent in the Western world since the first centuries AD which was such an extraordinary spiritual period following the death of Christ? Frances Yates, whose studies of the gnostic tradition in the Renaissance have been a spectacular contribution to modern history, writes in tracing back these roots:

> This world of the Second century was . . . seeking intensively for knowledge of reality, for an answer to its problems which the normal education failed to give. It turned to other ways of seeking an answer, intuitive, mystical, magical. Since reason seemed to have failed, it sought to cultivate the Nous, the intuitive faculty in man.[248:4]

Neoplatonism, as its name implies, was initially a development in the first centuries AD of Platonic thought, though later its hellenic roots became imbued with Christianity. The most well-known and remarkable writer was Plotinus who lived from AD 204 or 205 to 270 and whose work was within the Greek tradition. Later members of the school include Porphyry, Plotinus' disciple, and Iamblichus, who died in 326; the movement as such ended with the Athenian and Alexandrian Schools of the fifth and sixth centuries, with Proclus, Hypatia and Damascius, when orthodox Christian influences closed such heretic philosophical enquiry; however, this alternative river of thought has continued underground throughout the centuries.

Wallis, in his study of neoplatonism, comments that the movement 'stands out not as an abandonment of Greek rationalism, but as an adaptation of Greek thought to the world of inner experience'.[233:6] It was a philosophical school rather than a religion.

Neoplatonic thought rests on the assumption of an ordered cosmological reality, based in the One, the ground of all things, which is unity. As life comes more into form, as it moves further down the Chain of Being, it is more diversified, more in conflict, more fragmented. The individual soul can, however, if it so wishes, ascend to become more unified again with Unity through purification and simplification. Matter is relatively base, and spirit relatively pure. The One, in Plotinus' thinking, is both transcendent and immanent in living creatures. Creatures can be more creative and indeed more alive, the more they contemplate the One: the most perfect form of the world is multiplicity-in-unity. The worst sin is isolation from and ignorance of the Unity of the creative force. 'External evil and suffering take their place as necessary elements in the great pattern, the great dance of the Universe.'[191:24]

Plotinus wrote a specific tract *Against the Gnostics*, although later neoplatonic thinking and gnostic thought became intertwined. Unlike the gnostics, Plotinus did not believe that matter and the world are inherently evil. He believed the universe was good at root and that the gnostics were arrogant beyond belief to criticize the creator.

The man who censures the nature of the universe does not know what he is doing, and how far this rash criticism of his goes. This is because the Gnostics do not know that there is an order of firsts, seconds and thirds in regular succession, and so on to the last, and the things that are worse than the first should not be reviled; one should rather calmly and gently accept the nature of things, and hurry on oneself to the first, ceasing to concern oneself with the melodramas of the terrors, as they think, in the cosmic spheres, which in reality 'make all things sweet and lovely' for them.[191:275]

The gnostics believed that it was formidably difficult to seek the soul's true home: Plotinus that the nature of things became clearer, simpler, sweeter as the soul approached the One. Here is the age-old contrast between the immanent and transcendent views of God as discussed in the general chapter on mysticism.

The gnostic movement was a religious movement in the Christian tradition. Jonas comments that the gnostic insistence on the 'reception of truth either through sacred or secret lore or through inner illumination replaces rational theory and argument'.[126:35] Its major writers were Justin Martyr, who died in 165, Hepesippus died 180, Clement of Alexandria died 215, Iraneus died 202, Tertullian died 230, Hippolytus died 236, Origen died 254, and Epiphanius died 403, together with the writers of the Gnostic Gospels discovered in 1945 at Nag Hammadi. These latter are a series of books about the life of Jesus, whose origins seem to be not dissimilar to those of the gospels now contained in the Bible. There are fifty-two texts in the find, including the *Gospel of Thomas* and the *Gospel of Philip*: the *Gospel of Truth* and the *Gospel to the Egyptians*: the *Secret Book of James*, the *Apocalypse of Paul,* the *Letter of Peter to Philip*, and the *Second Treatise of the Great Seth*. The texts actually found are dated AD 350–400, but the originals were thought to be in Greek and about 120–150 at source. The most fascinating point that Elaine Pagels makes in her study of the Gnostic Gospels is that 'we now begin to see that what we call Christianity – and what we identify as the Christian tradition – actually represents only a small selection of specific sources, chosen from among dozens of others'.[182:31]

The gnostic material is different from orthodox Christianity in several fundamental ways, which continued to make gnosticism a heresy in relation to the church throughout the centuries. The gnostic material is dualistic. It postulates an ineffable and transcendent Godhead: and a Creator of the world who had fallen and represents evil, the Demiurge. Everywhere contains the footsteps of God, but Jehovah, the Creator, the Demiurge, created the world from jealousy. So there is an eternal world, and a world of evil in which we live and are constant strangers, shut off from God except dimly, as a remembrance. It is error and lack of knowledge that leads to suffering and evil: it is only by coming to understand the true nature of reality, through gnosis, that we can find our way home. This knowledge is realized by few. It includes a knowledge that the institutions of society and our everyday experience are 'at best shadowy perceptions of another and more fundamental reality'; that we are 'strangers in a strange country'[113:14] on this earth. Jonas comments that:

> Greek thought had been a grand expression of man's belonging to the world . . . and through knowledge that breeds love had striven to heighten the intimacy with the kindred essence of all nature: gnostic thought is inspired by the anguished discovery of man's cosmic solitude, of the utter otherness of his being to the universe at large.[126:251]

It is the self-consciousness, the existentialism of many modern writers, but with the doctrine of redemption through knowledge – inner knowledge – at the heart. In the *Gospel of Thomas*, Jesus is quoted as saying, 'I manifested myself to men in the flesh. I found them drunk, I found them blind, and none athirst among them. When they have slept off their wine they will repent.' This doctrine of mankind being asleep is found in many modern writers.

Some of the gnostics thought there were several kinds of people at any one time; the sarkikos, the people of flesh where carnal elements predominate; the psychikos, who are more self-determining and aware and whose lives can go any way; and the pneumatikos, the noetic, who are truly spiritual people, those who have the capacity for search and for knowledge. Real knowledge springs from the immediate perception of a transformed aware consciousness. With awareness comes the knowledge that 'all power is a source of alienation . . . all institutions, laws, religions, churches and powers are nothing but a sham and a trap, the perpetuation of an age-old deception'.[148:28] Gnosticism has been a perpetual threat to orthodox Christianity because it is deeply radical and anarchic.

Neoplatonism and gnosticism are in many ways deeply opposed. But both were very heterogeneous movements over the centuries, and many gnostics took a more favourable view of the universe, and the possibility of reaching through to ultimate truth, accepting and working through all the evil and suffering of existence. The similarity that the gnostics and the neoplatonists shared, in contrast to orthodox Christianity, once it had formed into a church, was radicalism. This was related to the emphasis on inner experience as the root of knowledge, and on search: 'gnostics tended to regard all doctrines, speculations and myths – their own as well as others – only as approximations to the truth.'[182:125]

There was a third important stream of belief and thought relevant to our search for this 'alternative current' of Western traditions, which is *hermeticism*. This was a series of writings originating about the same time, in the first centuries AD, though they were thought by Renaissance scholars, to whom they were very important, to originate in ancient Egypt, under the name of Hermes Trismegistus. As Frances Yates writes,

> Hermes Trismegistus, a mythical name associated with a certain class of gnostic philosophical revelations or with magical treatises and recipes, was, for the Renaissance, a real person, an Egyptian priest who had lived in times of remote antiquity and who had himself written all these works.[248:6]

We now know that these actually came from this immensely rich and speculative period after the death of Christ, in the first centuries AD, and that they form part of the alternative stream of Western culture.

Hermeticism shares the gnostic belief in the significance of inner knowing, and stresses the secret nature of this knowledge. Its key theme is that of transformation, the renewal of nature and the world, and is associated through the centuries with magic, the transforming quality of spirit in matter. Dualistic hermeticism, where spirit and matter are seen as very separate and indeed opposing entities, tends to be pessimistic about the nature of the world, but there is a more pantheistic influence which is more optimistic and benign, as well as more unitary.

These three most fascinating schools of thinking and belief, then, form a most significant and persistent 'other' element in the Western world. As Pagels comments, 'it is the winners who write history – their way,'[182:147] so that this particular kind of interpretation of the world is not found in ordinary history books; also much of what we know of these origins has only recently been discovered – through the Nag Hammadi Gospels, through the original and initiatory researches of Frances Yates into the hermetic school, and through a renewed interest in mysticism this century. The influence of these streams of thought appears in many guises in our culture. For instance, E. R. Dodds comments that in Plotinus:

converge almost all the main currents of thought that come down from 800 years of Greek speculation; out of it there issues a new current destined to fertilise minds as different as those of Augustine and Boethius, Dante and Meister Eckhart, Coleridge, Bergson and T. S. Eliot.[153:36]

There are many differences between the schools, and certainly it is likely that Plotinus would not have wished to have seen his *Enneads* grouped together with the *Poimandres* of Hermes Trismegistus, but from today's perspective, they are part of a common perception of the world which is in marked contrast to an orthodox church which worshipped a man-like God, which valued certainty and hierarchy, and which eventually led to a view of knowledge as being external rather than internal to the person.

A striking feature of gnostic thought, as has already been indicated, is the emphasis on self-knowledge. As interest is centred on inner knowing and the spirit and God within, and the bars to this knowledge, the gnostics were necessarily interested in a dynamic understanding of human nature. This makes for a remarkable similarity with modern depth psychology, particularly transpersonal psychology.

Hoeller traces the basic assumptions of gnostic thought relevant to their view of the person: that there is a potency dwelling within people, and true awakening and gnosis is dependent upon the awakening of this element: that symbolism is an important key to this potential and it can be reached through dreams and other means: that the existential condition of people is not only determined by the sins of the past but also by the possibility of wholeness: that the gnostic idea of the 'Demiurge' 'is not a mere weird and shocking invention of the Gnostics but an archetypal image universally present in the human psyche, and inevitably manifest in the various myths of enlightenment or liberation'[113:39] – the Demiurge is the law that is applicable to the unenlightened, but which can impede full awakening:

> that the alienation of consciousness, along with the attendant feelings of forlornness, dread and homesickness, must be fully experienced before it can be overcome . . . that those unaware of suffering are much more likely to have their development arrested at the level of shallow personalist concerns than their fellows who are aware of the facts of suffering. The neurotic personality, resentful and fearful of the growing pains of the soul, tends to seek refuge in self-deception and thus frequently

convinces itself that growth is really unnecessary, for things are
quite satisfactory just as they are at present':[113:39-40]

that growth comes from the conflict of opposites, male and
female, light and dark, unconscious and conscious, and by the
reconciliation of those opposites within the person:

that the wholeness, or Self, which is the end result of the
process of spiritual growth, is characterised by all the qualities
such as power, value, holiness which religious systems have
always attributed to God':[113:41]

and that

goodness is no substitute for wholeness . . . that in the long run
what matters is not goodness or obedience to moral laws, but
only and simply the fullness of being'.[113:42]

This whole process can be summarized by one of the sayings
from the gnostic *Gospel of Thomas*: 'if you bring forth what is
within you, what you bring forth will save you. If you do not
bring forth what is within you, what you do not bring forth will
destroy you.'[113:155] The gnostics believed that exploring the
psyche is a religious task: that ignorance, not sin, leads to
suffering: that most people live in oblivion and therefore have no
real fulfilment. It is necessary for human beings and the human
race to work through the darkness within and without in order to
become truly themselves. In the *Gospel of Thomas*, Jesus scorned
those who thought that the Kingdom of God is in a particular
place, like heaven in the sky – he reckoned that if you thought
that, the birds would get there before you:

rather, the Kingdom of God is inside of you and it is outside of
you. When you come to know yourselves, then you will be
known, and you will realise that you are the sons of the living
Father. But if you will not know yourselves, then you dwell in
poverty, and it is you who *are* that poverty. . . . [182:136]

. . . . that 'Kingdom', then, is a state of transformed
consciousness.[182:137]

There is then a fascinating paragraph, again from the *Gospel of
Thomas*:

Jesus saw infants being suckled. He said to his disciples, 'These infants being suckled are like those who enter the Kingdom.' They said to him, 'Shall we then, as children, enter the Kingdom?' Jesus said to them, 'When you make the two one, and when you make the inside like the outside and the outside like the inside, and the above like the below, and when you make the male and the female one and the same . . . then you will enter (the Kingdom).'[201:121]

And yet, as Elaine Pagels comments, the Christian church expects the Coming and the Kingdom as special events, with a particular time and place – a concept that Jesus in the *Gospel of Thomas* assumed to be naive.

In the work of Valentinus, one of the later gnostics, he maintained that all things originate in 'the depth', 'the abyss' (presumably the unconscious), and one of his disciples, the author of the *Gospel of Philip*, maintained that it was possible to contact this truth by symbol and by image; 'truth did not come into the world naked, but it came in types and images. One will not receive truth in any other way.'[182:140] But all this was through self-knowledge. According to the *Book of Thomas the Contender*, another of the Gnostic Gospels, 'whoever has not known himself has known nothing, but he who has known himself has at the same time already achieved knowledge about the depth of all things.' Simon Magus claimed that each human being is a dwelling place 'and that in him dwells an infinite power . . . the root of the universe'.[182:141]

In the beliefs of these gnostic, neoplatonic and hermetic thinkers in those early centuries after the death of Christ when our present Christianity was being formed, there continued the split between those who assumed the universe to be basically evil, and those, like Plotinus, who believed that awareness and self-perfection could lead to the ultimate salvation of all. Hans Jonas, whose book on the gnostic religion came out originally in 1958, emphasized the dualistic split between good and evil: 'the terrified gnostic glance views the inner life as an abyss from which dark powers vie to govern our being, not controlled by our will.'[126:283] Later on, however, he accepts that some gnostic teaching could accept that the transcendent God could become immanent – the aware person could become a Christ. And Elaine Pagels, in her later study which is based on the Nag Hammadi Gospels, emphasizes the possibility of true gnosis and transformation through self-knowledge, the acknowledgment of the female as well

as the male qualities in Christianity, and the potential joyfulness
of life:

> The gospel of truth is a joy for those who have received from
> the Father of truth the grace of knowing him. . . . For he
> discovered him in themselves, the incomprehensible,
> inconceivable one, the Father, the perfect one, the one who
> made all things.[201:38]

The gnostics were deeply concerned with evil, and different
schools came to different conclusions about the fundamental
nature of the world, whether it was good or evil, and at what
level.

There is a conception though, that fragmentation must become
unified as well as ignorance changed through knowledge if there is
to be any possibility of salvation. Porphyry wrote:

> Endeavour to ascend into thyself, gathering in from the body
> all thy members which have been dispersed, and scattered into
> multiplicity from the unity which once abounded in the
> greatness of its power. Bring together and unify the inborn
> ideas and try to articulate those that are confused and to draw
> into light those that are obscured.[126:61]

This is an excellent description of psychosynthesis. And from
orthodox Christianity, St Augustine in his *Confessions* writes, 'by
continence we are collected into the One, from which we have
declined to the many.'[126:62]

All these writers, within the framework of ideas about the Great
Chain of Being, struggled with the relationship of body (matter)
and soul (spirit) and saw human beings and society riven with
conflicts. Plotinus wrote that:

> the soul is many things, linked to the realm of sense by what is
> lowest in us, linked to the intelligible realm by what is highest.
> For each of us is an intelligible cosmos. By what is intellective,
> we are permanently in the higher realm; by our lower part we
> are prisoners of sense.[192:25]

From the other current of gnosticism comes the affirmation that
these splits can be healed. From the *Odes of Solomon* comes the
statement that 'he who possesses knowledge . . . . [is like] a person
who, having been intoxicated, becomes sober and having come to
himself reaffirms that which is essentially his own'.[182:71] Ordinary

human existence is spiritual death, and resurrection is the moment of enlightenment.

Gnostics believe that in knowing oneself, one knows the divine and the universe. Also that souls who are enlightened recognize one another – 'souls are responsive to one another because they all come from the same soul – the Soul'.[192:134] The concept is thus much closer to that of immanence than to transcendence:

> For Plotinus, the higher is not the more remote; the higher is the more inward. . . . Augustine's 'tu autem eras interior intimo meo et superior summo meo' (you were more inward than the most inward place of my heart and loftier than the highest), with its suggested identification of the inward and the higher, strikes an authentically Plotinian note. As the soul ascends to the One, it enters more deeply into itself; to find the One is to find itself.[153:40]

With the total reliance of all of these systems of thinking and belief on the authenticity of the Self and the God within, authority, including political authority, is clearly rooted far more in the individual than in an outside hierarchy. Plotinus regarded action as weak contemplation, but he did regard it as important to act in the world and make a contribution.

> The Gnostic is in fact not an antinomian (anti = against, nomos = law) but a seeker after autonomy (autos = self, nomos = law), inasmuch as he strives for a state of consciousness wherein his own law is declared to him day by day and moment by moment by his indwelling divine intuition. It is in the dusty, bloodied and tear-soaked arena of daily existential confrontations with life, and not in the library of Bibles, Korans and Gospels, that the Gnostic discovers the law that is applicable to his particular and individual condition.[113:103]

This is a view which has cropped up from time to time throughout religious history (the Anabaptists, Luther, the Quakers), even within the orthodox Christian church.

The similarity of psychosynthesis to gnostic and neoplatonic thought is obvious, even without the intermediary of Theosophy and Jungian psychotherapy. In the psychosynthetic insistence on the relationship with the 'I' and the Self can be traced the gnostic concept of self-knowledge and contact with the divine and the potential within the person. There is the importance of symbolism as a means to the truth, and the non-belief in a hierarchical church. Instead there is a vision of the unity that comes through the reconciliation of opposites both at a personal and at a social level, and a conviction that through being in touch with the soul all creatures are one, a dream that has emerged in many utopian attempts at a good society. This belief and experience that it is possible for people to relate to one another at the level of the soul is basic to psychosynthesis. A quotation from the *Second Treatise of the Great Seth*, one of the Gnostic Gospels, indicates this spirit: that what characterizes the true church is the union that members enjoy with God and each other, 'united in the friendship of friends forever, who neither know any hostility, nor evil, but who are united by my gnosis . . . in friendship with one another'.[182:118-19]

The gnostic tradition has been throughout its history a utopian tradition, a vision of how the world could be and a strong sense that the way the world is now is not the way it was meant to be. James Robinson points out in his introduction to the collection of Nag Hammadi Gospels:

> The focus that brought the collection together is an estrangement from the mass of humanity, an affirmity to an ideal order that completely transcends life as we know it, and a life-style radically other than common practice. This life-style involved giving up all the goods that people usually desire and longing for an ultimate liberation. It is not an aggressive revolution that is intended, but rather a withdrawal from involvement in the contamination that destroys clarity of vision.[201:1]

Although the psychosynthesis view is that a person truly in touch with themselves should make a contribution to society as it is now, but from a different, centred place, the element of a search for the *alternative* vision is there, even if only in potential, of the social and political world.

RELIGIOUS CONCEPTS.

12 The Kabbalah and the Jewish tradition

In Assagioli's library there are both scholarly books and modern journals on Jewish mysticism; the scholarly work includes writing by Buber, with whom he was personally in touch, and Gershom Scholem. As Martin Buber has himself commented, Scholem 'has created a whole academic discipline', that is, Jewish mysticism.

> Through his exhaustive investigations of the history of Jewish mysticism from the second to the eighteenth centuries, Scholem opened up a world of ideas which hardly anyone knew existed. . . . Scholem has shown that at the very heart of mainstream Judaism lie powerful forces of myth and mysticism.[43:1]

Within both the Kabbalistic and the Hasidic traditions there are many concepts similar to the gnostic and the neoplatonic schools. A classic Kabbalistic medieval book is the *Zohar*, which is in fact a series of gospels which are attributed by Scholem to Moses de Leon. Scholem also comments that 'the Kabbalah of the early thirteenth century was the offspring of a union between an older and essentially Gnostical tradition represented by the book *Bahir*, and the comparatively modern element of Jewish Neoplatonism'.[206:175] The *Zohar* was produced in Spain. At the same time in Italy Abraham ben Samuel Abulafia was composing a series of Kabbalistic books, inspired by the writings of the great Jewish philosopher Maimonides, who in his turn was influenced by Meister Eckhart. The thirteenth century was the great classic period of Kabbalistic writings, but they were based, of course, on a much older tradition, particularly the Italian Merkabah mysticism which contained many gnostic concepts, especially number mysticism, the centrality of Redemption and the sense of the 'cosmic veil' between mankind and the otherness of God. The Kabbalah has always been seen as part of the esoteric element in Jewish spirituality, available only to the few and the learned.

Assagioli was Jewish by birth, and of course an Italian, living in an area in which much of the Jewish mystical writing was formulated. The Kabbalistic and to a lesser extent the Hasidic doctrines pick up many of the themes of the mystical material discussed so far: also there is a remarkable similarity between the basic Kabbalistic diagram of the Sephirot – the pictorial representation of man's relationship to God – and the 'egg-shaped diagram' in psychosynthesis.

The Kabbalah was a secret doctrine – 'a school of mystics who are not prepared to hand their secret knowledge, their "Gnosis", to the public'.[206:47] Consistent with this secrecy is a reluctance of the writers to talk of themselves or to inject their own personalities into the spiritual writing; they write in an impersonal way. Scholem comments that 'Jewish mystics are inclined to be reticent about the hidden regions of the religious life, including the sphere of experience generally described as ecstasy, mystical union with God and the like', and that this attitude 'emanates from modesty and the feeling that a Kabbalist who had been vouchsafed the gift of inspiration should shun ostentation'.[206:120] He cites various instances of this tendency, and I certainly think we could add another name to this list, that of Roberto Assagioli, who in psychosynthesis produced a psychotherapy and a series of techniques based on a strongly mystical influence which is hardly acknowledged except in the most general outlines. His own personality remains quite hidden in his writing, all of which seems to emanate from an unknown source.

Kabbalism is about the movement away from God and the way back again to the spiritual. In Hasidic thought we forget what we were born knowing, because otherwise that knowledge would drive us mad in such an evil world. Jewish mystical writing is particularly aware of evil: 'they have a strong sense of the reality of evil and the dark horror that is about everything living'.[206:36] This awareness and concern with evil, together with the interest in magic and control, and the element of secrecy to be found in Kabbalism, account for some of the wariness with which the whole subject of Kabbalism is approached. From the beginning there has been 'the closest and most indissoluble union of religious fervour and mystical ecstasy with magical beliefs and practices',[206:51] as was also the case with hermeticism.

As with other kinds of gnosticism, there is a strong sense of God immanent in all things, that has already been quoted as a general comment: 'the infinite shines through the finite and makes it more and not less real.'[206:28] In medieval Hasidism 'one is . . . forced to recognise the existence of a religious mood with a strong tendency towards pantheism, or at least a mysticism of divine immanence.'[206:107] In the *Zohar*, the hidden God has neither qualities nor attributes,[206:207] but the image is that of a coal and a flame – 'that is to say, the coal exists also without a flame, but its latent power manifests itself only in its light.'[206:208]

> This divine Self, this 'I', according to the theosophical Kabbalists – and this is one of their most profound and important doctrines – is the Shekinah, the presence and immanence of God in the whole of creation. It is the point where man, in attaining the deepest understanding of his own self, becomes aware of the presence of God.[206:239]

This process is diagrammatically represented in the Sephirot.

The assumption is that the human being is deeply embedded in the matter and evil of the world. The Kabbalist considers evil as the bark of the cosmic tree or the shell of a nut, which has to be stripped or broken before the true person, the person who is in touch with God, can emerge.

> Abulafia's aim, as he himself has expressed it, is 'to unseal the soul, to untie the knots that bind it'. 'All the inner forces and the hidden souls in man are distributed and differentiated in the bodies. It is however in the nature of all of them that when their knots are untied they return to their origin, which is one without any duality and which comprises the multiplicity.' This untying is, as it were, the return from multiplicity and separation towards the original unity. As a symbol of the great mystic liberation of the soul from the fetters of sensuality the 'untying of the knots' occurs also in the theosophy of northern Buddhism.[206:131]

Again the similarity to the process of psychosynthesis hardly needs pointing out.

Scholem writes:

> Taken altogether, the spiritual outlook of the Zohar might well be defined as a mixture of theosophic theology, mythical cosmogony and mystical psychology and anthropology. God, the universe and the soul do not lead separate lives, each on its own plane.[206:243]

Instead, God is immanent in the universe. For the Kabbalist, everything mirrors everything else, every thing is a symbol of everything else.

But beyond that he discovers something else which is not covered by the allegorical network: a reflection of the true transcendence. The symbol 'signifies' nothing and communicates nothing, but makes something transparent which is beyond all expression.[206:27]

The path to be followed within the Kabbalistic system is, as has already been indicated, demonstrated by the Sephirot (Figure 12.1), which is generally known as the tree of life – the roots in the earth, the branches near to heaven, and containing a natural propensity to grow. The pattern of the Sephirot is seen as being true of divine attributes, of life on earth, and of the 'four worlds' in which we exist – Will, Intellect, Emotion and Action. It is the Kabbalistic method of delineating pure form behind the changing world of our existence, and as such is consistent with the general mystical tradition.

This pattern can be applied to many forms. But if it is applied to the picture of the person, like Assagioli's egg-diagram, there are the following likenesses.

(i) The Tiferet is the Self (the Higher Self):

With the emotional Sephirot of Hesod and Gevurah it forms the triad of the Divine soul; with the higher Sephirot of Hokhmah and Binah it forms the great triad of the Divine spirit. . . . In the human psyche Tiferet is the Self, the core of the individual, which lies behind the everyday ego: the 'Watcher' which focuses the largely unconscious influences of the higher centres of Mercy and Justice (Hesod and Gevurah), Wisdom and Understanding (Hokhmah and Binah).[104:7]

Thus, Assagioli's picture of the superconscious and the relationship to the Self is depicted somewhat more precisely in the Kabbalah. The Higher Self is shown in his diagram as being on the edge between the superconscious and the collective unconscious: in the Kabbalah the Tiferet is shown as organizing the higher qualities of the person and also as being in direct touch with Keter, the Crown, which is the source, the cause, the truth.

(ii) Yesod is the 'I', which is directly in touch with the Self, and with the active principle of Nezah and the passive principle of Hod. Halevi comments that it is a complex Attribute with many qualities:

First, it is generative: it is from this point, as will be seen, that further Trees manifest. Second it is reflective: here, directly

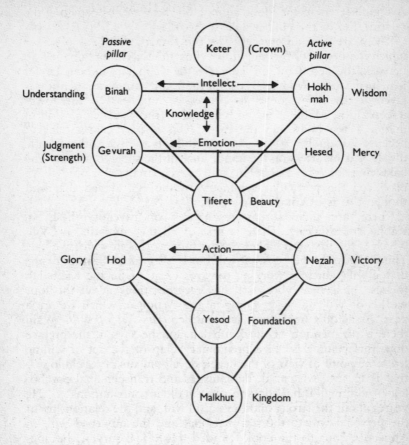

Figure 12.1 The Sephirot

below Tiferet, an 'image of the image' can be perceived, and the Tree sees itself; Yesod is the mirror within the Mirror. these two complementary functions mean that its constitution (or Foundation) must be clear and sound; hence the inner meaning of sexual purity associated with this Sephirah. In ourselves it appears as the ego, the lower place of consciousness, in which we see ourselves, and which projects a persona for others to see which may or may not (according to our state of balance and self knowledge) reflect the true nature of the self at Tiferet. Most of our perception of the world, and most of our implementation of Will, take place at Yesod.[104:7]

Assagioli refers to the moon shining on the water as depicting the relationship of the Higher Self to the 'I'.

There are also differences. The function of the 'I' as observer which is so basic to the map in psychosynthesis is more divided up between the Yesod and the Tiferet in the Kabbalah. In fact, Tiferet is named as 'the Watcher'. Also in the Kabbalah more attention is given to the superconscious processes, and less to the lower unconscious. Malkhut in the Kabbalah is the presence of God in matter – the body and the earth. This is particularly relevant because Assagioli's particular contribution to psychotherapeutic theory was his stress on the importance of the superconscious. The balancing of the Kabbalah and psychoanalysis would have produced the particular symmetry of the egg-shaped diagram: though this is of course guesswork.

There are many other resonances of psychosynthesis in Kabbalistic thinking. There is first of all the emphasis on Will, which is the first and highest of the four worlds in which we live. This is not only the personal will but is also the realization of the divine will which is working towards creation. In the Kabbalah the use of a clear good will has reverberations in all the four worlds of Will, Intellect, Emotion and Action of which we are a part. Assagioli's final book was entitled *The Act of Will*. Again there is no mention of the Kabbalah, but he says in the preface that 'this volume is . . . a preliminary map of the act of willing from the point of view of the newer developments in psychology – that is to say, existential, humanistic, and transpersonal psychology – although it has roots in various older contributions'.[2:iv] He writes about the strong and the skilful will, and the relationship of the personal will to the transpersonal and the universal will. In Appendix Four to the book, entitled 'Historical survey', he does cite older writers about the will – Raja Yoga, Zen Buddhist writers, Augustine and various nineteenth and twentieth century philosophers, before going on to examine assumptions made about the will in psychology. Perhaps all we could say about the significance of Kabbalistic thinking here is that all mystical writings tend to emphasize the path, the journey, and therefore the relationship of the personal to the divine will.

Similar things could be said about the emphasis on awakening in the Kabbalah and the development of awareness. We have already seen these as a main theme in Plato, Dante and Hasidism. These ideas are connected in the Kabbalah to the idea of reincarnation. Again there is the idea that we are born knowing many things, but we forget: 'the person begins to forget his memories of the upper Worlds as he becomes increasingly

COME BACK TO ME .....

involved in the physical life of being a baby'.[104:14] Halevi talks of the people who still vaguely remember:

> that other, freer, place, the dimly recalled homeland . . . such people, called outsiders by some, are still slaves, like all their fellows bound in the flesh, but they are particularly unhappy ones because they know they are enslaved and cannot, like their companions, simply lose themselves in the game of everyday life.[104:19]

The Kabbalah teaches that the seeker must be well grounded in ordinary life.

> Thus the Kabbalist does not withdraw from the lower Worlds and seek special conditions or isolation in which to develop, but uses the daily situation and ordinary events around him. . . . Only Man has the capability of perceiving both the superior and inferior Worlds. To acquire such an inner and outer faculty of sight is one of the aims of Kabbalah. . . . [104:27]

Here again is a similarity with Assagioli's insistence on acting in the real world, with true awareness.

Thus the Kabbalah is a spiritual path, concerned with developing personal self-knowledge and awareness. The assumption is that the higher worlds are simpler and purer; each level of the four worlds, of Will, Intellect, Emotion and Activity, 'contains the qualities of the one above, so that each descending level in turn is under more laws, is more complex, and is further from the source.'[104:9] In psychosynthesis, the personality level contains the greatest diversity and multiplicity, and the task is to contact the qualities of the superconscious which are clear and coordinating. In the Kabbalah, 'man's final purpose is to re-unite the divine and human wills.'[28:146]

Halevi quotes a classical Kabbalistic story from the *Zohar*, which illustrates the spirit of both the Jewish mystical search and of psychosynthesis:

> A certain young man once saw the figure of a veiled girl at a window of a palace. At first only curious, he went each day to catch a glimpse of her. After a while, she would look in his direction as if expecting him. Slowly he became involved in what appeared to be a relationship if only at a distance. In the course of time the girl lowered her veil to reveal something of her face. This so increased his interest that he spent many hours

at the palace hoping to see the fulness of her beauty. Gradually he fell deeply in love with her and spent most of his day at her window. Over time she became more open with him and they conversed, she telling of the secrets of the palace and the nature of her father the King. Eventually he could bear it no longer and wished only to be joined with her in marriage so that he might experience all she spoke of. The man in the allegory is the soul, the princess the spirit, the palace existence, and the King the King of Kings.[104:24]

13 The influence of Dante

Assagioli states quite categorically that 'the central symbolic meaning of the Divine Comedy is a wonderful picture of a complete psychosynthesis'.[1:211] The journey by Dante through Hell, Purgatory and Paradise is the journey of the spiritually aware person through life. This symbolism is present on many levels – Dante journeys through geographical space and counted time through the regions, in a kind of non-material world: the symbolism is allegorical, is moral and is an image of everyone's life on earth, as Assagioli saw it.

> The first part – the Pilgrimage through Hell – indicates the analytic exploration of the lower unconscious. The second part – the Ascent of the Mountain of Purgatory – indicated the process of moral purification and gradual raising of the level of consciousness through the use of active techniques. The third part – the visit to Paradise or Heaven – depicts in an unsurpassed way the various stages of superconscious realization, up to the final version of the Universal Spirit, of God himself, in which Love and Will are fused.[1:211]

Assagioli felt a most special connection with Dante Alighieri. Dante was born in Florence in 1265, and was exiled from there, for the rest of his life, in 1302. The *Divine Comedy*, his major work, is dated Easter 1300 in its events – the journey was made at that particular time, but most of it was actually written in political exile: Dante finished it shortly before his death in 1321. Assagioli lived much of his life in Florence, but must have often felt an exile in Mussolini's Italy. He felt completely identified with Dante, whose work he had known all his life, in following a spiritual path. He also particularly liked to work with symbolism, and many of the themes of Dante are reflected in psychosynthesis.

Dante the poet is also the main character in the story:

> Midway this way of life we're bound upon,

midway this life we are bound
upon

> I woke to find myself in a dark wood,
> Where the right road was wholly lost and gone. . . .
>
> How I got into it I cannot say,
> Because I was so heavy and full of sleep
> When first I stumbled from the narrow way.[61a]

— RENINCI
1956

The person until this time is pictured as half asleep, and it is not until well into life that this spiritual journey begins. From the dark and frightening wood, Dante can see a mountain which seems to him the right way, but he is stopped by a leopard, a lion and a she-wolf – self-indulgence, violence and maliciousness. It becomes clear that he has to go on the journey the long way round. At this point he meets Vergil, who is Dante's symbol of human reason and who offers to guide him through the alternative path through Hell and Purgatory to reach the mountain and the right way, which is at present blocked by the sins. So begins the long journey through all the torments of Hell to the centre of the earth and Lucifer, 'the ill Worm that pierces the world's core'.[61a:34.108] At this centre point, 'the point . . . toward which all weight bears down from everywhere',[61a:34.111] Dante and Vergil start to ascend to the antipodes and to Purgatory, where instead of punishment for sin being the predominant theme, the souls find hope and redemption through their suffering.

Hell, Purgatory and Paradise are all arranged in tiers – the concept is completely hierarchical – so the two travellers, having ascended into the nethermost reaches of Hell, begin to climb up through Purgatory; all the time, as in Hell, they meet and converse with souls in the various regions, until they reach the 'other wood' on the edge of Paradise – the one the human race should have started out at if sin and its subsequent suffering had not occurred; where, having cast aside sin, Dante has achieved again his real innocence.

At this point, human reason – Vergil – can take him no further, and eventually wisdom, for which he has been most earnestly seeking – Beatrice – appears to take him through Paradise. Beatrice and Dante rise through all the tiers of Paradise to God, where all qualities are merged and become whole. Here is the image of the 'rose of snow-white purity', where all Heaven gathers in a perfect shape and coherence.

This then is Dante's – Christian and Catholic, and medieval – picture of our task on earth:

Don't you see

That we are worms, whose insignificance
Lives but to form the angelic butterfly
That flits to judgment naked of defence?[61b:10.123-6]

In order to have the possibility of becoming a butterfly, the person must be looking for meaning and for God. He or she is likely to start the search after the experience of a 'dark wood'. The search involves becoming more and more one's unique self, centred in awareness, and related to all the different aspects of the personality, and then related to the Higher Self, to all of society, and to a search for spiritual meaning and purpose. But in order for this to happen, the person has to wake up to the necessity of the journey in the first place – many of the souls in Hell have never been prepared to be fully alive.

Again there is an implicit image of a worm changing into a butterfly – but each butterfly a unique, particular, irreplaceable being whose identity is not to be merged but who can add to the richness of reality. Barbara Reynolds quotes Teilhard de Chardin in her Introduction to Paradise: 'In and by means of each one of us ... an absolutely original centre is established in which the universe is reflected in a unique and inimitable way.'

Three major themes relevant to psychosynthesis emerge on the journey. These are the importance of reason, and also its limitations; the basis of love in the universe, and its relation to wisdom and to reason; and the significance of free will and of choice.

Reason and the search for truth is what drives us on in the search, and it will only be when we have found the truth that our reason will allow us to rest:

That nothing save the light of truth allays
Our intellect's disquiet I now see plain –
God's truth, which holds all truth within its rays.

Intellect, like a wild thing in its den,
When it has run and reached it, there can it rest,
As reach it must, else all desire were vain.

Hence, at the foot of truth, the undying quest
Springs like a shoot, and doubt is still the lure
That speeds us toward the height from crest to crest.[61c:4.124-32]

Thus the search for knowledge, being one of the ways to the Self, is the companion and the goad on this journey. But reason has its

limitations, and can only take us so far. Vergil, the representative
of human reason, can take Dante right through Hell and
Purgatory, up to the beautiful wood just outside Paradise. At this
point he says that they

>   . . . . have reached a place
> Where, of myself, no further I discern.
>
> I've brought thee here by wit and by address;
> Make pleasure now thy guide – thou art well sped
> Forth of the steep, forth of the narrow way.[61b:27.128-32]

The fundamental basis of love has been accepted throughout, even
in Hell and in Purgatory. In Purgatory, Vergil, in a long discourse
on the failures of weak or misapplied love, comments:

>   Never, my son, was yet
>   Creator, no, nor creature, without love
>   Natural or rational – and thou knowest it.[61b:27.91-3]

Beatrice, wisdom, in Paradise comments that at that point intellect
and love are fused, in the famous lines:

> Pure intellectual light, fulfilled with love,
> Love of the true Good, fulfilled with all delight,
> Transcending sweet delight, all sweets above.[61c:30.40-2]

This fusion is commented on by Assagioli in *The Act of Will* as
being part of the synthesis about which he is writing. The
combination here is also, of course, the personal fusion with
universal truth and love.

The final lines in the *Divine Comedy* also relate to this ultimate
fusion:

> Yet, as a wheel moves slowly, free from jars,
> My will and my desire were turned by love,
>
> The love that moves the sun and the other stars.[61c:33.143-5]

Choice and personal will are emphasized throughout the story.
Sayers comments that Dante shared:

> the belief of all Catholic Christians that every living soul in the
> world has to make the choice between accepting or rejecting
> God, and that at the moment of death it will discover what it

has chosen: whether to remain in the outer darkness of the alien self, knowing God as only terror and judgment and pain, or to pass joyfully through the strenuous purgation which fits it to endure and enjoy eternally the unveiled presence of God.[61a:14]

The strength not to give up but to go on being fully alive is debated interestingly in Dante's conversation with the spirit of Marco Lombardo on the second cornice of Purgatory. Dante expresses his despair:

> The world indeed is barren through and through,
> As thou hast said, of virtue and of worth,
> Sin-laden and sin-clouded – that's most true.

Marco replies:

> Light's given you to know right from wrong at need.
>
> And free will, so its stuff can stand the strain
> Of its first tussles with the stars, will fight,
> If nourished well, to win the whole campaign;
>
> For of a nobler nature, mightier might,
> You're the free subjects – might which doth create
> A mind in you that's no star's perquisite.
>
> So, if the world now goes with crooked gait
> The cause is in yourselves for you to trace.[61b:16.75-83]

The responsibility for the world's ills, particularly the political ills, is firmly with the human race, but some problems may spring from the individual and some from the society:

> Clear cause, then, why the world's so ill-behaved
> Is that it's governed after an ill mode.
> Not that the nature in you is depraved.[61b:16.104-6]

Dante, particularly with his own extensive political experience and suffering, is most aware of the social as well as the personal aspects of the meaning of suffering. As Dorothy Sayers writes:

Both loomed large in Dante's mind, and they interpenetrate and complete one another. For most of us it may be easier to understand Hell as the picture of a corrupt society than as a corrupt self. Whichever we start with, it is likely to lead to the other.[61a:19]

And Dante saw the allegory as being not only about the journey of the individual but also about the community of the world – it is the political way of salvation as well as the personal way.

The combination of personal and political, of knowledge and love, of the single will to the universal, is at the basis of psychosynthesis. Sayers comments on the universality of the vision that is opened to the reader – something that has become much more difficult in the modern Western world, where different branches of knowledge and understanding are fragmented. Talking of Dante's attitude, she writes:

> As for the mixture of passion, mysticism, and science in one and the same poem, he would highly approve it, as imparting an agreeable variety and comprehensiveness to the work. It would never occur to him that he ought to keep his head, his heart, and his religious experience in water-tight compartments, or that a poem might not properly appeal to all of them in turn. It is only the twentieth century reader who is disconcerted by having to break down the Victorian bulkheads in order that his partitioned-off personality may flow together again.[58b:12]

This combination is something which was both inspiring and difficult for Assagioli, as will be discussed in the next section. Synthesis is fundamental, but Assagioli also regarded himself as a scientist, which is, of course, an analytical rather than a synthetic activity. The first therapists in the twentieth century definitely saw scientific investigation as being very different from religion, and regarded reason rather than feeling as being the mainstay of their task. Assagioli's espousal of both Dante and Plato gave him a different and alternative framework for his work, though he was always very keen to say he was a scientist.

The final point that I would like to make about the relevance of Dante's framework to Assagioli is the very hierarchical nature of the pictures of Hell, Purgatory and Paradise. This is in accordance with the picture of the Great Chain of Being, which was a notion of the universe held by most people from neoplatonic times until the eighteenth century. He describes this in his *In Convivio* (The Banquet):

> The goodness of God is received in one way by substances separated (from matter), that is Angels, which have no material

goodness but are almost diaphanous through the purity of their form; differently by the human soul which, although it is in part free from matter, is in part impeded like a man under water except for his head and thus not entirely in or out of it; differently again by animals, whose soul is made entirely of matter but somewhat ennobled; by plants; by minerals; differently from all these by the earth which is the most material and therefore the most remote from and disproportioned to the first, simplest and noblest virtue which is entirely intellectual, that is God.[60:7.5]

As Holmes writes in his book on Dante, 'the highest beings in the universe were the most simple, the most spiritual and the most uniform. The lower parts of creation were increasingly diverse and material.'[114:34] This also is part of Assagioli's picture of the human being, a mixture of soul and personality, where the superconscious is the most pure and clear, and the diversity of the subpersonalities is the stuff that has to be worked with and resolved. There is definitely a sense of the 'higher' and the 'lower' forces, with the lower being attuned to and relating to the higher, but being to some extent different in quality.

Assagioli uses the work of Dante for his work with the superconscious. He suggests that suitable people should be given the task of reading the *Divine Comedy* as it represents so clearly the personal journey, looking carefully at the symbolic meanings and identifying with Dante. He also refers again to the guided daydream technique of Desoille, where the client is asked to descend into a cave or to climb a mountain.

> Desoille has found empirically that during the descent the images that are evoked in the imagination are related to the unacceptable or threatening powers of the unconscious and also to certain complexes and images related to parent figures with which negative emotions are connected. In contrast, in the ascent of the mountain there is the evocation of positive and constructive feelings; also newly experienced feelings of love and wisdom are often invoked by this technique.[1:212]

Assagioli was also most attached to the exercise of the blossoming of the rose, clearly a mystical symbol related to the white rose in Dante's Paradise, which he quotes among other referrals to the beauty and significance of the rose and which is symbolic of growth and 'livingness', the life force which is the spirit.

14

The alternative mystical tradition traced through the Renaissance and into the modern period

It would be inappropriate to spend too much time in this study of psychosynthesis in describing the truly fascinating history of the alternative mystical tradition, in alchemy, in astrology, in heretical Christian movements such as the Cathars and the Anabaptists, in the massive artistic and spiritual flowering of the Renaissance, in the work of Shakespeare, Vaughan, the great Italian painters, the utopian visionaries of Europe, William Blake and William Wordsworth, and the Romantic movements of the early nineteenth century. But some evidence must be given for the continuation of the gnostic strand through this long period, an alternative current that at times flowed very strongly into the main Western culture.

This current is, in Mannheim's definition, part of an alternative 'other' system of thought which he defined as 'utopian': 'we regard as utopian all situationally transcendent ideas . . . which in any way have a transforming effect on the existing historical-social order.'[157:185] Gnosticism is utopian in two senses, not only as being part of a whole different concept of 'knowing' in the later part of the period, but also being part of a largely unacceptable kind of spiritual knowledge. It is part of those 'complexes of ideas that tend to generate activities towards changes of the prevailing order'.[157:xxiii] But it has remained throughout this long period as part of the alternative, part of the utopian rather than in any way of the mainsteam ideology: so it remains potentiality rather than actuality.

All the streams of belief so far discussed came together in the Renaissance, particularly in Italy where the sense of transformation was strongest, and most particularly in Florence. Scholars came to have access to classical Greek thought, and brought to it a freedom of appreciation generally not found in the Middle Ages; Marsilio Ficino for instance, who lived from 1433 to 1499, founded a new Platonic Academy, backed by Cosimo de Medici. He translated hermetic material, was deeply involved in the Kabbalah, was a student of Dante, knew of Plotinus, and reckoned all this material could be absorbed in the Christian tradition. Also at that period, Eastern and Oriental work became available in the West, particularly Islamic Sufism, the Muslim mystical tradition, and even some knowledge of Hindu and Buddhist thought. This extraordinary and exotic mix of cultural experience concerning the nature of the universe and the place of the human race within it resulted in a blossoming of artistic and exploratory work which is unique in history. But Christianity remained the orthodox religion, split as it then became into Catholic and Protestant, and science later became the mainstream method of thought and the recognized basis of knowledge. Gnosticism remained 'the other'.

Alchemy, throughout the Middle Ages and afterwards, remained part of this unacceptable alternative. Jung regards alchemy as part of the constant psychological striving of mankind to get in touch with the ultimate. 'The point is that alchemy is rather like an undercurrent to the Christianity that ruled on the surface. It is to this surface as the dream is to the consciousness.'[132:23] Alchemists, in their attempt to make gold, and to induce spirit to appear in matter, were in Jung's view in an existential search similar to the more orthodox religious search, and perhaps in their attempt to control matter were following a similar path to the one which was a direct ancestor of modern science. Alchemy was part of the gnostic process – 'the alchemists ran counter to the Church in preferring to seek through knowledge than to find through faith'[132:35] – but this insight was part of the 'out there' knowledge that eventually led to science. Alchemy springs from gnosticism in its search for the philosopher's stone (the Higher Self?), but its methods eventually led to the split between science and mysticism with which we are concerned in studying the significance of psychosynthesis. Jung saw alchemy (and astrology) as human projection – 'such projections repeat themselves whenever man tries to explore an empty darkness and involuntarily fills it with living form':[132:245] the belief in the separate reality of the external – separate, that is, from the person projecting his understanding – would be Jung's explanation of the split in science and mysticism today.

Frances Yates writes that:

> the Hermetic science par excellence is alchemy; the famous *Emerald Tablet*, the bible of the alchemists, is attributed to Hermes Trismegistus and gives in a mysteriously compact form the philosophy of the All and the One. In the Renaissance, a new style 'Alchymia' becomes associated with the new Magia and Cabala . . . the *De harmonia mundi* (1525) of Francesco

> Giorgio, a Franciscan friar of Venice, develops to the full a
> theme which is implicit in all types of the Hermetic-Cabalist
> tradition, namely the theme of universal harmony, of the
> harmonious relationship between man, the microcosm, and the
> greater world of the universe, the macrocosm . . . to the native
> Pythagorean medieval tradition, Hermeticism and Cabalism
> added immense richness and complexity, swelling out the
> universal harmonies into a new symphony.[248:150-1]

The preoccupations of Plato and Plotinus, together with the
alchemical attempts to activate and control the basic energy of the
universe, come flooding into the origins of our modern period.

It was in the fifteenth century that the translations and original
work that were to be the foundation for the Renaissance started to
appear. The hermetic work had been brought to Florence from
Byzantium in 1460, and Ficino's translations of the *Corpus
Hermeticum* became available in the 1460s. He translated Plato's
Symposium in 1469, and another Platonic work within the next
decade. His own major work, the *Platonic Theology on the
Immortality of the Soul*, appeared in 1474. He subsequently
translated Plotinus, from 1484 to 1492, and also brought out his
other original work, *On Drawing Down the Life of Heaven*, in
1489, a book that was largely based on hermetic material. He
worked along with other scholars in Florence's Platonic Academy.

Pico della Mirandola (1463–94) was working in Florence at the
Academy at the same time. He also translated neoplatonic
material, and among his 900 productions included much
Kabbalistic material; he was 'the seminal figure who perceived the
structural similarities between the Kabbalah and the *Corpus
Hermeticum*'.[28:147] His own book, *Oration on the Dignity of
Man*, used neoplatonic ideas, particularly the ideas of correspondence of harmonies in the universe and man as microcosm of
the whole:

> that the good magic works through 'simpatia', through
> knowing the mutual rapports running through all nature, the
> secret charms through which one thing can be drawn to
> another thing, so that as the peasant marries the vine to the
> elm, 'so the Magus marries earth to heaven, that is to say, the
> forces of inferior things to the gifts and properties of supernal
> things.'[248:90]

Alchemical work at this time was particularly influenced by
Paracelsus (1493–1541), who could be seen as one of the major

forerunners to modern 'alternative' medicine. He held strongly that disease is evil or disharmony, linking up the hermetic ideas of the natural harmony of the universe. Ahern writes that he believed that 'crucial to success' in healing work 'are the physician's arcane understanding, self-knowledge and other, more Christian virtues'.[28:150] Again there seems to be a direct link here to modern depth psychology, carried underground into the twentieth century. The symbolic function of alchemy is again brought into the twentieth century transpersonal therapy movements by Burckhardt's notion that spiritually understood, the transmission of lead into gold is nothing other than the repairing of the original nobility of human nature: and again Ahern writes, 'gold and silver are the macrocosmic correspondence to the original condition of the soul'.[28:149]

Giordano Bruno, who also had strong Florentine connections, lived from 1548 to 1600, when he was burnt at the stake for his heretical views. He carried these earlier Renaissance views to many parts of Europe, and developed them. He is the subject of one of Frances Yates's major books, *Giordano Bruno and the Hermetic Tradition*. Bruno shed the Christianity to which the majority of other Renaissance writers had held, and believed truth was to be found directly from these alternative doctrines – a view of course completely unacceptable to the church of the time. He was interested in the relationship between spirituality and magic, that is, control and domination over natural phenomena.

Bruno adhered to the picture of the world in which the celestial images, the archetypal forms, are the true reality, which may be accessible to the human being. Yates quotes from a text, *Corpus Hermeticum* XI, which gives something of the aspirations of these beliefs, which were totally unacceptable to a hierarchical church and reckoned to be entirely blasphemous:

> Unless you make yourself equal to God, you cannot understand God: for the like is not intelligible except to the like. Make yourself grow to a greatness beyond measure, by a bound free yourself from the body; raise yourself beyond all time, become Eternity; then you will understand God. Believe that nothing is impossible for you, think yourself immortal and capable of understanding all, all arts, all sciences, the nature of every living being. Mount higher than the highest height; descend lower than the lowest depth. Draw into yourself all sensations created, fire and water, dry and moist, imagining that you are everywhere, on earth, in the sea, in the sky, that you are not yet born, in the maternal womb, adolescent, old, dead, beyond

death. If you embrace in your thought all things at once, times,
places, substances, qualities, quantities, you may understand
God.[248:198]

This is the most ambitious and risky method of experiencing the
world in the mind, the most powerful way of interpreting the
relationship of the microcosm to the macrocosm. It closely related
God to the nature of human thinking.

Bruno reflected the ambitions of the hermetic thinker, the
gnostic sense that the world is not as it should be, a conservative
sense of a paradise lost, and a radical sense of potential nowhere
realised. Plato's image of the cave is there, and the sense of a
knowledge not shared with the majority of mankind, who are
asleep and actively or passively trying to keep the human race
within the prison.

It is interesting to see that the modern alternative picture that
the earth is alive is present in Bruno's thought: 'the interior
principle in things is the cause of their movement. . . . Therefore
the earth and the heavenly bodies move in accordance with
individual differences in their intrinsic principle which is their
soul. . . .'[248:243] And everything, including all the differences of
the particular, is one: 'The summum bonum, the supremely
desirable, the supreme perfection and beatitude consists in the
unity which informs the all. . . . May the Gods be praised and may
all living things magnify the infinite, the most simple, the most
one, the most high, the most absolute cause, beginning and
one.'[248:248] The divine light, he believed, was in everything. In his
Eroici Furori, published in England in 1585 with a dedication to
Philip Sidney, Bruno writes of the divine light that shines through
all things and beats on our senses: 'behold he standeth behind the
wall, he looketh forth at the windows, showing himself through
the lattice.'[248:275]

In England, the neoplatonic and hermetic stream of thought was
represented in particular by such men as Robert Fludd
(1574–1637) and John Dee (1527–1608), who influenced Philip
Sidney and, as Tillyard indicates in his classic book *The
Elizabethan World Picture*, the whole extraordinary vitality of the
Elizabethan age – including, of course, Shakespeare and the great
playwrights and poets. The aim of such men as Dee and Fludd, in
line with the ambitions expressed by Bruno above, was to gather
together the whole of human knowledge, and to understand it and
experience it through the gnostic tradition. Poetry was so highly
regarded at that time because of, as Tillyard puts it, 'the Neo-
Platonic doctrine that poetry was man's effort to rise above his

fallen self and to reach out toward perfection'. He quotes Sidney on poetry:

> Neither let it be deemed too saucy a comparison to balance the highest point of man's wit with the efficacy of nature, but rather give right honour to the Maker of that maker, who, having made man in his own likeness, set him over and beyond all the works of that second nature; which in nothing he showeth so much as in poetry, when with the force of the divine breath he bringeth things forth far outpassing her doings, with no small argument to the incredulous of that first accursed fall of Adam, sith our erected wit maketh us know what perfection is and yet our infected will keepeth us from reaching unto it. [226:30]

This is a classic lament of the reach for the sun and the stars and a comment on the bridge of poetry that should make the journey possible. There is also, interestingly enough, a hint of the assumption of domination over nature that was to form one of the themes of 'natural magic' or science in the next centuries.

Over the next few centuries the neoplatonic and hermetic traditions continued even more underground. Frances Yates follows the story into the seventeenth century with the Rosicrucian movement in Europe. She ends her study *The Rosicrucian Enlightenment* with the words of Comenius (born 1592) in his *Via Lucis* which expresses the great hope of the alternative vision:

> If a light of Universal Wisdom can be enkindled, it will be able both to spread its beams throughout the whole world of the human intellect (just as the radiance of the sun as often as it rises reaches from the east to the west) and to awake gladness in the hearts of men and to transform their wills. For if they see their own destiny and that of the world clearly set before them in this supreme light and learn how to use the means which will unfailingly lead to good ends, why should they not actually use them?

The spiritual awareness that the Rosicrucians, as heir to the neoplatonic vision, had in mind was of the inward nature of people as well as that of the natural environment:

> This illumination shines inward as well as outward; it is an inward spiritual illumination revealing to man new possibilities in himself, teaching him to understand his own dignity and

worth and the part he is called upon to play in the divine
scheme.[250:277-8]

There is a direct link here through to the Theosophical and
Anthroposophical movements of the nineteenth and twentieth
century, and through to 'New Age' mysticism of the present day.
At intervals in this long period there was a considerable poetic
resurgence of the ideas of microcosm and macrocosm, a sense of
the spiritual nature of all life, a sense of rebirth and the soul
forgetting much that it was born knowing. The philosopher
Swedenborg had represented a hermetic strand in the eighteenth
century, but of course at the time of the Enlightenment rationality
was prized above all and mysticism was largely discredited.
However, at the turn of the eighteenth/nineteenth centuries there
is evidence of a renewed interest in Plato, Plotinus, hermeticism
and mysticism in both poets and philosophers in Europe.

William Blake was the great eighteenth century mystical poet,
expressing a sense of the correspondences and the relationship
between the microcosm and the macrocosm. His art and his
poetry represent the neoplatonic and the hermetic tradition in a
period that was largely unsympathetic. Goethe, as a philosopher,
was deeply impressed by Plotinus: 'Goethe had the need to feel
himself one with the totality of nature; the consciousness of this
unity, the unio mystica with the eternal and all-one, was his joy,
his religion.'[166:282] These strands from eighteenth century Europe
passed over into the nineteenth century Romantic movement. The
general philosophical movement towards Romanticism was supported by Spinoza and by Schelling. There is mention at the turn
of the century of a 'new religion'. Novalis at this time wrote:

In Spinoza . . . lives this divine spark of the understanding of
Nature. Plotinus, perhaps stimulated by Plato, was the first to
enter with the true spirit of this holy place, and even yet no one
has pressed further into it than he.

Schelling himself was writing:

The seed of Christendom was the feeling of a separation of the
world from God. . . . The new religion, which already
announces itself in isolated revelations . . . will make itself
known in the rebirth of Nature as the symbol of the eternal
Oneness; the first reconciliation and resolving of the old-age
discord must be celebrated in philosophy whose sense and

meaning is grasped only by him who recognises in such
philosophy the life of the newly originated Godhead.[166:104]

A sense of experience being knowledge was present in the early
nineteenth century Romantic poets and the whole movement of
Romanticism in art and in philosophy. This German Romantic
movement also rediscovered Giordano Bruno, as well as drawing
on the vision of the mystic Boehme. In an interesting and very
well-documented book about the English poet Coleridge and the
'pantheist' tradition, Thomas McFarland[166] traces Coleridge's
knowledge of Bruno. His neoplatonic interests were shared by
other English Romantic poets; these lines that are very familiar, from
Wordsworth's *Tintern Abbey*:

> . . . . and I have felt
> A presence that disturbs me with the joy
> Of elevated thoughts; a sense sublime
> Of something far more deeply interfused,
> Whose dwelling is the light of setting suns,
> And the round ocean and the living air,
> And the blue sky, and in the mind of man;
> A motion and a spirit, that impels
> All thinking things, all objects of all thought,
> And rolls through all the things.

Byron has similar lines in *Childe Harold* and Shelley in *Mont
Blanc*. The gnostic and the Plotinian spirit emerges with great
strength in this nineteenth century work. Walt Whitman and
W. B. Yeats are among later poets in the nineteenth and twentieth
centuries who draw on this same enduring vision. As Kathleen
Raine has put it in her essay 'Yeats' debt to William Blake', in a
passage that sums up the modern significance of the gnostic
stream in art:

> there is a universal language of symbolic discourse, age-old and
> world wide, but inseparable from the kind of knowledge which
> it embodies. The present difficulty in understanding this
> language – or even divining its presence – arises from the
> denial, by current philosophies coloured from positivism, of the
> reality of a spiritual order. In Europe spiritual knowledge is
> embodied and transmitted principally within that tradition
> which descended through Orphism to Plato, to the neo-
> Platonists and the Gnostic sects, and to their successors both
> within Christendom (Dionysius the Aeropagite and Dante were

of them) and outside it. It is the language of Alchemy and of the Cabala, and of all allied ways of thought whose foundation is what Blake calls the 'language of divine analogy', the teaching of the Smaragdine Table of Hermes, 'as above, so below'. The created world is, at every level, a manifestation (and therefore a symbol) of anterior forces. It is the language also of all symbolic art; or one might rather say that symbolic art is the natural language of such thought. The measure of its exactness is its conformity to the spiritual knowledge of the Perennial Philosophy. Just as the terms of mathematics must remain meaningless to those who do not comprehend number, so this symbolic language must remain hidden forever from those for whom its universe of discourse is as if non-existent. It might be called 'occult' or 'esoteric' since it is hidden from all but initiates; yet it is so hidden only in as far as its terms are incomprehensible except in the light of knowledge of a certain kind. To those who, like Yeats, are both by natural bent and by a fortunate environment, capable of discerning its traces, it is everywhere apparent throughout the entire range of imaginative art.[197:70]

15 Religion and mysticism at the turn of the nineteenth/ twentieth century

By the end of the nineteenth century, materialism, science, positivism and technology had transformed the Western world, as will be discussed further in the next chapter. Conventional religions had failed to convince, and indeed had repelled, many of the educated people within society. Then, as now, there was a sense of impending doom, and a growing atheism.

Darwin's *The Origin of Species*, published in 1859, had had a major impact on assumptions about the nature of mankind in the latter part of the nineteenth century. His work explained the evolution of the human race in a way which was independent of any divine agency. His basic premises of 'the survival of the fittest' in the evolution of species and the survival of individuals, and of 'natural selection' which postulated that the strongest strains would survive, could account for the development of the creatures of the world, including ourselves, by chance and by principle. This scientific framework, which depended upon twenty years of painstaking, thorough research and reflection, could explain the human situation in scientific, materialistic, non-divine terms.

The visionary Karl Marx, who protested against the ills of the Western economic way of life, saw his new communist revolutionary society in materialist terms, perceiving conventional religion as part of the power position he wished to destroy; Marx saw his view as perfectly consistent with Darwin's theories of the evolution of the human race. Many humanistic, ethical and socialist societies, largely grounded in agnosticism or atheism, were set up at the end of the nineteenth century. Budd maintains that the reaction against conventional religion, which she outlines so graphically as it occurred in England, was also a reaction against the authority of the churches.[52:139]

Stuart Hughes, in his interesting study of the consciousness of social thought in Europe at the turn of the century, describes the 'self-satisfied cult of material progress found at that time. Positivist systems thinking was paramount – thinking based on the predominance of science, the importance of empirical research and the 'objectivity' of knowledge.'[116] All thinkers of that time absorbed a notion of knowledge that was positivist, systemic, scientific. Freud thought of himself as an engineer or a technician, as did all the great sociologists working at that time; medicine and psychology were seen in much the same light as other kinds of technology.

But it is interesting that scholars also thought in terms of grand designs and great systems. It must have seemed to many that the whole existence would perhaps shortly be understood. Mathematicians at Cambridge:

> were carried away by a wave of Darwinian enthusiasm; we seemed to ride triumphant on an ocean of new life and boundless possibilities. Natural Selection was to be the master-key of the universe; we expected it to solve all contradictions. Among other things it was to give a new system of ethics, combining the exactness of the utilitarian with the poetic beliefs of the transcendentalist.[52:139]

Thus for some, the new kind of scientific precision could be used with, and not supplant, older modes of human awareness and more ancient kinds of knowledge.

In the latter part of the nineteenth century there occurred, slowly and marginally, a renaissance in spiritual awareness among certain groups. Spiritualism became known and even fashionable in both Europe and America. Eastern religions slowly became known to some aware people who were able to see countries such as India not only as Empire but also as repositories of ancient wisdom with much to offer the West. Many books, both before and after the turn of the century, investigated other periods of human experience very different from those of the materialistic West: William James, whose father was a disciple of Swedenborg, gave his lectures on the 'Varieties of religious experience' in 1901, publishing them a year later; Ralph Waldo Trine's *In Tune with the Infinite*, a book drawing on the experience of the mystics, came out in 1897; Ernst Haeckel's *The Riddle of the Universe*, of 1899, written in German, examined the relationship between science, conventional religion and a new religious and social/spiritual awareness in Germany and in Europe; R. M. Bucke's *Cosmic Consciousness*, published in 1901, was about the possible development of a new consciousness within the human race. Particularly relevant to Roberto Assagioli, though he knew all of this material, was the founding of the Theosophical Society, as his mother became a member. This was formed in America in 1886, in England in 1888, and in Italy in 1902, as well as in many other countries round the world in swift succession.

Thus, an alternative system to the materialistic one was developing; or rather, as H. P. Blavatsky, the founder of Theosophy, maintained, the 'new' spiritual awareness was an extension of Darwinism. She argued that Darwin had not gone far enough: he analysed the physical evolution of the human race, and in doing this lost his faith. She considered that he failed to see the possibility of a spiritual evolution. This was at the root of her philosophy, and was based on the age-old stream of mystical awareness, both Eastern and Western. This was the evolution that she was concerned to track in her difficult books *Isis Unveiled* (1877) and *The Secret Doctrine* (1888).

Hughes maintains that the new, or rather rediscovered, awareness of the irrational, 'non-logical, the uncivilised, the inexplicable' factors in human affairs occurred both at the level of grand and respected theory and at the more popular level of the spiritualists and the Theosophists, who would still not be seen by most conventional academics as serious contributors to thought.[116:35] There was some acceptance that rational thought could not on its own explain the human condition. It came from those people who would not quarrel with Darwin's work and its implications, and yet could not take for granted, as many atheists and agnostics did, that spiritual awareness had been dismissed once and for all by scientific knowledge and technology. The interest in the nature of consciousness, and the new work being done at the turn of the century, most notably by Freud, on the nature of unconsciousness, brought a new way to study not only the external world, but also the internal emotional nature of human beings. This was a first scientific attempt to study the non-rational in the social sciences, and led to the invention of psychology (a very positivistic science) and psychodynamics (a scientific 'school' studying the non-rational).

It was early in the nineteenth century that a Frenchman, Anguetil du Perron, brought back from India a collection of fifty Upanishads. In the latter part of the nineteenth century, more Eastern books were being brought to the West and seriously studied. Thus, as at the time of the Renaissance, a whole different way of seeing the world became available, though this time potentially to a much wider proportion of the population. At first this material was only seen by a few – for example the Upanishads, including the *Bhagavadgita*, which was obtained by Edward Carpenter in England in 1880 from a friend in the Ceylon Civil Service. In 1879, Sir Edwin Arnold published *The Light of Asia*, which was written in the form of a Buddhist poem and went into many editions. Theosophists from the beginning drew on Asian religious sources, particularly Tibetan. And gradually this interest, which at first had been mainly the prerogative of scholars, spread to groups of people in European countries and America which were large enough to form societies. In England the Buddhist Society was founded in 1907, with an understanding that the purpose was not only scholarship but practice and belief – 'the dual need, to study objectively and to practice subjectively'.[117] The Buddhist Society, especially through the great influence of such people as Christmas Humphries, had particular links with Theosophists: indeed, Theosophy was known by some as 'esoteric Buddhism'.

Buddhism contains the idea of an immanent God:

> God's light dwells in the self and nowhere else. It shines alike in every living being and one can see it with one's mind steadied. . . . If the world is what it is, it is because of tension. The world of time and change is ever striving to reach perfection.

Most people, in this view, do not become true individuals, but just live out their social roles:

> Any sense of satisfaction and security derived by submission to external authority is bought at the price of the integrity of the Self. . . . By developing our inner spiritual nature, we gain a new kind of relatedness to the world and grow into the freedom, where the integrity of the Self is not compromised. . . . The sense of insufficiency, of barrenness and dust is due to the working of the Perfection, the mystery that lurks at the heart of Creation. . . . Wisdom is direct experience which occurs as soon as obstacles to its realisation are removed.[196:44]

These are Radhakrishnan's words from a mid-twentieth century version of the *Gita*, but they sum up some of the universal messages of the long fable of the story – the fight between good and evil, the journey of each person, the problem of suffering and the possibility of wisdom – a choice not taken by many people. These were messages from another ancient culture that, at the turn of the century, came with great force to some individuals who were unconvinced of the ultimate wisdom of science and technology, and tired of the conventional authoritarian churches, fossilized into respectability. This Eastern strand remained relatively latent during most of the twentieth century, but of course re-emerged with considerable aplomb in the 1960s.

Hermann Keyserling, with whom Assagioli was in steady and respectful contact, wrote an interesting pamphlet, published by the Shanghai Mercury in 1912, on *The East and West and their Search for the Common Truth*. He spoke at that time of the 'extraordinary interest in all things Eastern – Eastern thought, art, religion and culture in general' that had arisen in the West in the last fifty years, and which did not exist before. He comments that 'modern nations are striving to bring happiness to mankind by improving environments, forgetting that happiness is the function of an inner attitude towards outer circumstances'. But though the East had almost certainly attained a greater wisdom than the West, just as the ancient Greeks had a greater sense of the universe of ethics, and a greater possibility of speaking directly from the soul than people do in modern society, neither of these civilizations had been effective at *doing* things. Keyserling comments:

> The East has been sitting within the sun, and so it was enlightened; but it had got there not by a gradual approach but by a sudden jump, and it could not understand its nature. As long as it did not move, it remained in the light. As soon as it moved at all, in whatever direction it be, it moved away from the sun, and the sun shone on its back, so finally it lost the light. So far we Westerners have never been in the sun, but we are slowly approaching it. And as the sun is before our eyes, and not at our back, we will not only reach it some day but we will know its intrinsic nature.

He believed that people in the West had lost track of their own roots; that they needed to tap the wisdom of the East, and also forgotten Western knowledge. The technology of the West, combined with ancient wisdom, could be the next step forward for human consciousness.

Several authors at this period began to collect evidence of mystical experience, and to develop a conviction that out of all the seeming chaos and cruelty of the external world could emerge a new consciousness that could be shared by all, and which would wondrously alter the conditions of life on earth. Marx had prophesied this on a material and social/economic/political plane only. But such a writer as Edward Carpenter in England combined socialist convictions with spiritual awareness, and understood that a new world could only emerge when the spiritual and the social were seen together. In his splendidly titled *From Adam's Peak to*

Elephanta, published in 1892, he compared the visions of East and West:

> The West seeks the individual consciousness – the enriched mind, ready perceptions and memories, individual hopes and fears, ambition, loves, conquests – the self, the local self, in all its local phases and forms – and sorely doubts whether such a thing as a universal consciousness exists. The East seeks the universal consciousness, and in those cases where its quest succeeds, individual self and life thin away to a mere film, and are only the shadows cast by the glory revealed beyond.[51:243]

But again he believed that the two sides of the world could together bring about one vision.

Ernst Haeckel, in his influential *The Riddle of the Universe*, published in German in 1899, tackled a theme that was later repeated by Assagioli – how science had progressed at an unprecedented rate throughout the nineteenth century, but that there was no advance, only barbarism, in social and moral arrangements. He commented that the greatest theories of the soul in the last two thousand years had sprung from introspection, and that the most neglected aspect of the study of the person was the soul. He saw the way forward to 'the Riddle of the Universe' in a greater understanding of the nature of mankind.

R. M. Bucke, in the preface to his well-known *Cosmic Consciousness*, published in 1901, believed that the possibilities for a new world were present at that time:

> The human race is in the process of developing a new kind of consciousness, far in advance of the ordinary human self-consciousness, which will eventually lift the race above and beyond all the fears and ignorances, the brutalities and bestialities which beset it today.

He thought three revolutions were about to happen – aerial navigation (planes), which would lead to the dissolution of barriers between nations; social and economic action that would lead to greater equality and the end of poverty; and a spiritual awareness based on renewed personal experience of the divine, which would develop into an entirely different experience of living for people. Most of the latter part of the book is taken up with case histories of men and women from different periods who had experience of 'cosmic consciousness'.

So the period at the turn of this century was full of

contradictions. There was hope in science, but awareness among some that science could probably only tackle relatively physical problems, with limited human awareness; a decline in conventional religions and churchgoing, and a scepticism about religion influenced most strongly by scientific theories of knowledge and the iconoclastic work of Darwin; and a strong sense of impending doom because of human inability to understand the great forces unleashed on the world by the human race. But simultaneously a small minority of people considered, and often fervently believed, that the human race was just at the beginning of what could be a completely new age and consciousness, when the physical evolution already analysed by Darwin could be followed by a social and spiritual awareness, the social being dependent on the spiritual.

So Theosophists, the group most relevant to this study, were part of a larger movement. Annie Besant was one of the most prolific and articulate writers in the Theosophy movement at that time, and one of its leaders. She insisted that the evolutionary idea was basic to the inspiration of Madame Blavatsky; that the 'secret wisdom' on which it was based had existed through the ages and rested on the mystical knowledge and insight of the Platonist, neoplatonist and Eastern streams; that the truth of things had always been experienced by a few, but now it was important that more people understood and experienced the basic unity of the human race and the human quest – this was why it was particularly important and significant to acknowledge the wisdom of other cultures; that wisdom is different from and superior to knowledge, however scientific; that individual awareness and growth is important but is only significant if it is used in service to others in the world; that mankind brings sorrow, but that basically 'life is not a cry but a song'.

The three aims of the Theosophical Society were: (i) to be the nucleus of a universal brotherhood; (ii) to promote the study of Aryan and other Eastern literatures, religions and sciences; and (iii) to investigate unexplained laws of nature and the psychical powers latent in man.

The society with these aims, and with the charge of being 'esoteric Buddhism', continued to be attacked as unscientific, putting forward 'abstract and unverifyable conceptions', eccentric and weird. It was often regarded as nonsense. The interest in psychic phenomena, the doctrine of Karma, reincarnation, the occult and the esoteric tradition have made it a marginal force in society, but the aims are grand and ambitious and always have been.

A modern academic, Theodore Roszak, considers Blavatsky 'among the most original and perceptive minds of her time, if also one of the most uneven', and Theosophy 'one of the most adventurous and intriguing bodies of nineteenth century thought'.[202:118-19] He writes that she got a glimpse of what might be called the higher sanity possible to the human mind, a sanity that had only existed before in the consciousness of a few outstanding individuals, but which might be possible for the whole human race – and indeed essential for its survival. The psychology then existing at the turn of the century, and still the most usual form taught in our universities, was experimental, physical, reductionist and secularized. A psychology 'grounded in the transcendent impulse' was only derived from this marginal thinking. William James, a psychologist of great repute, firmly split his standard psychological works *Principles of Psychology* from his *Varieties of Religious Experience*. The two aspects of the person, personality and soul, were then regarded as totally separate, and still largely are today. It was groups like Theosophists which were the only ones to see the legitimate connection.

Theosophists followed the gnostic split between spirit and matter, and paid great attention to spirit. But they also had a sense from the Buddhist tradition of the immanent God, the God within, available to all. All souls have connection with the World Soul. Various concepts relevant to psychosynthesis in a direct way can be found in Theosophy – the idea of the World-egg, the philosopher's stone, which represented unity, and which could at least be seen against Assagioli's 'egg-shaped diagram', the drawing of the nature of the person; and the idea of the seven rays, the seven basic forces in the universe, and the possible connection with the seven ways to the Self in psychosynthesis, a concept also found in Eastern religions.

Theosophy also contains the idea of division and unity within the person, and the connection between the two. 'Divided by separative desire we are our lower selves. Dominated by our perception of the universal harmony we become our higher selves.'[105:69] Annie Besant, in *A Study of Consciousness*, published in 1904, writes that the normal person's sense of 'I am' is restricted to ordinary consciousness. However, she continues to say that by working through what she calls the subconscious and its instincts and divisions, it is possible to contact 'the superphysical consciousness'; and she particularly comments on studies of dreams (Freud's *Interpretation of Dreams* came out in 1899), of intuitions, of creative artistry, which indicate to us something of its existence. Blavatsky herself wrote earlier that 'this grand universe is in reality but a huge aggregation of various states of consciousness'.[105:181]

So at the time that Assagioli wrote his first paper in 1906, on humour and smiling wisdom, many of the ideas which entered into psychosynthesis were already around, for those able and willing to perceive them. The creation of a new phenomenon such as psychosynthesis is of course always a mystery, but it is important to understand the atmosphere in which a person begins to work, the surrounding web of ideas and experience available to him or her. Assagioli created from his own religious experience and from a very wide cultural base; his roots in Italy, in Europe, at the exuberant turn of the century were undeniably part of the basis of his inspiration.

It is from these mystical ideas of the nature of reality, existing through the ages, that we turn to the scientific side of psychosynthesis. The mystical was already there, but in fuller measure through the movements at the beginning of the century, particularly Theosophy: the scientific study of the person, and specifically the unconscious, was just emerging, with Freud's publications coming with the new century. It is on the scientific side that we must now concentrate.

16 The nature of science in psychology and psychotherapy

In Chapter 8 on the split development of scientific and mystical thought in the last four hundred years, it was pointed out that science sprang from the mystical inspiration of the Renaissance, the 'natural magic' of the time. We have come to see, at this point in the twentieth century, that the 'objectivity' of natural science is objectivity within a paradigm, a framework of knowledge. This is most obviously true in the scientific study of the human being, that most complex of phenomena as seen by ourselves who *are* human beings. The development of the discipline of psychology illustrates the many-sided nature of that knowledge, not only in the intellectual discipline of psychology, but also in the associated fields of psychiatry based in medicine, and psychotherapy based in schools initially springing up outside the accepted knowledge of the universities.

A classic study of the history of psychology by Brett, written in 1912–20, well before the seminal work by Kuhn, states that 'it is more in keeping with the history of thought to describe science as the myths about the world which have not yet been proved to be wrong'.[188:37] This seems at first sight to accord with the well-known arguments by Karl Popper that science can only be known as true science by the possibility that its main assumptions *can* be disproved: that it is an open system of knowledge rather than a closed one. He defines a closed system of thinking – including Freud, Marx and Adler, as well as Plato – as a system that is so comprehensive that no happening in the world can disprove it. A Marxist would have her or his own interpretation for anything that occurred, just as the Freudian would have his or her quite different one: whatever happened, each would leave the scene with his or her conceptual world intact.

But maybe natural science, which seems so open, is a closed system of thought, too: that though a particular piece of evidence may be able to disprove a particular theory, the scientific way of conceiving the world persists: that underneath the modern framework of natural science there are also persistent, value-laden, hard-to-contact assumptions about the human situation. So what are the basic values of modern science that have entered into our conception of psychology and medicine – values and methods to which Assagioli wished to adhere?

The objective, empirical, materialist, analytical view of knowledge was applied first to the study of the physical universe, and then gradually to the social sciences. The first great sociologists, Comte, Spencer and Hobhouse, took the biological model of an organism as the most appropriate one for an analysis of societies. They attempted, as biologists did with organisms, to observe, to produce analyses of patterns, and to develop laws which could hopefully be predictive. Psychology was also seen as close to biology – more obviously close than sociology. The kind of study developed towards the turn of the century, both in the problem of madness and in the methods used in discovering general patterns of human functioning, was experimental and empirical.

The *sine qua non* of the Western view of science is measurement and quantity. To be able to define, to state 'facts', to categorize, and to establish connections between phenomena that can be observed is a large part of the search for certainty and control in this system. Bohm, the theoretical physicist, maintains that measure was originally a form of insight – it involved feeling and aesthetics as well as mathematics. But gradually roles about measurements and quantities became laws, and were learned as laws.

> They appeared to be absolute truths about reality as it is, which men seem always to have known, and whose origins were often explained mythologically as binding injunctions of the Gods, which it would be both dangerous and wicked to question. Thought about measure thus tended to fall mainly into the domain of unconscious habit and as a result, the forms induced in perception by this thought were now seen as directly observed objective realities, which were essentially independent of how they were thought about.[47:22]

David Bohm maintains that Western science tends to see measure as being the essence of reality, whereas Eastern thinking, on the contrary, takes our surface perception as being 'maya', illusion.

Clearly measurement, order, the deduction of laws from empirical material is useful and very effective. The problem about it as a method, however, is that it is limited, and, what is infinitely more serious, not always perceived to be so. It is a well-known experience for many students of the social sciences that the more accurately you can measure a thing, the less interesting, humanly speaking, it is likely to be. And yet it is also clear that there are many 'tendencies' in social events and facts, and that there are patterns of human behaviour, both psychological and sociological. Social science methods are useful but we can expect too much of them, just as the Victorians – and indeed many people today against all the twentieth century evidence – assume that science can solve the problems of the world, and by itself lead to more and more progress.

This same inflation of expectation can be seen in relation to the other characteristics of science. The careful rigorous study of the world has led to an immensely developed technology which has changed the Western world and is penetrating the rest. But its ostensible objectivity and rigour within the scientific world view can obscure the subjectivity of the objects studied: the object can completely overpower the subject, whether it be a human being, animal, social or the world at large. But more than this, the assumption that science is 'value-free' can make scientific knowledge seem like the only real knowledge. People can come to think 'that what science discovers somehow casts doubt on things it does not discover'.[241:21]

Modern scientific assumptions by themselves are one-sided; science cannot deal, except in the most mundane ways, with quality: 'values, life meanings, purposes, and qualities slip through science like sea slips through the nets of fisherman'.[241:27] This statement is contrary to the optimism about science held by many when it was thought that through study we should come to understand every thing, and to be able to control it and make the world better if not perfect.

This optimism was present at the turn of the century. William James, in his massive *Principles of Psychology*, published originally in 1890, is offering an overview of psychology as a natural science as it was known at the time. His is a particularly philosophical psychology, though he was especially careful to distinguish it from metaphysics, and to define his method as an objective one. At that point, he does mention the 'soul' but writes that most psychology, even at that stage, is 'soulless' (omitting spirituality), and that he was to discuss the spiritual nature of mankind in a quite separate and different framework, his lectures given in 1901 on 'The varieties of religious experience'. Psychology, as it developed, was rooted even more firmly in the empirical experimental and eventually behaviourist stream. Concentration from the beginning was on biology, on the physical workings of the brain, on perception physiologically defined, on memory, and on the measurement of feeling and emotion. Tests of many kinds were developed to study all these phenomena and to generate rules.

Freud himself, who did not really start to develop psycho-analysis until his forties, was trained in the empirical careful rational medicine of his day, being particularly impressed by the methods followed by Charcot and Janet in France. Several writers maintain that his original model of the human being was an engineering one – a tracing of the moving parts of the system, the dynamic effect of the drives, instinct and libido on the build-up of the personality. Wyss writes that Freud's dependence on the physiology and physics of the nineteenth century 'obliged him to work with concepts of models that originated in these sciences but which were both unbiological and unphysiological to a degree'. Wyss also makes the interesting point that the analogy between the function of the libido in the personality and the function of capital in the social system as seen by sociologists at that time is a striking one – both technical models of a process, emphasizing input and output, drives, conversions.[246:105] Wilber accepts the socio-biological basis of Freud's work, and calls it reductionist, but reckons his immense originality and genius was to follow a method which was not strictly scientific – indeed how could it be, in the work he was attempting – but rather was 'hermeneutic and phenomenological'.[241:178] It was scientific in that it was observa-tional, but Freud was prepared to deal in symbols and in meaning, which was to take him far outside the usual definition of Western science. These methods and their results could be tested, but only by those people 'willing to take up the discipline of introspective interpretation'.[241:179] Freud's work, as has been pointed out by many writers, was following an older school of knowledge – philosophical, artistic (as was indicated by Bleuler in the letter quoted in Chapter 1), metaphysical, in Popper's terms an obviously closed system. It was also clinically based and related to people's subjective experience.

Through the twentieth century, the assumption that 'real' knowledge is based in science and its methods has continued to dominate the social sciences and medicine, the fields in which psychology and psychotherapy are embedded. Capra defines the Western paradigm, derived from the Scientific Revolution, the Enlightenment and the Industrial Revolution, as comprising the following four values:

> the belief in the scientific method as the only valid approach to knowledge; the view of the universe as a mechanical system composed of elementary material building blocks; the view of

life in society as a competitive struggle for existence; and the belief in unlimited material progress to be achieved through economic and technological growth.[54:12]

The value basis in this paradigm is humanistic. Ehrenfeld quotes Webster's *Third International Dictionary* in defining humanism as:

> a doctrine, set of attitudes, or way of life centred upon human interests or values . . . a philosophy that rejects supernaturalism, regards man as a natural object, and asserts the essential dignity or worth of man and his capacity to achieve self-realisation through the use of reason and the scientific method. . . .[69:5]

It is assumed within this paradigm that human reason will eventually triumph, that it has achieved so much and will eventually conquer all problems. It is often assumed that the universe is arranged for the benefit of humanity. This is not a necessary basis for science, which could be humble, but these values seem to dominate the Western view of science.

Through this century also – and this is particularly relevant to the creation of psychosynthesis – there has been a considerable reaction against the modern scientific mode, particularly within the social sciences, culminating in a more phenomenological approach in the 1960s; this was particularly so in sociology, but to some extent also in psychology and the development of alternative psychotherapies. It is not that the scientific empirical mode and reason are discounted, but they are increasingly seen as a one-sided approach to the study of living beings. Robert Pirsig, in his cult book *Zen and the Art of Motor-Cycle Maintenance*, published in 1974, repeats Vico's eighteenth century warnings when he writes:

> Phaedrus remembered a line from Thoreau: 'you never gain something but that you lose something'. And now he began to see for the first time the unbelievable magnitude of what man, when he gained power to understand and rule the world in terms of dialectic truths, had lost. He had built empires of scientific capability to manipulate the phenomena of nature into enormous manifestations of his own dreams of power and wealth – but for this he had exchanged an empire of understanding of equal magnitude: an understanding of what it is to be part of the world, and not an enemy of it.[69:170-1]

Not only has the dream of power contained in our present world views been widely criticized, but also the fragmentary nature of the knowledge has met with sharp opposition. This is, as Maslow points out in one of his many books, of particular significance for psychology:

> The search for a fundamental datum (in psychology) is itself a reflection of a whole world-view, a scientific philosophy which assumes an atomistic world – a world in which complex things are built out of simple elements. The first task of such a scientist then is to reduce the so-called complex to the so-called simple. This is done by analysis, by finer and finer separating until we come to the irreducible. This task has succeeded well enough elsewhere in science, for a time at least. In psychology it has not.[161:3-4]

It is particularly in psychology, and more especially psychotherapy, that the essence of a person can be seen to be his or her whole being. It is relationship that forms the therapeutic element in therapy, from the centre of one person to the centre of another. It has already been noted that from the beginning Freud used relationship and symbols, personal meanings, in his therapeutic work. The whole thrust of psychotherapy as it has developed through this century has been a growing emphasis on listening, accepting, sharing.

This does not mean that the scientific mode has been excised from psychotherapy. Maslow throughout his work was keen to argue for a wider definition of science – a synthetic rather than an analytic science. Capra sees this newer approach to science as following the revised paradigm in physics, rooted in quantum theory and relativity, whereby the world is perceived not as static building blocks to be analysed, but as constantly changing, constantly being modified, and being understood better by studying relationships than by analysing discrete parts. It is now much more understood, particularly through Kuhn's work, how much we create our images of science and of reality itself: that the thing seen *cannot* be understood apart from the observer seeing it and the assumptions he or she makes. As Roger Jones writes in *Physics as Metaphor*, 'we are not the cool observers of the world, but its passionate creators.'[127:3] Scientists, those detached, white-coated observers, are in this equally passionate and equally the creators of what they see: we can only find what we are looking for.

Psychology, psychiatry and psychotherapy are of course in very different positions in this debate. Psychology is a mainstream social science, accepted in universities, in industry, and strongly biologically based. Psychiatry is part of medical science, based in the strongly scientific medical model, but in practice often using methods derived from psychotherapy. Psychotherapy has by and large developed outside the university system, always putting considerable emphasis on the relationship between the therapist and the client. It is psychotherapy that has been more influenced by the newer 'third' and 'fourth force' therapies put forward by Rogers, Maslow, Jung, Assagioli, May and others. These therapies put more emphasis on process and feeling and less on intellect, and are far more seen as essentially a relationship between two or more people, with far more equality between the participants.

Rollo May in his work reckons that he alternates between seeing his client subjectively and objectively, between perceiving the patterns in the life and 'seeing' and relating to the client as a whole. Transpersonal psychotherapies, where the basic relationship is perceived as existing not only between two personalities but also between two souls, again attempt to use techniques and analysis within what is really a spiritual framework. Here a balance is achieved between subjective experience and more objective checking of that experience, which was the balance deemed appropriate by Assagioli.

Jung and Maslow are the two psychotherapists – and they are both psychiatrists also – who have struggled most publicly with the issues of science and medicine in relation to an understanding of the nature of the individual which they see as essentially spiritual. Both fully take on board the assumption that each 'psychology' is unique and particular to its creator and proponent. Jung states quite specifically that in his view Freud created a psychology that represents more himself than the people he studied.[131:3] Jung considered that mechanical science *per se* is useless at the art of living and can only take us part of the way. At the same time he felt the basis of his own work in general was empirical psychology[133:4] rather than philosophy, and that observation, and learning through careful practice, is fundamental to the development of our understanding of human beings. (Popper would no doubt define this as 'closed system' thinking: but then again, is there any system that is not closed?) Both Freud and Jung used themselves and their own unconscious material as objects of study, and were willing to enter dark and uninvestigated areas of their own psyche.

In spite of the developments of understanding in this century, Jung's judgment was that we are only at the very beginning of study of the human being, either as an individual or in society. 'For the purposes of psychology, I think it best to abandon the notion that we are today in anything like a position to make statements about the psyche that are "true" or "correct".'[131:133] Maslow and Assagioli held that fundamentally people are good, though clearly that goodness can become highly distorted and lead to the sobering events we see around us daily. Jung was less sure of this; he believed good and evil forces are balanced and feared for the future of humanity. Freud was frankly pessimistic. All three perceived that each person and humanity as a whole must take into account and work through what Jung called the 'shadow' if the human race is to survive and create: a truly gnostic view.

In the areas in which all of these thinkers and practitioners were working, Western science was useful but could only take them so far. Maslow argued for 'enlarging and deepening its nature, goals and methods',[163:viii] and believed that his work on self-actualizing and self-transcending personalities could be used as a basis for good research. Jung believed that much of the evil in the world is due to the fact that most people do not understand what they do. Their actions are profoundly unconscious. Knowledge, insight and awareness are urgently needed for the future of mankind. He believed that the new movements of the twentieth century affecting psychotherapy were religious rather than mechanically scientific in character, and that, in fact, they had to be in order to work. Both believed that 'adjustment' to a greedy and one-sided society is not the aim of psychotherapy and our understanding of human nature that might lead to it: rather they put their belief into unrealized human potential and awareness, growing beyond our present attitude of control and power based in science, technology and Western humanism alone.

Assagioli was of course subjected to pressures, internally and externally, to be a scientist. These pressures meant for him, first and foremost, following a professionalism, pursuing an open frame of mind, assuming that what he put forward was 'not true', as is still maintained today in psychosynthesis, and being willing to go on learning through his lifetime, modifying his system as he did so. Second, because he was a doctor, a psychiatrist and a clinician, he was therefore trained in the empirical method, learning to adapt to what he learned of the human condition through patients. Third, an internal obligation for him was to trust and study his own subjective experience. This is of course not necessarily the view of the natural scientist, who tends to put empirical 'objective' findings before subjective conviction. The challenge was that Assagioli's subjective experience from early in his life was mystical, as an overriding wish to be present to his Self. It is in the mixture of these three definitions of science that the crux of the contradictions about the nature of knowledge in psychosynthesis lies.

The medical model of the person at the turn of the century was, and largely remains today, a very physical one. As was demonstrated in a previous chapter, the scientific view of the person had become the most widely accepted framework of serious knowledge.

> Three centuries after Descartes, the science of medicine is still based, as George Engel writes, on 'the notion of the body as a machine, of disease as the consequence of breakdown of the machine, and of the doctor's task as repair of the machine'.[54:118]

Engel was writing in 1977, and certainly these assumptions would have been true of the basis of scientific training Assagioli received at the beginning of the century. However, by the time he wrote his doctoral dissertation in 1910, he was already influenced by psychoanalysis, and was already in contact with Freud and Jung. They also were doctors, of course, and regarded themselves as scientists.

Assagioli regarded the whole of psychosynthesis as a science. He writes in his introduction to *Psychosynthesis*:

> May I emphasize the fact that the elements and functions, coming from the superconscious, such as aesthetic, ethical, religious experiences, intuition, inspiration, states of mystical consciousness, are *factual*, are real in the pragmatic sense . . . because they are *effective*. . . , producing changes both in the inner and the outer world. Therefore, they are amenable to observation and experiment through the use of the scientific method in ways suited to their nature: also they can be influenced and utilized through psycho-spiritual techniques.
>
>   At this point the question may arise as to the relationship between this conception of the human being on the one hand and religion and metaphysics on the other. The answer is that psychosynthesis does not attempt in any way to appropriate to itself the fields of religion and philosophy. It is a scientific conception, and as such it is neutral towards the various religious forms and the various philosophical doctrines,

excepting only those which are materialistic and therefore deny the existence of spiritual realities. Psychosynthesis does not aim nor attempt to give a metaphysical nor a theological explanation of the great Mystery – it leads to the door, but stops there.[1:6-7]

In these two paragraphs, it is possible to see Assagioli's struggles with being both a 'scientist', claiming the authority of science, and also drawing on mystical material. The whole system assumes that the person has a soul as well as a personality – which would hardly be accepted by most empirically based scientists. The central paradox of his position is that he denies materialistic philosophies, but believes himself to be following the scientific method, which over the last century has been totally materialistic. Inductive, empirical science would be against the formulation of such unprovable entities as 'the great Mystery'. Assagioli attempts to prove that spiritual experiences are 'facts' because they have discernible consequences, both to the inner life of the person and in the outside world, but his actual work is therapeutic and clinical, and as far as I know he showed very little interest in doing exclusively observational or experimental work. This same description also applies on the whole to Freud and to Jung. Both, however, were greater writers than Assagioli. Assagioli simply presents a therapeutic system, including mystical material, yet in a way that claims it to be scientific. In theory, his two worlds fit together only uneasily: combining them in practice appears to be less problematic.

Assagioli's presentation is both academic and polemical. He closes his Introduction by making 'a cordial appeal to all therapists, psychologists and educators to actively engage in the needed work of research, experimentation and application', but this appeal is related to 'the great need of healing the serious ills which at present are affecting humanity'. He felt he had the truth, or was near the truth; he felt it vital to act in the world, but conceived that this should be done within a scientific framework.

No one could read *Psychosynthesis*, even less *The Act of Will*, and least of all most of Assagioli's articles, and think that this was the work of a 'normal' scientist. His style is narrative and polemical. The first two chapters of *Psychosynthesis* were originally published in the prestigious *Hibbert Journal* in the 1930s, which is a journal devoted to philosophical and religious knowledge, and his style is consistent with this framework. However, Assagioli in the earlier part of his career also contributed to scientific journals, both in Italy and elsewhere.

The model that he took for himself was not that of the scientist, or the medical doctor, but that of the clinician. He writes:

> As is well known, in the course of the last seventy years a group of inquirers, which was at first small but which gradually grew more active, turned its attention to the investigation of the phenomena and mysteries of the human psyche. The most important results have not been achieved by academic psychologists, but by independent investigators. Nearly all of them were clinicians, driven by the practical needs of their patients and aided by the greater evidence that certain psychological phenomena acquire when they are accentuated by a morbid condition.[1.12]

His first reference and acknowledgment is to clinicians who were alive at some point in his own lifetime: Pierre Janet, Sigmund Freud, Alfred Adler, Melanie Klein, Carl Jung, Otto Rank, Karen Horney, Erich Fromm, Victor Frankl. All these therapists touched the medical and the academic fields but have only been accepted within them to some extent. Assagioli is pointing to something very significant when he writes that these investigators were often pushed more by the needs of their patients than by academic requirements alone. They were a somewhat maverick group of individualistic workers, because they were in touch with the real problems of people and had to attempt to solve the complex and muddled conflicts of the human psyche.

Assagioli lists the research which has influenced him – and the list is indeed formidable and very varied, and must often contain contradictions. At the beginning of *Psychosynthesis*, he lists psychosomatic medicine, and 'inter-individual and Social Psychology and Psychiatry and the Anthropological study of man' from the more conventional medical and social science disciplines; the psychology of religion, the investigation of the superconscious and 'creative understanding' from the more religious side – the psychology of religion being more within the academic mainstream, and the latter two more fringe knowledge; 'the holistic approach and the psychology of the personality, which includes humanistic and transpersonal psychology', founded on the 'holistic' idea first realized by Jan Smuts; parapsychology and psychical research, which has been a fringe study for several centuries, though it was in the mainstream before the eighteenth century – and perhaps is coming back in England now with the recently founded Chair in Parapsychology; Eastern psychology, which is tied in with Eastern religious thinking; and finally 'active techniques' for the treatment and development of the personality which relate to the older School of healing, of hypnotism, and through to guided daydreams (Desoille) and psychodrama (Moreno).

This is anything but a classical scientific approach. It is an immense hotchpotch of ideas available to the searcher in the twentieth century. There is no careful slow investigation of these ideas and how they relate – or not – to each other. Instead, Assagioli next describes his worked out structure of the nature of the person. He worked and thought intuitively, not analytically. It is up to the research worker to unravel some of the pieces.

He was, however, aware throughout that what he had developed was 'only a working hypothesis':[1.85] in relation to his picture of human nature, 'we must also guard against the danger of "indoctrination". We must keep in mind that, after all, we are giving the conception of man according to psychosynthesis *as it has been developed up to the present time.*'[1.85] This fits in with the practice in teaching psychosynthesis of writing 'this is not true' at the bottom of the teaching material. Assagioli left an open-endedness to his work which is definitely part of the scientific spirit.

Assagioli has a similarly pragmatic approach to values. He accepts that there is a hierarchic approach in his therapy; for instance in the terms 'superconscious' and 'lower unconscious'. He thinks, with most modern thinkers in the social sciences, that we inevitably make value judgments, however 'objective' we believe ourselves to be – 'many psychologists who refuse to accept valuation are making valuation judgments all the time, although blissfully unconscious of it. Surely it is better to do it consciously and deliberately.'[1.88] Some of his own values – for instance on the nature of women – are not at all acceptable in the modern climate today.

He quotes many of the classical psychological tests as part of his 'active techniques', although, in my experience, they are rarely used in psychosynthesis now – the association tests, projective techniques such as the Rorschach and the Thematic Aperception Test (TAT), and Happich's initiated symbol projection. He certainly felt himself to be working and thinking within a wide scholarly framework, particularly as it was relevant to clinicians. He continued to adapt his work and his thinking up to the end of his life, incorporating insights from Maslow, Rogers and Fromm in his later writing.

Two questions remain at the end of this chapter. The first is whether Assagioli is himself in any acceptable sense of the term a scientist? The second, related question is whether psychology, psychiatry and psychotherapy are scientific pursuits? The second question will be approached in the next chapter. The first question must wait until the conclusions of this book.

17 The development of psychotherapy and dynamic psychiatry: the scientific study of the unconscious

Henri Ellenberger's comprehensive and fascinating book *The Discovery of the Unconscious* is a model of the history of ideas in paying attention to the social and political bases of the ideas the author is concerned with. His tracing of the history of psychiatry from the earliest human societies necessarily uncovers the pattern discussed in a previous chapter, in which knowledge up to the beginning of modern Western society was seen to be all unitary; then, in the time between the seventeenth and nineteenth centuries, scientific and religious/spiritual theories became split. This process happened rather later with regard to notions about the nature of people than in the general views about the nature of the universe. In modern science, the primary discoveries were made by the classic natural sciences, physics and chemistry, and were only later applied to the social sciences.

Ellenberger's study, in contrast to L. L. Whyte's *The Unconscious before Freud* which has been discussed earlier, concentrates on the medical understanding of unconscious forces. This was the direct lead-in to Freud's work.

Earlier human societies had of course been greatly concerned about the nature of the person and the forces that affected a person's life. Theories of diseases were developed in each culture, particularly relating illness to the existence of evil, and remedial action, including therapy, was applied according to the understanding of the cause of disease; exorcism, magical rites, extraction of a wicked spirit through catharsis, restoration of a soul that had been lost, were all practices common throughout the world. Some understanding seems universal; an ancient Maori proverb could be used in any society: 'there is a well of dissatisfaction in the heart of man, and hence vexation and anxiety.' Great importance was placed in many societies on the Healer, who healed through his or her own person – through what he or she was. The equivalent practices can be seen today in the means that both industrialized and non-industrialized societies employ, though illness is now more routinely seen as the machinery of the body becoming faulty.

Ellenberger traces back some of the roots of modern psychiatric practice to classic beliefs – Stoic exercises in concentration and meditation, Galen's methods of individual therapy as evidenced by his treatise *On the Passions of the Soul*, and the religious cure of souls. Interestingly, too, he describes the setting up of the classical Schools of philosophy:

> The Pythagoreans, the Platonists, the Aristotelians, the Stoics, and the Epicureans, were not just adherents of 'philosophical systems' but members of organised 'schools', also called 'sects' that imposed on them a specific method of training and a way of life . . . members of each school were tied together by their common beliefs, the practice of the same exercises, the same way of life, and the cult of the founder – of his memory, more often probably, his legend and his writings.[79:41]

This, too, is a pattern common to twentieth century psychiatry and psychotherapy which has generally developed outside the university system. As Ellenberger comments later, 'with Freud begins the era of the newer dynamic schools, with their official doctrine, their rigid organisation, their specialised journals, their closed membership, and the prolonged initiation imposed upon their members'.[79:418] In fact, it is salutary to see from Ellenberger's detailed study that many of the features that we see in modern psychotherapy and that we take to be unique have old origins, and that many disputes and insights have always been around.

Ellenberger gives some interesting comparisons between what he calls 'primitive healing' and 'scientific therapy' (Table 17.1). A further point could be made, as it is by Ehrenreich and English in their book *For Her Own Good*,[70] that healers were often – though not exclusively – women, and that doctors, and therefore psychiatrists, have mainly been men.

In examining these contrasts between healing and modern scientific medicine, we must in the end ask where humanistic and transpersonal psychotherapies stand. Is there a tension between the two modes, or can they be combined? Is psychosynthesis truly a synthesis, as quoted from Keen in the Introduction to this study, a reworking of the best of the old healing and the new science, or still uneasily straddling the two?

Ellenberger states that 'the emergence of dynamic psychiatry can be traced to the year 1775, to a clash between the physician Mesmer and the exorcist Gassner'.[79:53] Gassner was a healer, working in the religious tradition. Following a great deal of controversy, official enquiries were held in Germany in 1775

Table 17.1

	Primitive healing		Scientific therapy
1	Healer much more than a physician: foremost personality of his social group.	1	Therapist a scientist amongst many others.
2	Healer exerts his action primarily through his personality.	2	Therapist applies specific techniques in an impersonal way.
3	Healer a psychosomatician: treats physical diseases through psychological means.	3	Dichotomy between physical and psychic therapy. Accent in psychiatry on the physical side of mental illness.
4	Healer's training is long and exacting: includes experience of severe emotional diseases that he has had to overcome in order to be able to heal others.	4	Training is rational and does not take into account the personal medical or emotional problems of physician.
5	Belongs to a 'school', with own traditions and teaching.	5	Therapist acts on basis of unified medicine which is a branch of science and not an esoteric teaching.[79:47]

about Gassner's work and activities, and he was compared unfavourably with Mesmer: Ellenberger sees the controversy as being a struggle between the Enlightenment and rationality on the one hand and Religion and healing (including such practices as exorcism) on the other. Science and Reason won: Gassner was pensioned off. Ellenberger comments that 'Gassner's downfall prepared the way for a healing method which retained no ties with religion'.[79:57]

Mesmer's theories of madness and sanity, called 'animal magnetism', became most influential over the first half of the nineteenth century, particularly as they led – through one of his followers, Puysegur – to the development of hypnotism. Mesmer's science, which was pre-positivist, was well mixed with magic. He had studied astrology, and he postulated that a 'subtle physical fluid fills the universe and forms a connecting medium between man, the earth, and the heavenly bodies and also between man and man'; that health, particularly mental health, depends on the equilibrium of this fluid being maintained. He worked through catharsis; his name is the origin of the word 'mesmerism'. He also set up a society of followers, the Société de l'Harmonie. His work drew on ancient systems rooted probably in Paracelsus and Van Helmont, and was closer to the ancient magician than to the twentieth century psychotherapist. But his belief in the therapeutic power of the healer, the importance of the relationship between healer and patient, and the foundation of hypnotism as a method of communication were all significant and used by Freud.

The borderline between magic and science was investigated again in the mid-nineteenth century through the development of 'spiritism' and the beginnings of parapsychology. Ellenberger dates the growth of spiritism from the 1850s, and many people claimed to be 'mediums', in touch with the unseen world. In 1882, the Society for Psychical Research was set up in England: one of the phenomena investigated was automatic writing, as a method of exploring the unconscious.

The mental hospitals and treatment centres set up in the nineteenth century still worked on uncertain and often conflicting grounds, poised between the newer positivist medicine, which had made little contribution so far to mental illness, and the older strands of treatment. Two famous Schools, Nancy and Salpêtrière, were founded in France in the late nineteenth century. Liebeault of the Nancy School used hypnotism, and worked mainly with the poor around Nancy, treating physical as well as mental illness. He was succeeded by Bernheim, a university professor and physician, who developed the use of hypnotism, believing, however, that it worked best with people used to passive obedience.

Gradually Bernheim developed a treatment called psychotherapeutics, which used suggestion as a method of tapping the unconscious with people in a waking state. Freud visited Bernheim and also spent some months with Charcot at the rival Salpêtrière School. Charcot, a most charismatic figure, also worked with the unconscious through hypnotic methods and paid attention to dreams and to faith healing. These two schools attracted considerable attention not only from doctors but also from novelists and the general public. They were part of what Ellenberger calls 'the emergence of dynamic psychiatry'.

He lists the main features of the first dynamic psychiatry:

(a) hypnotism was adopted as the main approach, the via regia to the unconscious;

(b) particular clinical pictures received great attention, including multiple personality, and, towards the end of the century, hysteria;

(c) it was taken that the human mind consisted of both conscious and unconscious elements. Later the picture developed to a model of 'a cluster of subpersonalities underlying the conscious personality';

(d) the idea of a universal fluid, as propounded by Mesmer, was replaced by the concept of mental energy;

(e) there was an emphasis on the rapport between patient and therapist (known in the eighteenth century as 'magnetiser' as the magnetic force was then held to be the seat of attraction and repulsion).[79:111]

The idea of multiple personalities and the subpersonalities attracted a great deal of attention by the end of the nineteenth century. The psychiatrist Cory notes in a particular case that 'the two selves were formed along the lines of the old conflict', and so it was perceived quite early that subselves could be formed to protect a person and to be a defensive system. There were famous cases of 'two people in one' (Dr Jekyll and Mr Hyde in fiction), but it also came to be seen that we may all be several people, existing simultaneously, 'that the human mind was rather like a matrix from which whole sets of subpersonalities could emerge and differentiate themselves', and that these subpersonalities could be named and recognized. Gardner Murphy concluded that 'most cases of multiple personalities appear essentially to represent the organism's effort to live, at different times, in terms of different systems of values'.[174:433-51] The translation of the notion into psychosynthesis was thus quite natural, though the particular contribution of Assagioli was their relationship to the 'I'. It is apparent that several Italian psychiatrists (including G. E. Morselli) continued to work with the idea into the twentieth century. This was linked to the study of hysteria, which was seen as the existence of two sets of consciousness in the mind of the hysterical person.

The idea had long been current in the nineteenth century that the 'benefits of civilisation and morals . . . had been acquired at the cost of man's natural happiness . . . that civilised man remains for ever an unhappy creature'.[79:183] It is possible to see the growth of therapy as a response to the effects of industrialization and materialism on the inner life of individuals – the personal and collective load that every child in touch with feeling and not fragmented has to bear in a society with such seemingly meaningless injustices and horrors, known to all through more and more efficient communications, is considerable; this is the import of some of Foucault's writing, tracing the relationship between civilization and madness. 'Look hard enough at reason,' Foucault seems to be saying, 'and you will find madness.'[210:15] And again, 'madness came to be seen as the reverse side of progress: as civilised man became further removed from nature, the more he exposed himself to madness.'[210:32]

It is not surprising that the acknowledgment of unconscious forces gained ground at the end of the nineteenth century, as a reaction to the materialism and positivism then dominant.

> The second half of the century belonged to science and the belief in science . . . under the combined influences of positivist philosophy, the concentration of scientific research in universities, and the trend of cultural optimism, Western science was pervaded by an almost religious faith in science which reached more and more layers of the population . . . the scientism trend went so far as to deny the existence of all that was not approachable by scientific methods, and it often merged with atheism.[79:226-7]

The significant thing is that Freud began to study the unconscious as a medical scientist, deeply distrusting religion.

One controversy, brought into being by Darwin's work on natural selection, is highly relevant to the assumptions underlying the development of psychiatry and psychotherapy: is the human race naturally competitive or naturally cooperative, naturally good or naturally bad? Many followers of Darwin stressed the competitive, aggressive features of human nature. Thomas Huxley made a famous speech in 1888 which summed up the assumed conclusions that could be drawn from Darwin's work which so shocked many thinkers:

> From the point of view of the moralist, the animal world is on about the same level as a gladiators' show. The creatures are fairly well treated, and set to fight . . . where . . . the strongest, the swiftest and the cunningest live to fight another day. The spectator has no need to turn his thumbs down, as no quarter is given. . . . In the cycle of phenomena presented by the life of man, the animal, no more moral end is discernible than in that presented by the life of the wolf and the deer. . . . So among primitive man, the weakest and stupidest went to the wall, while the toughest and shrewdest, those who were best fitted to cope with their circumstances, but not the best in any other

sense, survived. Life was a continuous free fight and, beyond the limited and temporary relations of the family, the Hobbesian war of each against all was the normal state of existence. . . . But the effort of ethical man to work toward a moral end by no means abolished, perhaps hardly modified, the deep-seated organic impulses which impel natural man to follow his non-moral code.[120:195-236]

The assumption that people are competitive and destructive of the weakest was important not only to the assumptions of human nature underlying much psychiatry but also led to political views of racial and personal superiority, to genetic engineering, and to a justification of both the free market economy and some of the fascist policies.

It is interesting that Alfred Russel Wallace, whose discoveries of natural selection were made almost simultaneously with Darwin's, developed quite different views about the nature of people. 'While he would agree that man's bodily form developed by the continuous modification of some ancestral animal form, he believed that some other agency came into effect in order to develop the higher intellectual and spiritual nature of man.' Wallace was by no means certain that human beings were developing for the better – he had 'seen a good deal of primitive societies and had always been impressed with the higher standards of communal and social morality in them compared to those which existed in the industrial society of his own country.'[58:23] He believed that mankind had developed little in a fundamental way from the earliest societies to the present ones – that in some ways we had regressed. He thought that 'spirit', an undefinable, ineffable force, was the essence of the human being – 'spirit is mind; the brain and nerves are but the magnetic battery and telegraphy, by which the spirit communicates with the outer world'.[58:191] Other scientists, including Kropotkin, the biologist and anarchist, disputed that neither animals nor human beings have competition as their foremost characteristic – cooperation could just as readily be demonstrated in all species. These views underlie Maslow's critique of early psychoanalysis – that it tended to study the worst and the weakest in the human being and to assume that that was all there was.

Psychiatry, as opposed to psychotherapy, became fully part of establishment medicine in the nineteenth century. Around the middle of the century, psychiatry came under the strong influence of positivism and scientism, and it has remained within that framework ever since – though most psychiatrists now use some psychoanalytic notions in their work. Psychiatry is based within the experimental field, is close to physical medicine, and to physical as well as some psychological methods of treatment.

In the 1890s, the new science of psychology was being developed. In 1890, William James's *The Principles of Psychology* was published, in two volumes. In the preface he made the following statement:

> I have kept close to the point of view of natural science throughout the book. Every natural science assumes certain data uncritically, and declines to challenge the elements between which its own 'laws' obtain, and from which its own deductions are carried on. Psychology, the science of finite individual minds, assumes as its data: (1) thoughts and feelings, and (2) a physical world in time and space with which they co-exist and which (3) they know. Of course these data themselves are discussable; but the discussion of them (as of other elements) is called metaphysics and falls outside the province of this book. This book, assuming that thoughts and feelings exist and are vehicles of knowledge, thereupon contends that psychology when she has ascertained the empirical correlation of the various sorts of thoughts and feelings with definite conditions of the brain, can go no further – can go no further, that is, as a natural science. If she goes further, she becomes metaphysical. All attempts to explain our phenomenally given thoughts as products of deeper-lying entities (whether the latter be named 'Soul', 'Transcendental Ego', 'Ideas', or 'Elementary Units of Consciousness') are metaphysical. This book consequently rejects both the associationist and the spiritualist theories; and in this strictly positivist point of view consists the one feature of it for which I feel tempted to claim originality. Of course this point of view is anything but ultimate. [123]

This statement is a classic affirmation that psychology as well as psychiatry has its exclusive base in natural science. William James was of course not willing to stay with this limited belief himself, twelve years later giving the lectures that came to be written up as *The Varieties of Religious Experience*. He was one of the relatively few people who were familiar with the worlds both of psychology and of religion – worlds which were by this time far apart.

Around the turn of the century, the first international conferences of psychology were being held, in French, German, English, and sometimes Italian. The first International Congress of

Psychology in 1886 had 160 participants: the fourth such Congress in Munich in 1896 had 503 attenders. At a similar period, the term 'psychotherapy' was first used by some of Bernheim's disciples (of the Nancy School). It had been recognized that the hypnotic techniques widely used were largely dependent on patients being passive. 'One had to find a psychotherapy for educated people; it would be a non-authoritarian method, which would keep personal liberty intact. . . .'[79:321]

Janet was already working in France, and in 1900 an 'Institut Psychologique International' was founded in Paris. He also had to attempt a compromise between his scientific and his religious tendencies, and explained his psychological vocation 'as a kind of compromise between his definite inclination for natural science and the strong religious feelings of his childhood and adolescence'.[79:348] Janet built up a vast psychological system which greatly influenced both Freud and Jung. He investigated unconscious and subconscious processes (the latter term being coined by him), and both he and Jung remained interested in considering the human mind as comprising a number of subpersonalities.

The next part of this book will discuss some of the specific contributions of Freudian theory, but at this point it is useful to pause and consider the nature of psychoanalysis, which was one of the key factors in the development of psychosynthesis. Innumerable books have been written on its status as an area of knowledge and practice, from Popper's condemnation of such theories as a 'closed system', unscientific because impossible to disprove, to devoted adherence by many practitioners.

Psychoanalysis certainly aims to be scientific, in the sense that it follows the medical technique of developing treatment from observation and the making of hypotheses: it is also scientific in the sense that it aims to understand, categorize and explore unconscious material – Western science intends to uncover the secrets of the unknown, to find out the rules and use them, and to make them public. Empirical, experimental methods are used in this exploration: they are shared by the scientists and are openly published, in as far as this is possible.

But psychoanalysis is also the erection of a system of thinking which explains all the phenomena it sees in its own terms and therefore cannot be wrong. It is a myth, a creation of reality. But then maybe all human knowledge has in the end only a myth-type status, including the powerful myth of science. It is in areas of knowledge such as psychoanalysis that the discrepancies between 'objective' science and theoretical knowledge created by one person begin to lessen. If both 'hard-line' scientists and creative imaginative thinkers are equally living in man-created worlds, then maybe the attempt to cut across some of those boundaries is not so illegitimate; it could perhaps be a new synthesizing, a reworking of old boundaries, drawing the lines in a different place – perhaps even getting back closer to the more comprehensive view of knowledge held routinely until the sixteenth century.

If this is the case for psychoanalysis, it is even more so for psychosynthesis. Assagioli equally maintained that he was a scientist. But from the beginning psychosynthesis was rooted in a different tradition, that of spirituality. At the time he developed his ideas, science was rooted in Newtonian physics, orthodox religion was based in the idea of a transcendental God, and the mystical traditions of immanence and his own mystical experience on which he drew were part of a largely unaccepted form of knowledge. What changed in the twentieth century, and is still changing, is a reworking of the relationship between these different sources of understanding, and this is the story that has to be traced in the final part of this study.

III

Developments in the Twentieth Century

Introduction

In the Introduction to this book, three major questions were raised. The first was on the origin of the ideas that lay behind the creation of psychosynthesis. We have seen in Part Two that these lay partly in Western and Eastern mysticism as well as Assagioli's own lifelong awareness of his Self, and partly in the impetus created at the beginning of the century by Freud and others in the empirical study and treatment of unconscious material. There is ample evidence of these twin sources both from his own writing and from a study of his still intact library in Florence.

The second question was on the nature of the knowledge in psychosynthesis. The search for the answer to this question has been implicit as well as explicit in Part Two, which has picked up the major themes of psychosynthesis described in Part One: the existence of the soul as well as the personality in the nature of the human being; the assumption that unconscious material is the source of creativity as well as of problems – indeed, that problems worked through in a transpersonal context are a source of creativity and transformation; finally the theory that collective material is part and parcel of the individual human position, and that the process of transformation for the individual is identical to the transformation of potential for the human race as a whole. In tracing the clear messages given by Plato, Dante, and the gnostic and neoplatonic writers, a pattern emerges which is a repetition of the themes behind psychosynthesis. One source of knowledge for Assagioli is certainly what Huxley called 'the perennial philosophy', repeated in twentieth century psychotherapeutic dress. The other source of knowledge certainly lies in the twentieth century techniques of psychology and psychoanalysis – both disciplines striving to be explicitly scientific, but only partially succeeding. This was the position at the time when the framework of theory and practice was formed.

The third question brings us on to the third part of this study. From the context traced in Chapter 15 it is possible to see how psychosynthesis, and Jungian therapy, could develop at the turn of the century. But tackling the question of the development of psychosynthesis brings us well into the twentieth century, and indeed to the present day. Because what is altering during the twentieth century is precisely our understanding of the nature of science: it is now much more accepted that science as a way of understanding the world is man-made, not objective in any more fundamental sense than that; and that our 'mechanical' view of science has changed to one that is seen by many modern writers as much closer to that of mysticism – the sense of interconnectedness of all things being at the root of both insights. The dramatic emergence of some of these views in the 1960s brought about a climate in which psychosynthesis could become international. And though the intoxication of that period has died away, continued work in both psychotherapy and 'new age' mysticism has brought a steady stream of material which supports the basis of psychosynthesis training internationally.

In Part Three there are only three chapters: the first on psychosynthesis and twentieth century psychotherapy: the second on psychosynthesis and 'new age' thinking: the third and concluding chapter then ties up, as far as possible, all the many strands of this evolving theory and practice, and attempts a deeper synthesis than was possible earlier in the study.

18 Psychosynthesis in the context of twentieth century developments in psychotherapy

It is not possible in the course of one chapter to give more than a sketchy outline of the history of psychotherapy in the twentieth century relevant to psychosynthesis. Nevertheless, it is important to delineate some of the major developments as they have been integrated into the theory and practice of psychosynthesis over this period. As we have seen, Assagioli was in touch with Freud and Jung from the beginning of his career, and was in continuing contact with Jungian developments. During the 1930s and 1940s, when Italy was cut off from developments in the rest of Europe and America, Assagioli continued to work within his practice, writing articles and papers during the less fraught times. When psychosynthesis started to expand internationally in the 1950s and become popular in the 1960s, Assagioli learned of the work of Fromm, Horney, Erikson, Frankl, Rogers, Maslow and many others. Fritz Perls's work in Gestalt became of considerable importance to psychosynthesis therapy and is now used extensively within the training. The technique of guided imagery, springing from work by Desoille, Happich, Leuner and others, was a natural tool for transpersonal psychotherapy. And the many humanistic techniques of the 1960s and 1970s – encounter, groupwork, methods relevant to personal growth – were all incorporated in psychosynthesis which is now well known for its huge range of techniques, both in the one-to-one client-guide relationship and in the training which is largely done in groups. For most of this time, psychotherapists have perceived the relevance of the study of the person to the state of the world – the daunting history of the twentieth century has been a continuing relevant backcloth to the study of personal therapy; there is the insistent question as to whether developing a more complete view of the person might be relevant to the kind of life that people can develop in society, and the question whether both individuals and societies can really change – the ever-present hope of Western culture and one of its main driving forces.

There have been four major schools of psychotherapy this century; positivist behaviourist psychology, which develops into psychotherapy with reinforcement and aversion techniques which relate, as the name suggests, mainly to behaviour; psychoanalysis itself and psychodynamic theory, based in the work of Freud and the Freudians; humanistic psychotherapy, known as the 'third force', following the work of Rollo May, Gestalt, Rogerian therapy and many individual and group techniques developed since the 1960s; and transpersonal psychology that assumes a person is a soul and has a personality – this is known as the 'fourth force' and includes Jung, Frankl, Maslow and Assagioli.

The psychoanalytic tradition

Many of the principles and concepts developed by Freud still stand, though with modifications even among the neo-Freudians. He was the first psychiatrist to study unconscious material systematically and scientifically through practice. All later psycho-therapies, except the behaviourist, have accepted the existence of unconscious forces, and have acknowledged that the laws governing the unconscious are different from those operating in everyday consciousness. It is in general accepted that we repress many unpleasant or disturbing experiences, building up defences against things we do not want to 'know': the size of the defence and the degree of hiddenness is likely to be in direct proportion to the unwantedness of the material. Freud wrote his first book on defences in 1894, *The Neuro-Psychoses of Defence*. It is to my mind most significant that this concept of what we allow ourselves to 'know' and 'not know' is fundamental here as well as in the spiritual and gnostic understanding of 'knowing'.

Freud discovered that material which is repressed may emerge in unlikely ways – most particularly through illnesses in the body, which was common among the patients he classified as 'hysterical'; he firmly linked together the processes in mind, feeling and body, which again has been a common assumption and has been greatly developed in Gestalt and in healing therapies. He postulated that *all* behaviour has a cause, however little or much that cause is understood by the person him- or herself or by the people around them. Nothing happens without a cause of some kind: but this cause may lie deep in the unconscious and be inaccessible without therapy.

Childhood, which had been often ignored as an experience in many cultures, was, and still is, regarded by psychoanalytic theory as a time of deep significance. Freud put forward the view, much against the values of his time, that childhood is a period of sexual significance, that relationships with parents are deeply sexual, and that material repressed then may skew the individual's later life to a crippling extent. Most people have what Gestalt therapists later came to call 'unfinished business' with their parents.

Freud traced the development of the person through his map of the 'id' (the strong unconscious forces), the 'ego' (the controlling centre of the person) and the 'superego' (the incorporation of family and cultural values, prohibitions and 'oughts'), and the conflicts between these three basic parts. Recently Bettelheim has written a book criticizing the way in which these elements of the map have been reified through translation – he argues that Freud's original analysis was far less firmly structured than it has become, and that he was not averse to the idea of a 'soul' at the root of the person. Certainly Freud saw us all as being driven by strong, repressed, often unknown forces, which were frequently in conflict with each other – one of the many reasons for repression.

The notion of the person being the outcome of many forces in conflict with each other is thus basic to Freudian theory: there are the strong instinctual drives and the attempts at control and rationality; the forces of society and those within the individual which may also incorporate social and familial patterns; and the pressures of Eros, the life and sexual instinct, and Thanatos, the drive leading to death and also to change – death of the old.

Two basic Freudian concepts that have been developed by many workers this century are those of projection – seeing in the external world an unacknowledgeable part of yourself – and introjection – taking into yourself those same elements from outside in an undigested form. These two concepts, together with much of the rest of Freud's work, demonstrate how the boundaries between the 'inner' and the 'outer' worlds are permeable, and it is often difficult to know what belongs to which area. It is an insight that has been developed in many ways, in Jung's notion of the relationship between the personal and the collective unconscious, in Assagioli's notion of permeability in his egg-shaped diagram, and in the Gestalt idea of 're-owning' repressed parts.

The techniques that Freud developed started with hypnosis and free association and developed into his emphasis on the relationship between the analyst and the analysand as being primary in the therapeutic process. In 1912 he published his *The Dynamics of Transference* where he considered that there was a therapeutic potential involved in the patient perceiving the doctor *as though* he were a significant person in the patient's own life: this could involve either 'positive' transference, with the patient likely to fall in love with the doctor, or 'negative' transference, when the patient cannot abide the doctor because he or she identifies the doctor as someone else. Again there is an acknowledgment here of the blurring of boundaries between 'inner' and 'outer' in how we tend to see the world. In his concept of 'counter-transference', Freud also acknowledged that the analyst could enter the same process.

One of the later criticisms of Freud's work is that it offers a strong and didactic picture of what is normal – a goal for which the patient should aim. However, Jung in particular protested at the goal of adjustment and normality, claiming that this could be just as restricting for an individual in an imperfect society as any other outwardly imposed rule. Assagioli, particularly in his earlier writing on the nature of women, accepted many conventional views of 'normality', but as psychosynthesis has developed it has become far closer to Jung, positing inward experience as the basic yardstick for growth. Another criticism is that Freud had on the whole a very poor opinion of human nature, both as manifested in the individual and in society: later therapists have tended to see human nature as either good at root (Rogers, Assagioli, Maslow), or at least in a position where good and evil are pretty evenly balanced (Jung).

From the beginning there was opposition to Freud, not only from the shocked population at large but also from within the ranks of psychiatry and psychotherapy. Many saw him as artistic and philosophical – for instance Bleuler, who was quoted in Chapter 1 – whilst Freud continued to see himself as scientific. Many over the years have disbelieved in the particularity of his symbolic interpretations and his overwhelming emphasis on early sexuality and the primacy of the sexual force in human life. But his massive and brilliant breakthrough to therapeutic work with unconscious material has been the undoubted basis for all subsequent therapy.

Since Freud's death in 1939, some Freudians have continued to develop ego psychology, which emphasizes the forces of reality in the individual which recognize and work with crisis and lead to adaptation rather than renewed defences, and also make unconscious material conscious. Rapoport, Lowenstein and Hartmann are among such workers. Other psychiatrists such as Klein, Bowlby, Fairbairn, Guntrip and Winnicott have worked in a field defined as 'object-relations theory'; their work has mainly been on the development of the ego in relation to significant others in early childhood. Studies have largely concentrated on the mother-child relationship and the ways that early upbringing can be damaging and is inevitably frustrating in part. Emphasis has thus been on the relationship of the child with significant other people, the processes of splitting good and bad as experienced by the child, and the effect on future relationships. Bowlby's work on attachment and loss has led to a widespread study of loss and mourning, and amongst some humanistic psychiatrists to a study of the creative use of pain, loss and failure. Again, healers have used much of this work in relation to the body's reactions to loss in illness and depression.

Fromm, Horney and Erikson are neo-Freudians who have expanded the narrow basis of Freudian theory and seen the individual in relation to his or her environment. Erich Fromm is a Marxist who has examined the work of these two iconoclastic thinkers, Marx and Freud, together. Both were working on the determinism of unconscious forces and the importance of the unconscious becoming conscious, whether at the social or at the individual level, and both were aware of the illusory and childish state of mankind at the present time and of the necessity of awareness, of facing the seeming inevitability of the given forces.

> Marx thought the basic reality to be the socio-economic structure of society, while Freud believed it to be the libidinal organisation of the individual. Yet they both had the same implacable distrust of the clichés, ideas, rationalisations, and ideologies which fill people's minds and which form the basis of what they mistake for reality.[95:14]

A transpersonal psychotherapy assumes the basis of reality to be spirit and would similarly be working to free people from the anachronistic rules that impede our contact with the Self – the old rubbish that we all carry around, and which only burdens us and keeps us asleep in life.

Karen Horney was part of the European escape to America during the Hitler years in Germany. She believed that both the individual and society could transform: that self-knowledge is the route to liberation: that disease is a form of self-expression and contains within it potential growth if it is recognized and related to. She emphasized a growing acceptance of bisexuality and homosexuality: and she was one of the first to spell out the psychic and social factors in the feeling of inferiority in being a woman. In *The Neurotic Personality of our Time* she emphasized the social forces in the production of neurosis – that in a society which is in many ways self-destructive, to be normal is to be neurotic: to be sane one should not aim at normality.

Erik Erikson also developed his theories of human nature with regard to a life-long process of learning in relation to society, and emphasized that learning continued to the end of life. He saw that choices are continually made by people, of trust as against distrust as a basic attitude to life, identity and integration as opposed to dependence on others, creativity as opposed to passivity. He studied the lives of several great men, including Luther and Gandhi, looking at the dynamics of creativity and originality in these people and at some of the costs of this creativity as well as its mainsprings. Jung, of course, was interested in these areas throughout his life, and most particularly in the growth and possibilities of the second part of life: and he investigated personally and professionally the necessity of facing the Shadow, the unconscious forces in our make-up, which he believed must be made fully conscious before the human race could be said to be fully grown up and could live through the destructive forces that seem to lie at the basis of our personal and social lives; he showed up the urgency of transforming these forces into creativity and wholeness, instead of maintaining the fragmentation and destructiveness that we all experience now.

Psychotherapy has been greatly influenced this century by existentialism and phenomenology. Both encourage the therapist to consider him- or herself as well as the client as subject rather than as object. Rollo May traces this influence back to Husserl. May was also much influenced by Binswanger, a Freudian who stayed loyal to Freud, but who stated in the celebrations of Freud's eightieth birthday that in his analysis Freud omitted much that is invaluable to the human race – art, religion, love in its fullest sense, and creativity. Freud believed that true knowledge of the nature of the person would be discovered through empirical means, whereas Binswanger and May maintained that what you discover in psychology depends on your original basic assumptions. May comments at one point that Carl Rogers's clients, who are listened to with 'unconditional positive regard', very rarely display anger: that to a very great extent the nature of the psychotherapy determines the nature of the problems that people bring to it.

It was because Freud was prepared to look into the abyss that the 'earthquakes that Freud produced in Western culture, earthquakes that shook the self-picture of modern Western man to its very base',[164:114] were produced. But existentialist psychiatrists believed Freud to have the balance wrong. As Blaise Pascal had written many years before:

It is dangerous to show man that he is equal to the beasts,

without showing him his greatness. It is also dangerous to show him too frequently his greatness without his baseness. It is yet more dangerous to leave him ignorant of both. But, it is very desirable to show him the two together.[184:111]

Taking into account our changed attitude to animals and to 'man', this has also been the message during this century of third- and fourth-force psychotherapies, including psychosynthesis. They have added an expectation of change.

Humanistic psychology

Irvin Yalom in his *Existential Psychotherapy*, published in 1980, traces the setting up of humanistic psychology as a discipline in 1950, whose intention was to address itself to 'those human capacities and potentialities that have little or no systematic place, either in positivistic or behaviourist theory or in classical psychoanalytic theory, e.g. love . . . growth . . . self-actualisation . . . becoming . . . responsibility. . .'.[247:18] The assumption behind this psychology is that the human being is more than the sum of the parts, that people are essentially aware creatures, have choices and can act with intention. This psychology concentrated on the optimistic side of things. Yalom comments in relation to this:

The existential tradition in Europe has always emphasised human limitations and the tragic dimensions of existence. Perhaps it has done so because Europeans have had a greater familiarity with geographic and ethnic confinement, with war, death, and uncertain existence. The United States (and the humanistic psychology it spawned) bathed in a Zeitgeist of expansiveness, optimism, limitless horizons, and pragmatism.[247:19]

Yalom is critical of the triviality of this paradigm for psychology, though he acknowledges that it has redressed the balance referred to earlier through Pascal. His own book addresses itself to the four major existential themes of death, freedom and responsibility, isolation and loneliness, and meaninglessness. These themes are clearly in contrast to the element of over-optimism of the humanistic school, but are also plainly very different from the basic Freudian assumptions of pathology and neuroticism. They are themes that are problems for any thoughtful person within any society, and they are also issues largely ignored in Western culture, where basic institutions do not address them directly.

Yalom's general messages in his huge book, which is richly illustrated by cases, are generally those of humanistic psychology, but with the depth of existentialism incorporated. In his work on death he argues that people unprepared to face their own mortality are also likely to be unprepared to be fully alive; in his work on responsibility and freedom he puts forward strongly the argument that we create our own worlds – that living is a creation if we do it with awareness; that isolation is basic to the human condition, but that we can both affirm and be affirmed by others – that it is maybe only from accepting one's basic aloneness that a person can truly relate; and that, in relation to meaninglessness, 'the more we fulfill some self-transcendent meaning, the more happiness will ensue'.[247:462] This form of psychotherapy, and Yalom's work in particular, is used as a basis by many psychosynthesis therapists.

A parallel development, and one very significant for psychosynthesis as it has developed, is Gestalt theory, which links existential philosophy with a holistic and dynamic understanding of the person. Fritz Perls completed his seminal book on Gestalt theory, *Ego, Hunger and Aggression: A Revision of Freud's Theory and Method*, in 1939, which was followed by many others. Its popularity soared in the late 1960s, and its almost 'magical' techniques (especially when they are seen by someone with no previous knowledge of the theory) are well known and well used in the humanistic field.

The holistic view of the person is in direct opposition to that of analysis. It is assumed that a person throughout his or her life is attempting to make sense and meaning out of the combined inner and environmental sources of which he or she is aware. The significant factor is the perception, and that might change: a sudden insight, an 'aha', is a clear, new, unexpected vision, a realignment of an old pattern, a new Gestalt. Reason is important in this process, but overemphasis on thinking can prevent the insight being available: feeling and seeing, all that we can experience through our total being, can be lost. Perls saw many people as rather like those obsessional photographers who pay so much attention to the technical appearance of their pictures that they fail almost entirely to see the world as it is: 'because you are busy with your computer, your energy goes into your thinking and you don't see and hear any more.'[186:22] This emphasis on experience is important also in the process of therapy. Perls did not believe that a person can be 'cured' through talking and through intellectual understanding only; he insisted instead on working with the 'here and now', in the therapeutic situation, in a face-to-face relationship between therapist and client, and using catharsis, objects such as cushions and chairs representing inner elements in the person that can be externalized and then worked with. Significant people can also be represented by cushions and chairs. Of course they will stand for the client's internalized image of those people rather than for their 'actual' personalities, representing often only selected and exaggerated aspects of them that have a strong emotional impact or meaning for the client. Through this kind of work, characteristics that have been disowned and projected out on to the outside world – such as power, vulnerability, attractiveness – can gradually be re-owned.

Gestalt theory is concerned with recognizing, knowing and accepting the present, because it is only with such an attitude that it is possible to be who you are.

> 'Being' is the inner light through which we become aware of our meaning, of what reality is for us. In gestalt therapeutic work, the client is the sole arbiter of his world; 'Knowing' what is true for himself at any moment is the only valid basis for the ongoing therapeutic process . . . the gestalt therapy approach affirms the aware person as the 'chooser' of his or her own responses.[230:24]

In this the philosophy is close to that of Yalom, especially in the emphasis on personal responsibility. It is also close to psycho-synthesis in its clarity about the person as decision-maker, working from a centre of being and knowing with awareness and lack of naivety and self-deception. Gestalt also lays emphasis on re-owning neglected or projected parts of oneself – often seen as subpersonalities in psychosynthesis terms. The major difference is that Gestalt is not a transpersonal therapy – it does not postulate a soul.

Gestalt is about the personal process of alienation and identity. It assumes that we all only identify partly what we are and the potential within us, and we look to find from others what we cannot mobilize in ourselves, and therefore become drawn down into alienation – 'what a dependency if you want everyone to love you.'[186:33-4]

> Objectively speaking, it may be possible for someone to identify strongly with all aspects of the world and, thus, to accept and appreciate whatever enters experience. However, this condition of acceptance, according to Maslow . . . , is a rarity, occurring only during 'peak experiences' in a person's life . . . to actualise

one's own set of values, inner wisdom, power, love and potential – to develop one's own inner support system – is one of the goals that is central in what gestalt therapists consider as health.[230:50-4]

There is thus a great emphasis on projection in Gestalt – again the importance placed on the false perception of 'what is' that most people carry around. Perls wrote:

> I suggest we start with the impossible assumption that whatever we believe we see in another person in the world is nothing but a projection. Might be far out, but it's just unbelievable how much we project, and how blind and deaf we are to what's really going on. So, the re-owning of our senses and the understanding of projections will go hand in hand.[186:67]

Gestalt is used directly as an integral part of psychosynthesis training and therapy at the present time. Its many techniques and insights are an intrinsic part of the framework now taught.

Transpersonal psychotherapy

One of the earlier psychotherapists to tackle the problem of meaning in the materialistic West was Victor Frankl. His school of logotherapy was born in a concentration camp in the Second World War. He wrote strongly against the sort of statement made by Freud in *Future of an Illusion*: 'religion is the universal compulsive neurosis of mankind . . . like that of a child, it derives from the Oedipal complex, from the relationship to the father.'[86:69] Frankl, however, speculated whether compulsive neurosis was not diseased and unexpressed religiousness: whether 'once the angel in us is repressed, he turns into a demon' – a phenomenon with which he was all too familiar in the concentration camp, which was itself an aspect of the distorted vision of the National Socialists. He disagreed with Jung's views of the collective unconscious and said that 'unconscious religiousness stems from the personal centre of individual man rather than an impersonal pool of images shared by mankind'.[86:65] He agreed with Yalom that 'the door to happiness opens outward'. He also had a sense that, as he put it, 'life is a task'. It is a job to be done with meaning, with the person potentially being an aware decision-maker and chooser. His work has led to a great deal of research and is in substantial agreement with Assagioli's view, although his theory and techniques are less specific.

But it is Jung, of course, who is the great scholarly transpersonal psychotherapist. Assagioli knew Jung throughout his working life until Jung's death, and wrote in his 1966 lectures on 'Jung and psychosynthesis' that 'Jung is one of the closest and most akin to the conceptions and practice of psychosynthesis'.[4(14)] His major differences with Jung were that Jung did not regard the Self as a <u>living experience</u>, but as an unprovable concept; as psychosynthesis is based on Assagioli's own experience from the beginning, this is a key point to him. Also Assagioli, as has been commented before, made a firm distinction between transpersonal and lower unconscious, and felt that Jung was too fascinated by the collective unconscious. But given these reservations, he always felt close to Jung.

The theory of the collective unconscious, together with that of the archetypes, is used in psychosynthesis training and is graphically represented as part of the egg-shaped diagram. 'The collective unconscious is the whole spiritual heritage of mankind's evolution born anew in the structure of each individual.'[129.8:158] This means that all human beings potentially have access in a direct personal way to everything that has ever happened in the history of mankind. Much of this material we make conscious by dreams, myths and fairy-stories. As has already been mentioned, Jung investigated much of the spiritual wisdom of the world, both Eastern and Western, and he thought spirituality was naturally basic to our experience of living. In *Modern Man in Search of a Soul*, one of his best known books published originally in 1933, he showed most vividly how strongly a person living in the twentieth century must be aware of the 'shadow', the dark side of human nature: and that the facing of this 'shadow' is vital. If it is just lived out unconsciously, as was already happening on a collective scale in the Europe of 1933, it is dangerously destructive; but if it is repressed, not acknowledged, life becomes meaningless, tasteless, and again potentially dangerous. And if spirituality and soul are denied, then there is no vehicle for the modern person to see and come to terms with the shadow. This is as true of the individual as it is of society; the religious quest Jung believed to be particularly essential in the second half of life of the individual, as well as the basic problems in the twentieth century for all human beings, are about the search for meaning.

Jung's term for the process of growth and becoming, the purpose of therapy, was 'individuation':

Individuation means becoming a single homogenous being, and, in as far as 'individuality' embraces our innermost, last and incomparable uniqueness, it also implies becoming 'one's own self'. We could therefore translate individuation as 'coming to selfhood' or 'self-realisation'. The aim of individuation is nothing less than to divest the self of the false wrappings of the persona (mask) on the one hand and the suggestive power of primordial images on the other.[129.7:171-2]

In describing this process, Jung introduced several concepts that are widely used in therapy, and indeed in ordinary society. In a man there is assumed to be an 'anima', an unconscious female element, that the man may be in touch with or which he may repress; this internal feminine aspect may be projected on to women in his life and/or it may be made more conscious within his own functioning. A woman is assumed to have an unconscious 'animus', a comparable male element, which can be both used and projected. In putting forward these concepts, Jung was saying once again that there are likely to be largely unexpressed elements in people, which are only lived out unconsciously. The acceptance and knowledge of both 'masculine' and 'feminine' traits – which are, however, socially determined – are understood as part of the process of individuation, giving us all the possibility of androgeny, of not having to play set roles.

Jung also developed a typology of people which is widely used, particularly the terms 'introvert' and 'extrovert' – in other words, the person most in tune with a subjective inner experience of living as opposed to the person more related to external events and people, and to the collective. Again, as in the distinction between male and female, there is the possibility for all people of developing neglected aspects of themselves, of extending into the areas of thinking, feeling, sensation and intuition, which Jung took as being fundamental to all, but differentially developed.

Jung's significance can hardly be exaggerated, not only in relation to psychotherapy but also in the twentieth century as a whole. He acknowledged both the personality and the spiritual side of the person within an enormous scholarly historical framework. He saw very clearly the relationship of the personal journey to the process of the human race as a whole, and he proffered this material to people in a way that made it accessible to all. He thought that as people learned to take back into themselves the projections they make, then – and only then – would the world become viable. As Laurens van der Post writes in his affectionate book *Jung and the Story of our Time*:

I remember him saying clearly that the individual who

withdraws his shadow from his neighbour, and finds it in himself and is reconciled to it as an estranged brother, is doing a task of great universal importance. He added that the future of mankind depended on the speed and extent to which individual men learnt to withdraw their shadows from others and integrate them honourably within themselves.[231:231]

There may be an analogy here with the picture of the gnostic Demiurge, the shadow and the creator, with which the human race must come to terms before the God behind can at last be found.

This is the preoccupation of Erich Neumann, particularly in his controversial *Depth Psychology and a New Ethic*, published in 1949. His book is about the need of people to break out of the imperative to be 'good' and therefore to repress large elements of themselves, into the need to be 'whole', to face everything in themselves. He writes that the person truly in touch with the Self will have faced most of the issues in him- or herself, have faced the shadow and the potentiality for evil, grown through this process and become 'non-infectious' to others and to society as a whole. He wrote this within the massive context of his work on the origin and history of human consciousness, and believed that in the twentieth century the personal and spiritual awareness could – and urgently needed to – come together.

> Slowly but surely, the human race is withdrawing the
> psychological projections by which it had peopled the
> emptiness of the world with hierarchies and gods and spirits,
> heavens and hells; and now, with amazement, for the first time,
> it is experiencing the creative fullness of its own primal psychic
> ground.[176:135]

With the more recent work of Maslow, Jung, Hillman and many others, psychosynthesis is in perhaps the most hopeful current of thinking and perception at the present time, which combines individual therapy with concern for the future of the human race. Depth psychology has branched into many directions since *The Interpretation of Dreams* appeared in 1899. It is the development of this theory and practice of working with the individual which gives an entirely new dimension to spiritual awareness, and though these two worlds are often ignorant of each other, in transpersonal psychotherapy they have come together: if spiritual awareness can widen psychotherapy into the social and environmental dimension, and if therapy can enable any individual to particularize his or her own personal searching, and ground her concern without losing the width, then this particular combination, only really possible in the twentieth century, could be of the greatest significance.

In this process, psychosynthesis has a strong part. Its weakness is that Assagioli as a writer can in no way compare with Jung. He made his therapy available mainly through practice, and though he was a scholar, was not able to attract people by the strength of his exposition, because of the boundaries he drew between his clinical and his mystical interests. On the other hand, as the century has progressed, psychosynthesis has taken on board many of the insights and the techniques described in this chapter, so that the therapy is open, changing and accessible. For some critics, as was clear from Keen's comments in the Introduction to this study, there is a too-facile optimism in psychosynthesis, an unpreparedness to stay with the depths, a lack of rigour; and it is also criticized for taking on board too many techniques and becoming an 'eclectic mishmash'. Psychosynthesis is not yet well known. Its openness, from a limited theoretical basis, to the changing perceptions described in both this and the next chapters is both a strength and a weakness. But the reason for its international development from the 1960s onwards has been its utility as a 'fourth force' psychotherapy in a rapidly changing world.

19 Psychosynthesis in relation to twentieth century mysticism

There have been two periods in the twentieth century in Europe and America when recoil from our materialistic, scientific, atheistic world has brought about a reaction in the shape of religious and spiritual awareness and mysticism. The first was at the turn of the century, when Western confidence was in many ways at its zenith, when it seemed that real human progress was possible and happening, and that human knowledge would triumph; this period has already been discussed as the time at which psychosynthesis was founded. The second period was in the 1960s, when psychosynthesis became internationally known. Then, a reaction against many of the values of Western civilization, its misuse of nuclear energy, the arrogance and wealth which impoverished the rest of humanity, its assumption of dominance and control, brought about a movement of counter-culture, a movement towards simplicity and respect for the environment, towards spirituality and an acceptance that humanity is only one element in the universe and must, if it is to survive, become part of nature, instead of striving to be master of the universe. In both periods, the religions of the East played an important part.

In the movements of the 1960s, the knowledge of psycho-therapy which had developed over the century laid more emphasis than in the earlier period on transformation of the inner life of the individual. It was recognized that the change of consciousness required in the world could only come through a change within each person: it seemed that the possibility of redemption for the world and the possibility of redemption for each person were part of the same process; one could not happen without the other. This is why psychosynthesis as a transpersonal psychotherapy, which taught the importance of becoming whole, relating to the still 'I', contacting the Higher Self and the potentiality for benign change, became particularly significant. Assagioli had worked out for the individual a way of possible transformation, using effective techniques, which he declared could be enlarged in relation to the whole of humanity; the process is about recognizing and working with fragmented parts of the greater whole, whether they are subpersonalities or nations, and working with these parts in the context of this larger perspective. As has been seen in this study, this process was based on spiritual philosophy that is many thousands of years old, but which in all those centuries has only been known to a few. Transpersonal psychotherapy makes that ancient wisdom concretely available to any who care to use it, though Assagioli himself was somewhat reticent about his sources.

These statements do not intend to inflate the limited achievements of increased spiritual, personal and environmental awareness so far, or the purity of its manifestation! The materialistic West in the 1980s proceeds unabated, in spite of many protests on all sides about its destructive potential environmentally and the alienation of many, if not all, of its citizens which has been vigorously protested since Marx. 'Alternative' lifestyles, medicine, food and movements for personal growth develop around the world, but it is difficult to see how significant they are: they still seem marginal. They are also, inevitably, full of contradictions themselves. For instance people often remain interested in their personal growth without seeing it as part of a much larger contribution to the world – the narcissism of American movements has been well commented on by Lasch (*The Culture of Narcissism*, 1978); and it is not easy to change the competitive egocentric and materialistic conditioning of a lifetime.

People who have contributed to this alternative vision of humanity this century include Bergson, Aurobindo, Keyserling, Jung, Gurdjieff, Ouspensky, Teilhard de Chardin, Steiner and Krishnamurti. Recent writers are Fritjof Capra, Peter Russell, Ken Wilber and Theodore Roszak, among many others. Several of these – for example Teilhard and Capra – are scientists whose understanding of the changed nature of the scientific paradigm with the coming of quantum physics has led to a picture of the universe which is closer to Eastern religions than to the image of the 'great machine'.

It is interesting that the old insight that there is a direct relationship between the macrocosm and the microcosm is used increasingly in both Western and 'alternative' thinking. Peter Russell begins his book with a comparison between the cancer of the body – a disease most specifically of Western lifestyles and attitudes – and the cancer of the environment, implying the damage that Western technology is doing to the earth: 'technological civilization really does look like a rampant malignant growth blindly devouring its own ancestral host in a selfish act of consumption'.[205:20] And he argues that the only hope of preventing either of these is through a major change of consciousness, at both macro and micro levels. In this view, it becomes increasingly clear through the work of such writers that we are part of a personal, social and spiritual whole, and how lethal the present fragmentation is.

It is Wilber's contention that we have lost, over the last four hundred years or so, the 'third eye' of knowledge. We have used extensively the 'eye of the flesh' which studies matter, and also the 'eye of reason' which values logic and philosophy, but we have lost the 'eye of contemplation' or spiritual awareness. Without that eye the person cannot perceive spiritual reality. With it, 'the knowledge of God is as public to the contemplative eye as is geometry to the mental eye and rainfall to the physical eye.'[241:34] Without it, we have lost our deepest source of knowledge.

Most of the writers in this stream in the twentieth century use the metaphor of evolution in their attempt to trace, as Blavatsky did in the nineteenth century, the historical development of *spiritual* consciousness, in addition to the physical evolution of the human race as depicted by Darwin and the social and economic development as analysed by Marx. Teilhard de Chardin considered that humanity is somehow involved with God in creation: that the struggle with evil and suffering is part of the necessary task: 'the fact is that creation has never stopped. The creative act is one huge continual gesture, drawn out over the totality of time. It is still going on.'[224:130] His view, which was influenced like that of many writers by Bergson's *Creative Evolution*, published in 1907, was that humanity had emerged from a basic preconscious entity (similar to that found in a foetus, baby and small child before the development of self-consciousness) and could develop towards a fully conscious unity, when all the potential which is at present unconscious is made fully conscious and available, at what he called the Omega Point. He wrote that awareness of this future possibility could reach some people and had done over the centuries. Teilhard believed, however, that in the twentieth century we are rapidly approaching this point, because soon mankind as a whole has to make a choice between destruction and fulfilment. This Omega Point could of course apply to the individual person's fulfilment as well as to that of the human race as a whole, and once again the two are seen as related.

Teilhard, who lived from 1881 to 1955, was a geologist and paleontologist, and as such was deeply and consciously related to 'matter', which he saw as 'spirit' or 'soul' in a different form. In *The Heart of Matter* he describes their relationship:

You can well imagine . . . how strong was my inner feeling of release and expansion when I took my first still hesitant steps into an 'evolutive' Universe, and saw that the dualism in which I had hitherto been enclosed was disappearing like the mist before the rising sun. Matter and spirit: these were no longer two things, but two *states* or two aspects of one and the same cosmic Stuff, according to whether it was looked at or carried further in the direction in which (as Bergson would have put it) it is becoming itself or in the direction in which it is disintegrating.[222:26]

Again an analogy could be drawn here with the individual, with the physical body which is disintegrating and eventually dying and the soul which has the potential to 'become itself'.

Teilhard believed, in trying to unite the concepts of mysticism and evolution, that only when the human race became sufficiently evolved as a whole would it be able to meet the transcendental God. In 1951, just before he died, he wrote:

. . . as time goes by, I have a curious impression of liberation and simplification . . . the moment one realises that the Universe flows (and always has flowed) in the direction of 'ever greater order and consciousness', a whole group of values is introduced into things which . . . give everything an extraordinary savour, warmth and limpidity: a superior and synthetic form of 'mysticism' in which the strengths and seductions of Oriental 'pantheism' and Christian personalism converge and culminate! Impossible for me not to pursue this vision in a series of essays that keep getting longer without me yet having managed to grasp exactly and fully what I feel. . . .[223:115]

Like most twentieth century mystical writers Teilhard saw that mysticism must be deeply related to action. The sense of urgency about the need to change the world and the consciousness of the human beings within it is felt by many writers this century. The evolution that is being written about is not perceived by anyone as inevitable. There is also the choice of destruction, which will occur, in the understanding of these writers, if people stay 'asleep', unconscious, 'not knowing' in the gnostic sense.

The conviction that the human race is asleep is part of the message of Gurdjieff and Ouspensky. Gurdjieff typically asks:

How many times have I been asked here whether wars can be

stopped? Certainly they can. For this it is only necessary that people should awaken. It seems a small thing. It is, however, the most difficult thing there can be because this sleep is induced and maintained by the whole of surrounding life, by all surrounding conditions.[181:143]

He thus maintained, like Jung, that the *ordinary* state of life is for people to be asleep. Again, in this analysis, evil springs not so much from rational ill-will as from ignorance: as Jesus said, 'they know not what they do.'

Gurdjieff has a particularly clear analysis of the different states of consciousnes that could occur through spiritual evolution, and it is worth quoting him here for this analysis is relevant to the basic relationship of individual awareness (through the consciousness of self and contact with the Higher Self) to the evolution of humanity.

The two usual, that is, the lowest, states of consciousness are first *sleep*, in other words a passive state in which man spends a third and often a half of his life. And second, the state in which men spend the other part of their lives, in which they walk the streets, write books, talk on lofty subjects, take part in politics, kill one another, which they regard as active. . . . The third state of consciousnes is self-remembering or self-consciousnes . . . our science and philosophy have overlooked the fact that we do not possess this state of consciousness and that we cannot create it in ourselves by desire or decision alone . . . the fourth state . . . is called the objective state of consciousness. In this state a man can see things as they are. Flashes of this consciousness also occur in man. In the religions of all nations there are indications of the possibility of a state of consciousness of this kind which is called 'enlightenment' . . . but the only right way to objective consciousness is through the development of self-consciousness . . . the fourth state of consciousness in man means an altogether different state of being; it is the result of inner growth and of long and difficult work on oneself.[181:141-2]

Gurdjieff maintains that it is only in the fully awakened state, which would be like Wilber's 'eye of contemplation', that true knowledge can be attained. Now the vast majority of people live in states one and two.

Thus, in this view, the evolution of humanity would lead

through self-awareness to a transformation both of the individual and the world.

This same theme of evolution is the basis of a post-1960s 'new age' book, Wilber's massive *Up from Eden* which is subtitled 'A transpersonal view of human evolution'. He traces the evolutionary thesis to Hegel who postulated that consciousness in the human race arose first with bodily awareness; then human beings developed self-consciousness, just as a child does, and at that point the possibility of alienation arose; he predicted that finally there would be a synthesis of objectivity and subjectivity – the thesis, antithesis and synthesis that lay at the root of Marx's materialist analysis. Wilber, as other mystical writers, says that there is a difference between the average mode of consciousness, which is still at the alienation stage, and the more advanced mode that can be perceived as yet by relatively few, though it is important that this knowledge no longer remains esoteric but is shared by many. Wilber also, in a similar way to other twentieth century writers, refers to the ancient concept of the Great Chain of Being, which he says describes the hierarchy of consciousness which is possible for human beings. Again the importance of a transpersonal psychology is seen in relation to and as a vehicle for human evolution. He describes the immanent God, the Higher Self, the God within, who needs to be realized to meet the transcendent God who is the unity in the world but not the only active and creative spirit.

Wilber's *Up from Eden*, like Neumann's *The Origins and History of Consciousness* which was published originally in German in 1949, is a grand attempt to trace through history human consciousness and spirituality. Both follow the by now familiar pattern from unity through self-consciousness and alienation to the possibility of synthesis. Russell's book *The Awakening Earth* is subtitled 'Our next evolutionary step', looking for a spiritual renaissance and a society with a high degree of synergy – where the interests of the individual and those of society *and* the natural environment can be seen as one: 'our task,' said Einstein, 'must be to free ourselves from this prison by widening our circle of compassion to embrace all living creatures and the whole of nature in its beauty.'[8] At this point there is an inner consistency between relationships between people, relationships within social institutions and relationships with the natural environment, and the true spiritual reality of the universe, more basic than the forms through which this reality manifests itself: all these are dependent on each person living from his or her soul rather than his or her personality: 'the enlightened person begins to experience a spontaneous love for every creature and every thing, whatever their qualities or attributes'.[205:138-9] However, this is in marked contrast to the way in which most people live now: Russell reports that 'some psychologists estimate that as much as 80% of our interactions with other people come from the need for self-reinforcement',[205:105] because people in general are so little in touch with themselves and have little sense of their own identity. Our alienated and self-centred world *is* the root of the problem. The problem of the person *is* the problem of evil and suffering on the earth. If we lived from our souls rather than from our personalities, 'we would begin to feel for the rest of the world in much the same way as we *feel* for our own bodies. This would almost certainly have a profound effect on how we treat the environment.'[205:183]

The key to all these theories of spiritual evolution is that there is a fundamental difference between the original unity that human beings enjoyed with the universe and the new active fruition that is possible to us. The first is the unity before the Fall, in Biblical terms, the unity that animals live in, without self-consciousness. Wilber writes that 'modern anthropological research (from Levy-Bruhl to Gebser to Cassirer) has established as highly likely the fact that primitive men and women lived in a type of participation mystique, a vague indissociation of self and group, self and nature, self and animals',[241:227] which is akin to the experience of a baby or small child, with little differentiation between 'me' and the rest of the world. This is the preconscious, prepersonal state. There is always a tendency for people to attempt in all sorts of ways to revert to this state, by refusing in many ways to grow up, by refusing to take lonely personal responsibility in the way that is brilliantly analysed by Fromm in *Fear of Freedom*, or most particularly by unquestioningly sticking to their predetermined roles. In all these states there is no connection with the personal 'I' and certainly no recognition of the soul.

This is in direct contrast to the vision of a transpersonal world which is the common goal of twentieth century mystics; this is a world in which people are truly awake and do realize what they do, and where the unity between people, society and universe will be completely conscious, and the uniqueness of each creature will be enhanced by the unity of the whole. At that point, most personal and collective unconscious material, of both heaven and hell, will have become conscious.

Wilber comments that Maslow and Assagioli do not confuse the prepersonal and the transpersonal in the way he thinks Jung does (whilst Freud of course does not allow for the transpersonal at all). Assagioli makes a firm distinction between the lower unconscious – the prepersonal, and the higher unconscious – the transpersonal. The collective unconscious is not divided in his 'egg-shaped diagram', yet this is probably because he was attempting to indicate it only in relation to the individual.

Jung's works have of course made a significant, indeed extraordinary contribution to this vision of the future, and he has been particularly interested in tracing back the roots of mystical experience in the past, through gnosticism, alchemy, Eastern religions, myths and legends. In his well-known book *Modern Man in Search of a Soul*, published originally in 1933, he comments on the extraordinary interest in mysticism and spiritual awareness over the last fifty years or so:

> The world has seen nothing like it since the end of the seventeenth century. We can compare it only to the flowering of Gnostic thought in the first and second centuries after Christ. The spiritual currents of the present have, in fact, a deep affinity with Gnosticism. . . . The modern movement which is numerically most impressive is undoubtedly Theosophy, together with its continental sister, Anthroposophy; these are pure Gnosticism in Hindu dress.[131:238]

He believed, with all the other mystical writers of the twentieth century, that reason is not enough in assisting with suffering: what is needed is wisdom, and that has been a quality largely ignored in the West.

That Jung himself was deeply rooted in Gnosticism is maintained by Hoeller in his *The Gnostic Jung and the Seven Sermons to the Dead*. In 1915 Jung produced the 'Seven Sermons' after a long and dangerous period of self-examination. Both Jung and others have maintained that his work has been based on this period, particularly on the 'Seven Sermons' and on his notes in his Red Book and Black Book. He, like the gnostics, was conscious of a search for a lost wholeness – a search impeded by the conventions of society where all insight is likely to be fossilized or bureaucratized. Hoeller writes that Jung saw depth psychology as being a natural descendant of the gnostic position that searches for self-knowledge above all.

> The fact remains that Jungian depth psychology is more than a therapeutic discipline, just as Gnosticism is more than an ancient religion. Both are expressions at their particular levels of existential reality of a Gnosis, a knowledge of the heart

directed towards the inmost core of the human psyche and having as its objective the essential transformation of the psyche.[113:33]

Psychosynthesis is in exactly the same position, attempting to reconcile the opposites, recognize the fragments of the whole, and see them in the light of the soul. Gnosis is true consciousness, the state to which most mystics aspired, in the long gnostic tradition already traced.

Thus, twentieth century 'new age' mysticism has built on the nineteenth century evolutionary theories and has transcended them: it also emphasizes the relationship between the possible transformation of the individual from a state of sleep and the possible saving of the world from the many destructive forces of the time. It is an attempt to bring back an active spiritual awareness, an understanding that the life we see around us is only an outward form of the spiritual processes that are the basis of reality. In a materialist age, spiritual or mystical writers are in the minority, but theirs is a position based in the whole history of the human race. It is on this long tradition that, as we have already seen, psychosynthesis was founded, and it is in the light of this renewed awareness that it has developed so far in the latter part of the twentieth century.

20 Summary and conclusion: a deeper synthesis

The gods did not reveal, from the beginning,
All things to us; but in the course of time,
Through seeking we may learn, and know things better.

But as for certain truth, no man has known it,
Nor will he know it; neither of the gods,
Nor yet of all the things of which I speak.
And even if by chance he were to utter
The final truth, he would himself not know it;
For all is but a woven web of guesses.

XENOPHANES

Impetus for this study sprang from a curiosity about the ideas lying behind psychosynthesis. My curiosity has taken me back to the past, to Plato, to the early gnostic and Christian writers, to the origins of modern Western society, and to the turn of this century as key periods: it also led me to an awareness of the constant change in the bases of knowledge, particularly in science, during this century. Each period in history must rework old ideas with new experience, constantly creating a new synthesis. To trace the origins of psychosynthesis, it is necessary to look back; to offer a critique of it, one must look forward at its present and future relevance.

There are many aspects to criticize in psychosynthesis. Its origins are obscure, its framework hardly justified in any systematic way by its founder. It was created in a magpie fashion. It may be wildly over-optimistic and sometimes superficial. From the scientific point of view, it is founded on experience and belief, and Assagioli showed relatively little interest in testing his framework. From the religious point of view, its personal and spiritual origins are not well described. And yet in some fashion psychosynthesis can really justify its name: its model and its techniques do offer a coming-together of inner experience and outer events, of the personal and the social, of past wisdom and present science, of psychotherapy and theology, in a way not precisely achieved by any other form.

Looked at in one way, it could now seem irrelevant that psychosynthesis should wish to be considered as a science at all. To whom does that matter? Contemporary science in any case may claim no more existential 'objectivity' than spiritual knowledge. The modification of our views of science, particularly through Kuhn's work, and work on the actual nature of scientific thinking itself, makes the old split between mechanical science and religious mysticism, felt so keenly earlier in this century, a rather out-of-date dichotomy. The very social and intellectual movements that encouraged the development of psychosynthesis from the 1960s onwards render the questions that were raised in my Introduction slightly anachronistic. In answering those questions, it is necessary to look at their actual validity as well as the replies.

The question of the 'authenticity' of psychosynthesis, raised in 1974 by Sam Keen who is quoted in the Introduction, no longer seems so real. The ideas of psychosynthesis now so obviously seem part of many ongoing streams of knowledge, and Assagioli created a distinct psychotherapeutic system out of them: it is a new creation but it is based on very old, often esoteric knowledge.

In Part One of this study, the ideas that were to be explored in psychosynthesis were presented. These are of course not the whole of psychosynthesis but rather some of the key areas – the assumption that we are souls, which are the context of our lives, with personalities that are the content, and that this pattern is repeated in the human race as a whole, over time: the assumption that the conscious personality is a relatively small part of the whole of our being – that the personal and collective unconscious is the framework of our lives and is expressed through myths, dreams and fairy-tales, which are a source of real knowledge in our search to understand our situation: and the assumption that the methodical, observational, empirical study of unconscious material is part of the psychosynthesis approach as it has been for most psychotherapeutic frameworks in the twentieth century.

Within this overall structure are concepts and assumptions that require further investigation. For instance, how, in a world so patently harsh and sorrowful, can we assume that basic reality, that a spiritual framework is fundamentally good? What would it imply if each destructive characteristic were at root a benign quality, perverted through defence mechanisms which often have already ceased to serve the person? This was the question raised in the Introduction about the idea of brokenness and its relationship to wholeness. How did the image of human beings as being asleep come about? And what would it be to wake up, as a person and as a species, and work through to the potential by way of facing our own destructiveness, evil and sin, and perhaps achieve 'what we may be'? What is the root of all these concepts?

In tracing back the early influences on Assagioli, it is possible to see these ideas recurring as a pattern over and over again. In Plato's earliest intellectual studies, there is the notion of the soul awakening in the dark cave, seeing that the world it had taken for granted is an illusion, a shadow (the archetype that Jung was to use to describe the unconscious aspects in ourselves we must work through), and finding its way, painfully, slowly, to the sunlight and the colours that are there — and always have been, though they could not be seen in the darkness. In Dante, the story is of the soul's journey through Hell, where there is no hope, down to the centre of the deepest darkness, and then slowly up through Purgatory, where, through purging, the people there could hope for light: onwards, then, guided by wisdom (Beatrice) rather than reason (Vergil), to Paradise. In the Jewish mystical tradition, the Kabbalah, the Sephirot represents a similar system, and as a diagram is akin to Assagioli's symbolic picture of the person. The gnostic tradition, through its emphasis on 'knowing' and realization, influenced Jung directly and Assagioli through Theosophy: here the Good is the context, but is obscured through the creative Demiurge which is evil as well as good: and the spiritual sense here is transcendental, the idea of the soul being 'homesick', searching for the goodness that is far away. The neoplatonic tradition emphasizes the immanent spiritual self — the 'I' and the Higher Self within, which can be realized through 'inner knowing', contacting the One that is the foundation of everything. Behind all these pictures is a sense of the evolution that is possible, though certainly not inevitable, both for the individual person and for the species. This evolutionary sense was graphically developed in the nineteenth century by several great thinkers — Feuerbach, the spiritual precursor of Marx, Marx himself in his model of the material possibilities for the human race, Darwin in his theory of physical evolution of the species, and Freud in his scientific study of the unconscious. This theme has continued in the present century in Jung, in Teilhard and in present-day 'new age' thinkers such as Wilber and Russell.

A major theme throughout this study has had to be the nature of the knowledge lying behind psychosynthesis. The earlier pictures of the soul's journey have been by definition mystical: this has been true of Eastern as well as Western religions. They have been glimpses by remarkable people of a model of human life known to and accepted by only a few: esoteric knowledge. But what has been noteworthy in this century is that gradually some thinkers in the scientific tradition, which itself sprang from the mystical tradition of the Renaissance as 'natural magic', have returned to these spiritual areas. The split between science and mysticism traced through Part Two is in some ways healing – though perhaps only marginally at the moment when we look at the whole of society and what is happening to it, but the potential may be there. Science itself is changing towards a view more consistent with the religious sense – the newer picture of reality is more about relationships, about change, about organic systems, and paradox and balance being held through consciousness. Scientists are now much more ready to acknowledge that the characteristics of the knower are as important as those of the known in the way that any situation is perceived; and that – following Kuhn – any science must be a 'myth', a model, a paradigm, about how things are. This means increasingly that there is more room for alternative myths of reality to be taken seriously. All, as Xenophanes indicates in the poem quoted at the beginning of this chapter, are 'but a woven web of guesses'.

This has been a study in the history of ideas – which is of course always speculative. Although Assagioli gave a list of the areas of study which had most influenced him, as recounted in my Introduction, he was most inexplicit about anything but the general outline of those areas. He emphasized the scientific framework, and played down the spiritual – representing those areas as being *about* the study of religion rather than being the religious experience itself. This perception of Assagioli is partly modified by an examination of his library in Florence, which has many specifically mystical books, and by his notes. And the impression from talking with people who knew him was that he was clearly a 'wise person' rather than simply an academic.

The two periods when he founded psychosynthesis and when it developed internationally are suggestive. The beginning of the twentieth century was able to provide the soil both for the scientific study of unconscious material and for relating to the Eastern (and Western) spiritual knowledge then current in educated circles in the West. Theosophy was known in Italy, and to Assagioli's family. From the beginning he wrote on mystical material – in 1908 he gave a paper on the German mystic Hamann and the American transcendentalist Emerson at an international philosophical conference, and he always worked in the area of medicine in relation to education and religion. His Italian background was of course particularly steeped in that synthesis, and in the relationship of ideas to art and to living.

It does seem that this is the first time in history that we can truly have a transpersonal psychotherapy. Psychotherapy as such has only really developed this century: and as has been traced in Part Three, the understanding of the unconscious and the techniques for working with unconscious material have developed out of all recognition in these last eighty years. Psychosynthesis relies on a large number of techniques – not an 'eclectic mishmash' but held together by a firm and still developing framework. The mystical tradition is of course old, but at this point in time – more perhaps even than at the beginning of the century – the unsatisfactoriness of an entirely material framework is increasingly recognized, and scientific study itself has brought about a greater understanding of the relativity of all of our ways of 'seeing' the world. In the last chapter, something of the development of holistic spiritual thinking in this century has been traced.

There are still many criticisms that can legitimately be made of psychosynthesis. It can be seen as too superficially optimistic, too ungrounded in real intellectual discipline. But when its long and important theoretical roots are uncovered, it could come to be grounded in richer earth than it has been so far. It has such a rich ancestry which could give it greater strength and override the doubts raised by Keen in his 1974 article.

But more than that, psychosynthesis can be seen as representing one significant strand in our search for meaning, in relating the inner life to outer reality, the spiritual path of the individual to the search for the potential of the human species through consciousness. It had seemed that science was the way to truth, but science then meant that any spiritual vision was 'nothing but' a dream, an illusion. One of the saddest pictures I hold from my reading for this study is Darwin's confession of his loss of faith – how the wonder of his first sight of South America had gradually been lost, and how the world had come to seem to him mundane, two-dimensional; Marx, too, assumed that when a human being took back the power which he or she had projected into religious, industrial or political institutions, there would then be no magic, and only material progress would then be possible. For both Darwin and Marx, though each had started off as a visionary, the result of their theories could only be materialistic, non-religious, certainly non-mystical. But perhaps now, at this point in the twentieth century, we can see that our older visions are not necessarily invalid, that science and religion, psychology, politics and theology can be re-united, and that in this a presently rather obscure praxis such as psychosynthesis may play a part. The very term 'synthesis' represents what many thinkers are presently searching for, as a correction to analysis. Perhaps, after all, the individual, and the world we live in, may be 'a soul'.

IS

Epilogue

I know that without me
God can no moment live;
Were I to die, then He
No longer could survive.

I am as great as God,
And He is small like me;
He cannot be above
Nor I below Him be.

In me God is a fire
And I in Him its glow;
In common is our life,
Apart we cannot grow.

He is God and man to me,
To Him I am both indeed;
His thirst I satisfy,
He helps me in my need.

God is such as He is,
I am what I must be;
If you know one, in truth
You know both Him and me.

I am the vine, which He
Doth plant and cherish most;
The fruit which grows from me
Is God, the Holy Ghost.

Angelus Silesius
(Johann Scheffler,
1624–1677)

Bibliography

To use the reference system:
There are two bibliographies: one is of books mainly internal to psychosynthesis, together with Assagioli's published and unpublished work, the other is of published books. All works are numbered.

The first reference number in the text refers to the number of the book as given in the two bibliographies. Sometimes bracketted letters or numbers are used with the main number – for instance, all Assagioli's unpublished writings are given the number of 4 and then a specific reference number, e.g. 4(14), and Dante's Hell, Purgatory and Paradise are given as 58(a), 58(b) and 58(c) respectively. If more than two texts are referred to, the reference is written 16/42, i.e. referring to texts numbers 16 and 42. In *Collected Works* (such as Jung's), the particular reference is given as, e.g., 126.9.1, i.e. Jung's *Collected Works*, volume 9, part 1.

The number after the colon in bibliographical references is the page (or occasionally paragraph) number.

Psychosynthesis bibliography

Apart from the two published books by Dr Assagioli, most of these works are articles printed internally by the Psychosynthesis Research Foundation of New York, the Psychosynthesis and Education Trust, London, or the Institute of Psychosynthesis, London. Other psychosynthesis books published commercially are listed in the general bibliography.

Books by Roberto Assagioli

1   *Psychosynthesis*, Turnstone Press, 1980 (originally 1965).
2   *The Act of Will*, Wildwood House, 1974.
3   *Psychosynthesis Typology*, Institute of Psychosynthesis (previously unpublished material, posthumously printed in book form).

Selected articles by Roberto Assagioli

These are in alphabetical order. They are internally printed or duplicated by the different Institutes: some are photocopied articles on general topics and some are on specific therapeutic techniques. Almost all are undated and unsigned.

4 (1) 'The balancing and synthesising of opposites'.
4 (2) 'Cheerfulness'.
4 (3) 'The conflict between the generations and the psychosynthesis of the human ages'.
4 (4) 'Dynamic psychology and psychosynthesis' (originally *Hibbert Journal* 1933 article, enlarged, vol. 32, October 1933–July 1934).
4 (5) 'The education of gifted and super-gifted children'.
4 (6) 'The Evening Review'.
4 (7) 'Evoking and developing desired qualities'.
4 (8) 'Exercises on the subpersonalities'.
4 (9) 'From the couple to the community'.
4(10) 'Guidelines for writing a psychosynthesis autobiography'.
4(11) 'Ideal model exercises'.
4(12) 'Identification Exercise'.
4(13) 'The Inner Dialogue'.
4(14) 'Jung and psychosynthesis' (Psychosynthesis Research Foundation 1967: three lectures).
4(15) 'Life as a game: and stage performance'.
4(16) 'Loving understanding'.
4(17) 'Meditation'.
4(18) 'The mystery of self'.
4(19) 'Psychological Workbook'.
4(20) 'Psychosynthesis: individual and social'.
4(21) 'The resolution of conflicts'.

4(22) 'The self as unifying centre'.
4(23) 'The seven ways to spiritual realisation'.
4(24) 'Spiritual development and its attendant maladies' (from *Hibbert Journal* article, vol. 36, October 1937–July 1938).
4(25) 'The superconscious and the self'.
4(26) 'Symbols of transpersonal experience'.
4(27) 'Talks on the self: a conversation'.
4(28) 'The technique of evocative words'.
4(29) 'Techniques of interindividual psychosynthesis'.
4(30) 'Training'.
4(31) 'Transpersonal inspiration'.

Internally printed articles by other psychosynthesis writers: a selection. Most of these articles are undated.

5   Alberti, Alberto, 'The Will in psychotherapy'.
6   Assagioli, Roberto, and Whitmore, Diana, 'The breadth and scope of psychosynthesis'.
7   Atreya, J. P., 'Psychosynthesis and Indian thought' (1965).
8   Brown, George Isaac, 'I have things to tell' (1973).
9   Cirinei, Gabriello, 'Psychosynthesis: the way to inner freedom'.
10   Crampton, Martha, 'Psychological energy transformation'.
11   Crampton, Martha, 'Towards a psychosynthesis approach to the group'.
12   Crampton, Martha, 'The use of mental imagery in psychosynthesis' (1968).
13   Ferrucci, Piero, 'Guiding and clienting'.
14   Ferrucci, Piero, and Whitmore, Diana, 'What is psychosynthesis?'.
15   Harovian, Frank, 'The repression of the sublime'.
16   Kull, Stephen, 'Evolution and personality' (1972).
17   Leuner, Hanscarl, 'Guided Affective Imagery (GAI)' (reprinted from *American Journal of Psychosyntherapy*, vol. 23, January 1969).
18   Lofgren, Ruth, 'The school as a living organism' (1959).
19   Maslow, Abraham, 'The creative attitude'.
20   Palombi, Edie, 'Short biography of Dr Roberto Assagioli'.
21   Patman, Sue, 'Childhood and the lower unconscious'.
22   Vargieu, James, 'Global education and psychosynthesis'.

Journals

23   *Synthesis*, vols 1 (23a), 2 (23b), 3–4 (23c), 1977 (3 volumes only). Available at the Psychosynthesis and Education Trust and the Institute of Psychosynthesis.
24   Institute of Psychosynthesis *Yearbooks*, London, annual: 1981 (24a), 1982 (24b), 1983 (24c), etc.

25   *Psychosynthesis*, Los Angeles, Annual: 1981, 1982, 1983, 1984, 1985.

Other

26   *Notes* by Roberto Assagioli, in the Psychosynthesis Library, Florence, catalogued by Piero Ferrucci.
27   *A Short History of Psychosynthesis*, undated and unsigned, also in the Florence library.

Main bibliography

The books listed below are those which have influenced the production of this present book. Some are quoted in the text, others are not.
Some of the older books are available in the British Library.

28 Ahern, Geoffrey, *Sun at Midnight*, Aquarian Press, 1984.
29 Aresteh, A. Reza, *Growth to Selfhood: The Sufi Contribution*, Routledge & Kegan Paul, 1980.
30 Arnold, Edwin, *The Light of Asia*, Routledge & Kegan Paul, 1971.
31 Bailey, Alice, *Education in the New Age*, Lucis Trust, 1981.
32 Barnes, B., *T. S. Kuhn and Social Science*, Macmillan, 1982.
33 Belotti, Elena, *Little Girls: Social Conditioning and the Effects on the Stereotyped Role of Women During Infancy*, Hazell, Watson & Viney, 1975.
34 Bergson, Henri, *Dreams*, trans. E. E. Slosern, B. W. Huebach, 1914.
35 Berlin, Isaiah, *Against the Current: Essays in the History of Ideas*, Hogarth Press, 1979.
36 Bertholf, Robert J. and Levitt, Annette S. (eds), *William Blake and the Moderns*, State University of New York Press, 1982.
37 Besant, Annie, *'The Riddle of Life' and How Theosophy Answers It*, Theosophical Publishing House, 1913.
38 Besant, Annie, *A Study in Consciousness*, Theosophical Publishing House, 1904.
39 Besant, Annie, *Theosophy and the Theosophical Society*, Theosophical Publishing House, 1913.
40 Besant, Annie, *Why I Became a Theosophist*, Theosophical Trust, 1889.
41 Bettelheim, Bruno, *Freud and Man's Soul*, Hogarth Press, 1983.
42 Bettelheim, Bruno, *The Uses of Enchantment*, Penguin, 1982.
43 Biale, David, *Gershom Scholem: Kabbalah and Counterhistory*, Harvard University Press, 1982.
44 Bibby, C., *T. H. Huxley: Scientist, Humanist and Educator*, Watts, 1959.
45 Blake, William, *Poems*, ed. W. H. S. Stevenson, Longman, 1973.
46 Boehme, Jacob, *The Signature of All Things*, James Clarke, 1981.
47 Bohm, David, *Wholeness and the Implicate Order*, Routledge & Kegan Paul, 1980.
48 Brown, Molly Young, *The Unfolding Self: Psychosynthesis and Counselling*, Psychosynthesis Press, 1983.
49 Buber, Martin, *Between Man and Man*, Routledge & Kegan Paul, 1947.
50 Buber, Martin, *Israel and the World*, Schocken Books, 1948.
51 Bucke, R. M., *Cosmic Consciousness*, Dutton, 1969.
52 Budd, Susan, *Varieties of Unbelief*, Heinemann, 1977.
53 Burrow, J. W., *Evolution and Society: A Study in Victorian Social Theory*, Cambridge University Press, 1966.
54 Capra, Fritzjof, *The Turning Point*, Wildwood House, 1982.

55 Carter-Haas, B., and Miller, S., 'The meeting of East and West', *Synthesis*, vol. 1, no. 2.

56 Cirlot, J. E., *Dictionary of Symbols*, Routledge & Kegan Paul, 1978.

57 Clark, R. W., *Freud: The Man and the Cause*, Granada, 1982.

58 Clements, Harvey, *A. R. Wallace*, Hutchinson, 1983.

59 Cousins, J. H., *A Study in Synthesis* (dedicated to Anne Besant), Ganesh, 1934.

60 Dante Alighieri, *The Banquet*, trans. E. P. Sayer, Routledge, 1887.

61 Dante Alighieri, *The Divine Comedy*: (a) *Hell*, 1980; (b) *Purgatory*, 1981; (c) *Paradise*, 1982; trans. Dorothy Sayers and Barbara Reynolds, Penguin.

62 Darwin, Charles, *The Origin of Species*, ed. J. W. Burrow, Penguin, 1978.

63 Davies, Paul, *God and the New Physics*, Penguin, 1983.

64 Desoille, R., *The Directed Daydream*, trans. Haronian.

65 Dostoevsky, Feodor, *Letters from the Underworld*, J. M. Dent, 1913.

66 Dukas, H. and Hoffman, B. (eds), *A. Einstein, The Human Side*, Princeton University Press, 1978.

67 Easlea, Brian, *Witch-hunting, Magic and the New Philosophy: An Introduction to the Debates of the Scientific Revolution 1450–1750*, Harvester Press, 1980.

68 Eastcott, Michal, *The Silent Path*, Samuel Weisler, 1973.

69 Ehrenfeld, D., *The Arrogance of Humanism*, Oxford University Press, 1978.

70 Ehrenreich, B. and English, D., *For Her Own Good*, Pluto Press, 1979.

71 Eiseley, Loren, *Darwin and the Mysterious Mr. X*, J. M. Dent, 1979.

72 Eliade, Mircea, *Images and Symbols*, University of Chicago Press, 1952.

73 Eliade, Mircea, *Mephistopheles and the Androgyne*, University of Chicago Press, 1970.

74 Eliade, Mircea, *Myth and Reality*, Harper & Row, 1963.

75 Eliade, Mircea, *The Myth of the Eternal Return*, Routledge & Kegan Paul, 1974.

76 Eliade, Mircea, *Myths, Dreams and Mysteries*, Collins, 1976.

77 Eliade, Mircea, *The Quest: History and Meaning in Religion*, University of Chicago Press, 1969.

78 Eliade, Mircea, *No Souvenirs: Journal 1957–69*, Routledge & Kegan Paul, 1973.

79 Ellenberger, H. F., *The Discovery of the Unconscious*, Basic Books, New York, 1970.

80 Ferguson, Marilyn, *The Aquarian Conspiracy*, Tarcher, 1980.

81 Ferrucci, Piero, *What We May Be*, Turnstone, 1983.

82 Feuerbach, Ludwig, *The Essence of Christianity*, trans. George Eliot, Harper & Row, 1957.

83 Firth, Raymond, *Symbols, Public and Private*, Allen & Unwin, 1973.

84 Fisher, Seymour and Greenberg, Roger, *The Scientific Credibility of Freud's Theories and Therapy*, Harvester Press, 1977.

85 Frankl, Victor, *The Doctor and the Soul*, Vintage, 1973.

86 Frankl, Victor, *The Unconscious God*, Simon & Schuster, 1947.

87 Frankl, Victor, *The Unheard Cry for Meaning*, Simon & Schuster, 1978.

88 Fransella, Fay (ed.), *Personality*, Methuen, 1981.

89 French, Peter J., *John Dee: The World of an Elizabethan Magus*, Routledge & Kegan Paul, 1984.

90 French, R. K., *Robert Whytt, the Soul and Medicine*, Wellcome Institute of History of Medicine, 1969.

91 Freud, S., *Collected Works*, Hogarth Press, London, 1952.

92 Freud, S., 'Psychoanalysis and psychosynthesis', in *Healthy Life Magazine*, 1928.

93 Freud, S., *The Interpretation of Dreams*, Allen & Unwin, 1967.

94 Fromm, Erich, *The Anatomy of Human Destructiveness*, Penguin, 1974.

95 Fromm, Erich, *Beyond the Chains of Illusion*, Abacus, 1962.

96 Fromm, Erich, *The Forgotten Language*, Holt, Rinehart & Winston, 1951.

97 Fromm, Erich, *Psychoanalysis and Religion*, Yale University Press, 1972.

98 Fromm, Erich, *To Have Or To Be?*, Abacus, 1976.

99 Gigante, Michael, 'Synthesis of the Nation', unpublished PhD, Ryoken College, Los Angeles, 1982.

100 Gimello, Robert, 'Mysticism and meditation', in Katz, *Mysticism and Philosophical Analysis*, op. cit.

101 Gittings, John, *John Keats*, Penguin, 1985.

102 Gosling, J. C. B., *Plato*, Routledge & Kegan Paul, 1973.

103 Haekel, Ernst, *The Riddle of the Universe*, Watts & Co., 1913 (originally published 1899).

104 Halevi, Z'en ben Shimon, *Kabbalah*, Thames & Hudson, 1979.

105 Hanson, V. (ed.), *H. P. Blavatsky and the Secret Doctrine*, Theosophical Publishing House, 1971.

106 Happold, F. C., *Mysticism*, Penguin, 1984.

107 Harovian, Frank, *The Repression of the Sublime*, Psychosynthesis Research Foundation, 1967.

108 Harré, R., *The Philosophies of Science*, Oxford University Press, 1972.

109 Heard, Gerald, *The Third Morality*, Cassell & Co., 1937.

110 Heilbron, Carolyn G., *Towards Androgeny*, Gollancz, 1973.

111 Hillman, James, *The Dream and the Underworld*, Harper & Row, 1979.

112 Hillman, James, *Re-visioning Psychology*, Harper Colophon, 1975.

113 Hoeller, Stephen, *The Gnostic Jung and the Seven Sermons to the Dead*, Quest, 1982.

114 Holmes, G., *Dante*, Oxford University Press, 1980.

115 Horowitz, Mark, 'Psychology in the global area', *Institute of*

Psychosynthesis Yearbook III, 1983, London.

116 Hughes, H. Stuart, *Consciousness and Society: The Reorientation of European Social Thought, 1890–1930*, Harvester Press, 1979.

117 Humphries, Christmas, *Sixty Years of Buddhism in England, 1907–1967*, Buddhist Society, 1968.

118 Husik, I., *History of Jewish Medieval Philosophy*, Jewish Publications of America, 1944.

119 Huxley, Aldous, *The Perennial Philosophy*, Chatto & Windus, 1980.

120 Huxley, Thomas, 'The struggle for existence in human societies', *Nineteenth Century*, vol. 23, no. 161, 1888.

121 Jaffe, Aniela, *The Myth of Meaning in the Work of Jung*, trans. R. F. C. Hull, Hodder & Stoughton, 1970.

122 Jahoda, Marie, *Freud and the Dilemmas of Psychology*, Hogarth Press, 1977.

123 James, William, *The Principles of Psychology* (2 vols), Dover, 1950.

124 James, William, *The Varieties of Religious Experience*, Collins, 1982.

125 St John of the Cross, *Poems*, trans. Roy Campbell, Penguin, 1960.

126 Jonas, H., *The Gnostic Religion*, Beacon Press, 1958.

127 Jones, Roger, *Physics as Metaphor*, Abacus, 1983.

128 Julian of Norwich, *Revelations of Divine Love*, Penguin, 1973.

129 Jung, C. G., *Collected Works*, Routledge & Kegan Paul, 1959.

130 Jung, C.G., *Man and His Symbols*, Picador, 1978.

131 Jung, C. G., *Modern Man in Search of a Soul*, Routledge & Kegan Paul, 1981.

132 Jung, C. G., *Psychology and Alchemy*, Routledge & Kegan Paul, 1980.

133 Jung, C. G., *Psychology and Religion*, York University Press., 1938.

134 Jung, C. G., *Symbols of Transformation, Collected Works*, op. cit., vol. 5, 1959.

135 Jung, C. G., *Two Essays on Analytic Psychology, Collected Works*, op. cit., vol. 7, 1917.

136 Katz, S. T. (ed.), *Mysticism and Philosophical Analysis*, Sheldon Press, 1978.

137 Keats, John, *Poems*, ed. J. Stillinger, Heinemann Educational, 1978.

138 Keller, Carl, 'Language, epistemology and mysticism', in Katz, *Mysticism and Philosophical Analysis*, op. cit.

139 Keyserling, Hermann, 'The East and the West and their search for a common truth', *International Institute of China Pamphlets*, Shanghai Mercury, 1912.

140 Keyserling, Hermann, *Immortality*, Oxford University Press, 1938.

141 Kidman, Brenda, *A Gentle Way with Cancer*, Century, 1983.

142 King, Preston (ed.), *The History of Ideas*, Croom Helm, 1983.

143 King, Ursula, *Towards a New Mysticism: Teilhard de Chardin and Eastern Religions*, Collins, 1980.

144 Kirk, G. C., *Myth: Its Meaning and Function*, Cambridge University Press, 1971.

145 Koch, Astrid, *All But One?*, unpublished MA thesis, Antioch University, 1984.

146 Kretschmer, W., 'Meditative technique in psychosynthesis', in Assagioli, *Psychosynthesis*, op. cit.

147 Kuhn, Thomas, *The Structure of Scientific Revolutions*, University of Chicago Press, 1973.

148 Lacarrière, Jacques, *The Gnostics*, Peter Owen, 1977.

149 Langer, S., *The Philosophy of Ernest Cassirer*, Evanston, 1949.

150 Leggett, Trevor, *The Chapter of the Self*, Routledge & Kegan Paul, 1978.

151 Leuner, Hanscarl, *Guided Affective Imagery*, Thieme-Stratton, 1984.

152 Leuner, Hanscarl and Kornadt, H. J., 'Initiated Symbol Projection', trans. W. Swartley, in Assagioli, *Psychosynthesis*, op. cit.

153 Louth, A., *The Origins of the Christian Mystical Tradition*, Clarendon Press, 1981.

154 Lovejoy, Arthur, *The Great Chain of Being*, Harvard University Press, 1978.

155 Lovelock, James, *Gaia: A New Look at Life on Earth*, Oxford University Press, 1979.

156 Malinowski, *Myth in Primitive Society*, London, 1926.

157 Mannheim, Karl, *Ideology and Utopia*, Routledge & Kegan Paul, 1979.

158 Manuel, Frank E., *Shapes in Philosophic History*, Allen & Unwin, 1965.

159 Markley, O. W. and Harman, W. W., *Changing Images of Man*, Pergamon Press, 1982.

160 Martin, Wallace, *The New Age Under Orage*, Manchester University Press, 1967.

161 Maslow, Abraham, *The Psychology of Science*, Harper & Row, 1966.

162 Maslow, Abraham, 'Theory Z', *Journal of Transpersonal Psychology*, Fall 1969, vol. 1, no. 2.

163 Maslow, Abraham, *Towards a Psychology of Being*, Van Nostrand, 1968.

164 May, Rollo, *Psychology and the Human Dilemma*, Norton, 1979.

165 McClelland, David C., *The Roots of Consciousness*, Van Nostrand, 1964.

166 McFarland, Thomas, *Coleridge and the Pantheist Tradition*, Clarendon Press, 1969.

167 McGuire, William (ed.), *The Freud-Jung Letters*, Hogarth Press and Routledge & Kegan Paul, 1974.

168 Medcoff, J. and Roth, J., *Approaches to Psychology*, Open University Press, 1979.

169 Mehta, Ved, *Mahatma Gandhi*, Penguin, 1977.

170 Merchant, Carolyn, *The Death of Nature*, Wildwood House, 1982.

171 Midgeley, Mary, *Evolution as a Religion*, Methuen, 1985.

172 Miller, Stuart, 'Dialogue with the Higher Self', *Synthesis*, vol. 1, no. 2, 1975.

173 Moustakas, C. E. (ed.), *The Self*, Harper & Row, 1956.

174 Murphy, Gardner, *Personality*, Harper & Row, 1947.

175 Needham, Joseph, *The Grand Titration: Science and Society in East and West*, Allen & Unwin, 1979.

176 Neumann, E., *Depth Psychology and a New Ethic*, Harper & Row, 1973.

177 Neumann, E., *The Origins and History of Consciousness*, Routledge & Kegan Paul, 1973.

178 Oldroyd, D. R., *Darwinian Impacts*, Open University Press, 1980.

179 Orage, A. R., *On Love*, Unicorn Press, 1932.

180 Orage, A. R., *On Love, With Some Aphorisms*, Janus Press, 1957.

181 Ouspensky, P. D., *In Search of the Miraculous: Fragments of an Unknown Teaching*, Routledge & Kegan Paul, 1983.

182 Pagels, Elaine, *The Gnostic Gospels*, Penguin, 1982.

183 Parkes, M. G., *Introduction to Keyserling*, Jonathan Cape, 1934.

184 Pascal, Blaise, *Pensées*, Penguin, 1984.

185 Pearce, Joseph C., *The Bond of Power, Meditation and Wholeness*, Routledge & Kegan Paul, 1982.

186 Perls, Fritz, *Ego, Hunger and Aggression: The Beginning of Gestalt Therapy*, Random House, 1969.

187 Perls, F., Hefferline, R. and Goodman, P., *Gestalt Therapy*, Penguin, 1979.

188 Peters, R. S. (ed.), *Brett's History of Psychology*, Allen & Unwin, 1953.

189 Plato, *The Complete Texts of the Great Dialogue*, trans. W. H. E. Rowse, New American Library, 1961.

190 Pirsig, Robert M., *Zen and the Art of Motorcycle Maintenance*, Bodley Head, 1974.

191 Plotinus, *Plotinus*, trans. and preface by A. H. Armstrong, 2 vols, Harvard University Press, 1966.

192 Plotinus, *The Essential*, trans. by E. O'Brien, Blackwell, 1964.

193 Popper, K. R., *The Open Society and its Enemies*, 2 vols (1 *The Spell of Plato*; 2 *The High Tide of Prophecy: Hegel, Marx and the Aftermath*), Routledge & Kegan Paul, 1973.

194 Progoff, Ira, *The Symbolic and the Real*, Coventure, 1963.

195 Rachman, Stanley J., *Fear and Courage*, W. H. Freeman, 1978.

196 Radhakrishnam (ed.), *The Bhagavadgita*, Harper Torch, 1973.

197 Raine, Kathleen, *Defending Ancient Springs*, Golgoonza Press, 1985.

198 Ramacharaka, Yogi, *Raja Yoga on Mental Development*, Yoga Publishing Society, 1905–6.

199 Ransom, Josephine (compiler), *A Short History of the Theosophical Society, 1875–1937*, Theosophical Publishing House, 1938.

200 Robertson, Chris, *Changing the Concept of Change*, Institute of Psychosynthesis *Year Book III*, 1983.

201 Robinson, J. M., *The Nag Hammadi Library*, E. J. Brill.

202 Roszak, Theodore, *Person/Planet*, Granada, 1979.

203 Roszak, Theodore, *Unfinished Animal*, Faber & Faber, 1976.

204 Rubins, J. L., *Karen Horney*, Weidenfeld & Nicolson, 1978.

205 Russell, Peter, *The Awakening Earth: Our Next Evolutionary Leap*, Routledge & Kegan Paul, 1982.
206 Scholem, Gershom, *Major Trends in Jewish Mysticism*, Schocken Books, 1961.
207 Seton, Anya, *The Winthrop Woman*, Hodder & Stoughton, 1968.
208 Sheehy, Gail, *Passages: Predictable Crises of Adult Life*, Bantam, 1977.
209 Sheldrake, Rupert, *A New Science of Life*, Granada, 1981.
210 Sheridan, A., *Michel Foucault: The Will to Truth*, Tavistock, 1984.
211 Simonton, Carl and Stephanie, *Getting Well Again*, Bantam, 1982.
212 Sinclair, J. R., *The Alice Bailey Inheritance*, Turnstone, 1984.
213 Singer, Jerome, *Daydreaming and Fantasy*, Oxford University Press, 1975.
214 Smith, Huston, 'The religions of man', in J. Weiser and T. Yeomans (eds), *Psychosynthesis*, Ontario Institute for Studies in Education, 1986.
215 Smuts, Ian, *Evolution and Holism*, Macmillan, 1926.
216 Sorokin, Pitrim A., *The Ways and Power of Love*, Beacon Press, 1954.
217 Stafford-Clark, D., *What Freud Really Said*, Penguin, 1965.
218 Steiner, Rudolph, *The Philosophy of Freedom*, Rudolph Steiner Press, 1964 (originally published 1894).
219 Steiner, Rudolph, *Theosophy*, Rudolph Steiner Press, 1965 (originally published 1922).
220 Stevens, A., *Archetype: A Natural History of the Self*, Routledge & Kegan Paul, 1982.
221 Tart, Charles (ed.), *Transpersonal Psychologies*, Routledge & Kegan Paul, 1975.
222 Teilhard de Chardin, Pierre, *The Heart of Matter*, Collins, 1978.
223 Teilhard de Chardin, Pierre, *Letters to Two Friends, 1926–52*, ed. R. d'Ouince, London, 1970.
224 Teilhard de Chardin, Pierre, *Writings in Time of War, 1916–19*, Collins, 1968.
225 Thomas, Keith, *Religion and the Decline of Magic*, Penguin, 1982.
226 Tillyard, E. M. W., *The Elizabeth World Picture*, Penguin, 1982.
227 Trine, R. W., *In Tune with the Infinite*, C. Bell & Sons, 1965.
228 Tyrrell, G. N. M., *Personality of Man*, Penguin, 1947.
229 Underhill, Evelyn, *Mysticism*, New American Library, 1974.
230 Van de Riet, Vernon, Korb, Margaret and Gorrell, John, *Gestalt Therapy*, Pergamon Press, 1980.
231 Van der Post, Laurens, *Jung and the Story of our Time*, Penguin, 1979.
232 Walker, Benjamin, *Gnosticism: Its History and Influence*, Aquarian Press, 1983.
233 Wallis, R. T., *Neoplatonism*, Duckworth, 1972.
234 Watts, Alan, *The Meaning of Happiness*, Rider, 1978.
235 Weiser, J. and Yeomans, T. (eds), *Readings in Psychosynthesis*, Ontario Institute for Studies in Education, 1985.

236 Welwood, John, *The Meeting of the Ways: Explorations in East/West Psychology*, Schocken Books, 1979.
237 White, Victor, *God and the Unconscious*, Element Books, 1982.
238 Whitmont, Edward C., *Return of the Goddess: Femininity, Aggression and the Modern Grail Quest*, Routledge & Kegan Paul, 1983.
239 Whyte, L. L., *The Unconscious Before Freud*, Julian Friedmann, 1978.
240 Wickes, Frances, *The Inner World of Choice*, Chaucer Press, 1963.
241 Wilber, Ken, *Eye to Eye*, Anchor Books, 1983.
242 Wilber, Ken, *Up from Eden*, Routledge & Kegan Paul, 1983.
243 Wilhelm, R./Jung, C., *The Secret of the Golden Flower*, Routledge & Kegan Paul, 1979.
244 Wordsworth, William, *Poems*, Penguin, 1977.
245 Wynn, Walter, *Theosophy: A Criticism*, Tract, 1892.
246 Wyss, Dieter, *Psychoanalytic Schools*, Jason Aronson, 1973.
247 Yalom, Irvin, *Existential Psychotherapy*, Basic Books, 1980.
248 Yates, Frances A., *Giordano Bruno and the Hermetic Tradition*, Routledge & Kegan Paul, 1982.
249 Yates, Frances A., *The Occult Philosophy in the Elizabethan Age*, Routledge & Kegan Paul, 1983.
250 Yates, Frances A., *The Rosicrucian Enlightenment*, Granada, 1975.

Recent addition

251 Whitmore, Diana, *Psychosynthesis in Education: The Joy of Learning*, Turnstone, 1986.

Index

FOR THE BEST IN PAPERBACKS, LOOK FOR THE

In every corner of the world, on every subject under the sun, Penguin represents quality and variety – the very best in publishing today.

For complete information about books available from Penguin – including Pelicans, Puffins, Peregrines and Penguin Classics – and how to order them, write to us at the appropriate address below. Please note that for copyright reasons the selection of books varies from country to country.

In the United Kingdom: Please write to *Dept E.P., Penguin Books Ltd, Harmondsworth, Middlesex, UB7 0DA*

If you have any difficulty in obtaining a title, please send your order with the correct money, plus ten per cent for postage and packaging, to *PO Box No 11, West Drayton, Middlesex*

In the United States: Please write to *Dept BA, Penguin, 299 Murray Hill Parkway, East Rutherford, New Jersey 07073*

In Canada: Please write to *Penguin Books Canada Ltd, 2801 John Street, Markham, Ontario L3R 1B4*

In Australia: Please write to the *Marketing Department, Penguin Books Australia Ltd, P.O. Box 257, Ringwood, Victoria 3134*

In New Zealand: Please write to the *Marketing Department, Penguin Books (NZ) Ltd, Private Bag, Takapuna, Auckland 9*

In India: Please write to *Penguin Overseas Ltd, 706 Eros Apartments, 56 Nehru Place, New Delhi, 110019*

In Holland: Please write to *Penguin Books Nederland B.V., Postbus 195, NL–1380AD Weesp, Netherlands*

In Germany: Please write to *Penguin Books Ltd, Friedrichstrasse 10–12, D–6000 Frankfurt Main 1, Federal Republic of Germany*

In Spain: Please write to *Longman Penguin España, Calle San Nicolas 15, E–28013 Madrid, Spain*

In France: Please write to *Penguin Books Ltd, 39 Rue de Montmorency, F–75003, Paris, France*

In Japan: Please write to *Longman Penguin Japan Co Ltd, Yamaguchi Building, 2–12–9 Kanda Jimbocho, Chiyoda-Ku, Tokyo 101, Japan*

FOR THE BEST IN PAPERBACKS, LOOK FOR THE 🐧

PENGUIN HEALTH

Acupuncture for Everyone   Dr Ruth Lever

An examination of one of the world's oldest known therapies used by the Chinese for over two thousand years.

Aromatherapy for Everyone   Robert Tisserand

The use of aromatic oils in massage can relieve many ailments and alleviate stress and related symptoms.

Chiropractic for Everyone   Anthea Courtenay

Back pain is both extremely common and notoriously difficult to treat. Chiropractic offers a holistic solution to many of the causes through manipulation of the spine.

Herbal Medicine for Everyone   Michael McIntyre

An account of the way in which the modern herbalist works and a discussion of the wide-ranging uses of herbal medicine.

Homoeopathy for Everyone   Drs Sheila and Robin Gibson

The authors discuss the ways in which this system of administering drugs – by exciting similar symptoms in the patient – can help a range of disorders from allergies to rheumatism.

Hypnotherapy for Everyone   Dr Ruth Lever

This book demonstrates that hypnotherapy is a real alternative to conventional healing methods in many ailments.

Osteopathy for Everyone   Paul Masters

By helping to restore structural integrity and function, the osteopath gives the whole body an opportunity to achieve health and harmony and eliminate ailments from migraines to stomach troubles.

Spiritual and Lay Healing   Philippa Pullar

An invaluable new survey of the history of healing that sets out to separate the myths from the realities.

FOR THE BEST IN PAPERBACKS, LOOK FOR THE 🐧

A CHOICE OF PENGUINS

Metamagical Themas Douglas R. Hofstadter

A new mind-bending bestseller by the author of *Gödel, Escher, Bach*.

The Body Anthony Smith

A completely updated edition of the well-known book by the author of *The Mind*. The clear and comprehensive text deals with everything from sex to the skeleton, sleep to the senses.

How to Lie with Statistics Darrell Huff

A classic introduction to the ways statistics can be used to prove *anything*, the book is both informative and 'wildly funny' – *Evening News*

The Penguin Dictionary of Computers Anthony Chandor and others

An invaluable glossary of over 300 words, from 'aberration' to 'zoom' by way of 'crippled lead-frog tests' and 'output bus drivers'.

The Cosmic Code Heinz R. Pagels

Tracing the historical development of quantum physics, the author describes the baffling and seemingly lawless world of leptons, hadrons, gluons and quarks and provides a lucid and exciting guide for the layman to the world of infinitesimal particles.

The Blind Watchmaker Richard Dawkins

'Richard Dawkins has updated evolution' – *The Times* 'An enchantingly witty and persuasive neo-Darwinist attack on the anti-evolutionists, pleasurably intelligible to the scientifically illiterate' – Hermione Lee in Books of the Year, *Observer*

A CHOICE OF PENGUINS

The Literature of the United States   Marcus Cunliffe

The fourth edition of a masterly one-volume survey, described by D. W. Brogan in the *Guardian* as 'a very good book indeed'.

The Sceptical Feminist   Janet Radcliffe Richards

A rigorously argued but sympathetic consideration of feminist claims. 'A triumph' – *Sunday Times*

The Enlightenment   Norman Hampson

A classic survey of the age of Diderot and Voltaire, Goethe and Hume, which forms part of the Pelican History of European Thought.

Defoe to the Victorians   David Skilton

'Learned and stimulating' (*The Times Educational Supplement*). A fascinating survey of two centuries of the English novel.

Reformation to Industrial Revolution   Christopher Hill

This 'formidable little book' (Peter Laslett in the *Guardian*) by one of our leading historians is Volume 2 of the Pelican Economic History of Britain.

The New Pelican Guide to English Literature   Boris Ford (ed.)
Volume 8: The Present

This book brings a major series up to date with important essays on Ted Hughes and Nadine Gordimer, Philip Larkin and V. S. Naipaul, and all the other leading writers of today.

A CHOICE OF PENGUINS

Adieux Simone de Beauvoir

This 'farewell to Sartre' by his life-long companion is a 'true labour of love' (the *Listener*) and 'an extraordinary achievement' (*New Statesman*).

British Society 1914–45 John Stevenson

A major contribution to the Pelican Social History of Britain, which 'will undoubtedly be the standard work for students of modern Britain for many years to come' – *The Times Educational Supplement*

The Pelican History of Greek Literature Peter Levi

A remarkable survey covering all the major writers from Homer to Plutarch, with brilliant translations by the author, one of the leading poets of today.

Art and Literature Sigmund Freud

Volume 14 of the Pelican Freud Library contains Freud's major essays on Leonardo, Michelangelo and Dostoyevsky, plus shorter pieces on Shakespeare, the nature of creativity and much more.

A History of the Crusades Sir Steven Runciman

This three-volume history of the events which transferred world power to Western Europe – and founded Modern History – has been universally acclaimed as a masterpiece.

A Night to Remember Walter Lord

The classic account of the sinking of the *Titanic*. 'A stunning book, incomparably the best on its subject and one of the most exciting books of this or any year' – *The New York Times*

FOR THE BEST IN PAPERBACKS, LOOK FOR THE 🐧

A CHOICE OF PENGUINS

The Informed Heart Bruno Bettelheim

Bettelheim draws on his experience in concentration camps to illuminate the dangers inherent in all mass societies in this profound and moving masterpiece.

God and the New Physics Paul Davies

Can science, now come of age, offer a surer path to God than religion? This 'very interesting' (*New Scientist*) book suggests it can.

Modernism Malcolm Bradbury and James McFarlane (eds.)

A brilliant collection of essays dealing with all aspects of literature and culture for the period 1890–1930 – from Apollinaire and Brecht to Yeats and Zola.

Rise to Globalism Stephen E. Ambrose

A clear, up-to-date and well-researched history of American foreign policy since 1938, Volume 8 of the Pelican History of the United States.

The Waning of the Middle Ages Johan Huizinga

A magnificent study of life, thought and art in 14th and 15th century France and the Netherlands, long established as a classic.

The Penguin Dictionary of Psychology Arthur S. Reber

Over 17,000 terms from psychology, psychiatry and related fields are given clear, concise and modern definitions.

ARKANA – NEW-AGE BOOKS FOR MIND, BODY AND SPIRIT

A selection of titles already published or in preparation

A Course in Miracles: The Course, Workbook for Students and Manual for Teachers

Hailed as 'one of the most remarkable systems of spiritual truth available today', *A Course in Miracles* is a self-study course designed to shift our perceptions, heal our minds and change our behaviour, teaching us to experience miracles – 'natural expressions of love' – rather than problems generated by fear in our lives.

Medicine Woman: A Novel Lynn Andrews

The intriguing story of a white woman's journey of self-discovery among the Heyoka Indians – from the comforts of civilisation to the wilds of Canada. Apprenticed to a medicine woman, she learns tribal wisdom and mysticism – and above all the power of her own womanhood.

Arthur and the Sovereignty of Britain: Goddess and Tradition in the Mabinogion Caitlín Matthews

Rich in legend and the primitive magic of the Celtic Otherworld, the stories of the *Mabinogion* heralded the first flowering of European literature and became the source of Arthurian legend. Caitlín Matthews illuminates these stories, shedding light on Sovereignty, the Goddess of the Land and the spiritual principle of the Feminine.

Shamanism: Archaic Techniques of Ecstasy Mircea Eliade

Throughout Siberia and Central Asia, religious life traditionally centres around the figure of the shaman: magician and medicine man, healer and miracle-doer, priest and poet.

'Has become the standard work on the subject and justifies its claim to be the first book to study the phenomenon over a wide field and in a properly religious context' – *The Times Literary Supplement*

ARKANA – NEW-AGE BOOKS FOR MIND, BODY AND SPIRIT

A selection of titles already published or in preparation

The I Ching and You Diana ffarington Hook

A clear, accessible, step-by-step guide to the *I Ching* – the classic book of Chinese wisdom. Ideal for the reader seeking a quick guide to its fundamental principles, and the often highly subtle shades of meaning of its eight trigrams and sixty-four hexagrams.

A History of Yoga Vivian Worthington

The first of its kind, *A History of Yoga* chronicles the uplifting teachings of this ancient art in its many guises: at its most simple a beneficial exercise; at its purest an all-embracing quest for the union of body and mind.

Tao Te Ching The Richard Wilhelm Edition

Encompassing philosophical speculation and mystical reflection, the *Tao Te Ching* has been translated more often than any other book except the Bible, and more analysed than any other Chinese classic. Richard Wilhelm's acclaimed 1910 translation is here made available in English.

The Book of the Dead E. A. Wallis Budge

Intended to give the deceased immortality, the Ancient Egyptian *Book of the Dead* was a vital piece of 'luggage' on the soul's journey to the other world, providing for every need: victory over enemies, the procurement of friendship and – ultimately – entry into the kingdom of Osiris.

Yoga: Immortality and Freedom Mircea Eliade

Eliade's excellent volume explores the tradition of yoga with exceptional directness and detail.

'One of the most important and exhaustive single-volume studies of the major ascetic techniques of India and their history yet to appear in English' – *San Francisco Chronicle*

ARKANA – NEW-AGE BOOKS FOR MIND, BODY AND SPIRIT

A selection of titles already published or in preparation

Weavers of Wisdom: Women Mystics of the Twentieth Century Anne Bancroft

Throughout history women have sought answers to eternal questions about existence and beyond – yet most gurus, philosophers and religious leaders have been men. Through exploring the teachings of fifteen women mystics – each with her own approach to what she calls 'the truth that goes beyond the ordinary' – Anne Bancroft gives a rare, cohesive and fascinating insight into the diversity of female approaches to mysticism.

Dynamics of the Unconscious: Seminars in Psychological Astrology Volume II Liz Greene and Howard Sasportas

The authors of *The Development of the Personality* team up again to show how the dynamics of depth psychology interact with your birth chart. They shed new light on the psychology and astrology of aggression and depression – the darker elements of the adult personality that we must confront if we are to grow to find the wisdom within.

The Myth of Eternal Return: Cosmos and History Mircea Eliade

'A luminous, profound, and extremely stimulating work . . . Eliade's thesis is that ancient man envisaged events not as constituting a linear, progressive history, but simply as so many creative repetitions of primordial archetypes . . . This is an essay which everyone interested in the history of religion and in the mentality of ancient man will have to read. It is difficult to speak too highly of it' – Theodore H. Gaster in *Review of Religion*.

Karma and Destiny in the I Ching Guy Damian-Knight

This entirely original approach to the *I Ching*, achieved through mathematical rearrangement of the hexagrams, offers a new, more precise tool for self-understanding. Simple to use and yet profound, it gives the ancient Chinese classic a thoroughly contemporary relevance.

Neal's Yard Natural Remedies Susan Curtis, Romy Fraser and Irene Kohler

Natural remedies for common ailments from the pioneering Neal's Yard Apothecary Shop. An invaluable resource for everyone wishing to take responsibility for their own health, enabling you to make your own choice from homeopathy, aromatherapy and herbalism.

The Arkana Dictionary of New Perspectives Stuart Holroyd

Clear, comprehensive and compact, this iconoclastic reference guide brings together the orthodox and the highly unorthodox, doing full justice to *every* facet of contemporary thought – psychology and parapsychology, culture and counter-culture, science and so-called pseudo-science.

The Absent Father: Crisis and Creativity Alix Pirani

Freud used Oedipus to explain human nature; but Alix Pirani believes that the myth of Danae and Perseus has most to teach an age which offers 'new responsibilities for women and challenging questions for men' – a myth which can help us face the darker side of our personalities and break the patterns inherited from our parents.

Woman Awake: A Celebration of Women's Wisdom Christina Feldman

In this inspiring book, Christina Feldman suggests that it *is* possible to break out of those negative patterns instilled into us by our social conditioning as women: confirmity, passivity and surrender of self. Through a growing awareness of the dignity of all life and its connection with us, we can regain our sense of power and worth.

Water and Sexuality Michel Odent

Taking as his starting point his world-famous work on underwater childbirth at Pithiviers, Michel Odent considers the meaning and importance of water as a symbol: in the past – expressed through myths and legends – and today, from an advertisers' tool to a metaphor for aspects of the psyche. Dr Odent also boldly suggests that the human species may have had an aquatic past.

"fossilized into
   respectability